Thous away, hundreds into the past . . .

His was a journey through time.

Soul-sick of the world around him, Michael Holzach fled to America and plunged into another life. In the communal colonies of the Hutterites he sought to discover what deprivation of the flesh could do to enrich the spirit. He found much, much more – the hoarded wisdom of centuries, the universal human folly, and . . . Rachel.

Here at last is a stunning translation of the poetic best-seller that so absorbed German readers. With the skill of a novelist Holzach provides an inside look into the "God's arks" that dot the prairie from South Dakota to the foothills of the Canadian Rockies.

We see and hear close-up the people who walk among us like stern strangers from a distant past. We suffer with them centuries of persecution and exile. We learn the unexpected rewards of day-long labor, prayer, and love. We exalt in the surprising and ironic glimpses into the human psyche and the more than human heart.

"I do not remember ever having read a book dealing with a subject matter so far removed from the background of an author who could nevertheless tell the story with such a love and dedication and in such an unusually attractive style that **I could not resist reading without a stop.**" — Cornelius Krahn, on *Das vergessene Volk, Mennonite Weekly Review, 3/19/81*

"Once I picked up the book I was mesmerized. I could not put it down again until I had read the last word on the last page." — Mary Wipf, former Hutterite, on *Das vergessene Volk*

Michael Holzach

The
FORGOTTEN PEOPLE
(Das vergessene Volk)
A Year Among the Hutterites

Translated from the German by Stephan Lhotzky

with an Introduction by Reuben Goertz

and Photos by Timm Rautert

Ex Machina Publishing Company
Sioux Falls, South Dakota

The Forgotten People is translated from *Das vergessene Volk: Ein Jahr bei den deutschen Hutterern in Kanada*, by Michael Holzach, Copyright © Hoffmann und Campe Verlag, Hamburg 1980.

Photos by Timm Rautert, © GEO, Verlag Gruner + Jahr, Hamburg.

Published by Ex Machina Publishing Company, Box 448, Sioux Falls, SD 57101.

First Printing, July 1993.
Second Printing, June 1994.
Printed by Pine Hill Press, Inc., Freeman, SD 57029.

Library of Congress Cataloging-in-Publication Data

Holzach, Michael, 1947-

   [Vergessene Volk. English]
    The forgotten people : a year among the Hutterites / Michael Holzach : translated from the German by Stephan Lhotzky : with an introduction by Reuben Goertz : and photos by Timm Rautert.
    p. cm.
   Translation of: Das vergessene Volk.
   ISBN 0-944287-10-7 (hardbound) : $21.95 − ISBN 0-944287-11-5 (softcover) : $14.95
   1. Hutterite Brethren − Alberta. 2. Holzach, Michael, − 1947-   I. Title.
BX8129.H8H5913 1993
298.7'7123 − dc20   93-13218
ISBN 0-944287-10-7 (Hardcover)   CIP
ISBN 0-944287-11-5 (Paper trade)

DEDICATION
(by Michael Holzach)

I want to thank Eta, Evelyn, Freda, and Niko

PUBLISHER'S
ACKNOWLEDGMENTS

The publisher wishes to thank the following institutions and individuals for invaluable help in preparing this volume:

Stephan Lhotzky.
Hoffmann und Campe, German publishers., Ingeborg Rose, foreign rights.
Mennonite Historical Library, Goshen, Indiana, John D. Roth, Director.
Reuben Goertz.
Gayle Emmel.
Mary Wipf.
Pine Hill Press

INTRODUCTION

"I was willing to integrate myself totally into the community, to share in the work, the prayers, the songs—in short, to experience everything first hand in order to some day maybe write a book about my experiences."

This promise, freely given to the leaders of the Wilson Hutterite Colony in Alberta, Canada, by Michael Holzach, journalist, writer and adventurer from Germany gained him the desired admission. The resultant book is historically and theologically correct and offered in an interesting way. It entices us to enter the colony with him for close scrutiny.

The influence of the Hutterite lifestyle on Mr. Holzach during the ensuing year is a story within the story. It reveals the subtle nuances of their ancient teachings in a way a clinical analysis never could. He learns to love his hosts and respect their commitment to their commune. There are moments when he is beset with doubts and he addresses these with straightforward candor. Never does he let disagreement become virulent, neither has he allowed a sympathetic understanding of this people to cloud objectivity with sentiment.

The book is replete with historical and Biblical references to explain contemporary Hutterite thought. So skillfully are these woven into the fabric of the story you never get the feeling that you are being preached to or that you are reading a history text.

Historical nuggets are gleaned from old writings. *The Great Chronicle* is the oldest and most revered. Probably the most used is the 894-page *The Songs of the Hutterian Brethren.* The youngest child commits the songs to memory by hearing them sung over and over by the community at work or at worship. Selected verses are included and have been skillfully translated. The suffering of the martyrs is commemorated. Michael Sattler, one of the two thousand victims of bloody persecution seems to be Martyr in residence. The cruelty of a hostile world is mourned, the glory of a heavenly eternity is celebrated.

The ancient teachings of venerable patriarchs, Jakob Hutter, Peter Riedemann and Peter Walpot are sacrosanct. The older a document is, the more meaningful and valid is its content. The occasional reference to books of the Apocrypha indicates that even older Bibles are the books of choice. This somber material is respected by Holzach, but he doesn't allow it to become melancholy. He rescues it from the pits of gloom by injecting his own comparisons to current situations outside the community. He makes it all seem rather contemporary.

Mr. Holzach uses his considerable language skills to augment historical accounts of Hutter places of origin and migration routes by the language they speak, the loan words they use.

Colony life is closely scrutinized. This book is not a dreary recital of details and minutia. It is a chorus of souls united in communal harmony as they strive for heaven in a belligerent world.

Mr. Holzach is made to go to school where he and the children are taught with emphasis that colony life is being, not having. Songs and Bible verses for every contingency are learned, sermons are analyzed and discipline is strictly enforced. The older children are slowly involved in the work force, helping where they can, learning by doing and listening.

Work is done according to the seasons, but the cadence of colony life never falters and the reasons for communal living are constantly stressed in all they do. You are taken into the fields, the cattle lots, the kitchen, but you are never outside the confines of the church. Catechism and baptism as well as courtship, engagement and marriage are conducted under the watchful eye of the commune — and of course you are there. The selection of ministers and their ordination are examined. Because the portals of heaven are in the colony, you celebrate death at the wake and funeral. Hutterite existence is always aware of its heavenly mission. "Life and death are always connected to each other; one reflects the other, and the community is the link between heaven and earth. 'We live in the outer courtyard of Paradise,' Jakob keeps saying." The celebration is genuine.

The approach of winter signals the end of the author's planned stay in the colony. The inner conflict of unresolved questions create an inner turmoil. Should he stay? Should he go?

To Dr. Stephan Lhotzky, a hearty "Thank You" for making this sensitive and useful book available to us with an excellent translation. He has made a significant contribution to our understanding of a little-known and much maligned people. They and we have benefited from Dr. Lhotzky's dedicated work.

Reuben Goertz
Freeman, S.D.
1992

Michael Holzach   As a Hutterite

THE AUTHOR

Michael Holzach was born on April 8, 1947 in Heidelberg, Germany. He majored in Social Studies at the University of Bochum. When he worked as a reporter for the news magazine *Die Zeit* in Hamburg, his main interest included the problems of minorities in West German society. After 1978 he worked as a free lance writer. He lived with the German Hutterites in North America for one year and wrote his first book about this experience, *Das vergessene Volk—The Forgotten People* (1980). In 1983 his book *Ich heiße Feldmann und bin ein Hund—My Name is Feldmann, I am a Dog* (written together with Freda Heyden) was published. The author died on April 21, 1983 of an accidental drowning. Holzach's book *Zeitberichte—Reports About the Present Time* (in collaboration with Timm Rautert) was published posthumously in 1985.

THE PHOTOGRAPHER

Timm Rautert was born in 1941 at Tuchel, West Prussia. He studied with Otto Steinert at the Folkwang school in Essen. He became a free lance photographer in 1971. The photos in this book were taken during two visits to Michael Holzach at the Hutterite colonies during Holzach's yearlong stay.

TRANSLATOR'S PREFACE

Michael Holzach's book *The Forgotten People* is one of the most interesting and readable works dealing with the Hutterites. In the course of the translation, I was fortunate to get first-hand information about the sect through various contacts I made with its members and former members. In that sense, translating Holzach's account was much more challenging than many other translation projects I have undertaken: It was a truly enriching experience through which I was able to familiarize myself with the Hutterite way of life and Hutterite beliefs and values.

Unfortunately, no translation will ever reach the flavor and style of the original; it will always remain a copy which can only attempt to preserve some of the original words, phrases, and sentences. In this translation, some of the truly interesting and, at times, very entertaining, elements were lost in the English version. I did not even attempt to find an English equivalent of the Hutterite German dialect. However, I was as faithful as possible in preserving the original text in all other aspects. In some places, for example, the use of slang may not seem appropriate to the American reader; however, it does add an ironic perspective to the account through which the author attempted to establish a certain distance between himself and the Hutterites.

All factual errors, though few, were left untouched as they appear in the German original. The best example of the author's misunderstanding of the Hutterite language is an old Hutterite story which Holzach describes in great detail: A disobedient daughter is taken by the devil through a hole in the ground. The city in which this tragic story takes place is Hamburg, as the author, himself from Hamburg in northern Germany, understood the Hutterites to say. According to the Hutterite story, "Hamburg" is located in Hesse in central Germany. Holzach uses this example to illustrate the Hutterites' ignorance of German geography. Holzach was right in that Hamburg is not in Hesse, but, in all likelihood, the Hutterites were talking about "Homburg", which is in Hesse—from their pronunciation the author inferred that the seaport of Hamburg was meant.

Those readers familiar with the Hutterite people will, in all likelihood, detect some words in the book with a spelling different from what some Hutterites would expect. From a linguistic point of view, however, these differences can be overlooked, and I chose the spelling as it appears in the original German version. Such differences include the name *Walpot* vs. *Walbot,* the word *Kukurutz* vs. *Gugurutz,* and the like. One source told me that the ship on which the first Hutterite settlers sailed to America was named "Hammonia" instead of "Harmonia" as it appears in Holzach's book. I assume "Hammonia" is a printing error and thus left "Harmonia" the way it is spelled in the German original.

One of the problems I faced dealt with quotations taken from the Bible. In English, I used the King James version in order to preserve the antiquated flavor of the original passages. At times, however, I had to select entirely different verses so that the original meaning could still be conveyed.

References and quotations from English-language scholarly research dealing with the Hutterites do not always follow the original English version; I took the liberty of re-translating most of them from the German. Even in cases in which the original meaning may have been changed, I left the re-translation in order to show exactly with which passages Holzach himself was working. However, for the most important work (the work which also sparked Holzach's interest in the Hutterites—*To Have or To Be?* by Erich Fromm), I used the original version published in the United States.

Finally, the translation was in need of a suitable title in English. *The Forgotten People* actually refers to the Hutterite people's being forgotten by those who share common ancestors with them, i.e. the people who live in present-day Germany. Given the fact that few Americans and Canadians know much about their Hutterite neighbors, the direct translation of the original German title seemed appropriate.

I would like to thank the following persons without whom the translation of *Das vergessene Volk* would not be a reality today:

Gerhard Martin Schmutterer, Professor Emeritus of Augustana College, from whom I borrowed Holzach's book three years ago; Sibylle Meyer-Chory, Rights Manager at Hoffmann und Campe, who supported the project through many encouraging letters; Freda Heyden, Michael Holzach's friend, who also corresponded with me; Christina Reimer, a student at Augustana College, who worked with me on the translation; Ron and Margaret Robinson, who found interest in the translation and considered it worthy of publishing; Gayle Emmel, who made the numerous corrections that rendered the translation readable; and my wife, Monica Oyen, who, three years ago, suggested that I translate the book.

Stephan Lhotzky
Sioux Falls
1992

THE TRANSLATOR

Stephan Lhotzky is a native of Lindau, Germany. He received his Abitur diploma from Johann-Sebastian-Bach-Gymnasium in Windsbach. He moved to the United States in 1978 and received his B.A. from Luther College with majors in French and German and his M.A. and Ph.D. in German Literature from the University of Colorado. He taught at North Central College, Naperville, Illinois, before moving to South Dakota in 1987. He lives with his wife Monica Oyen and his daughter Kara in Sioux Falls, where he has been Chair of the Modern Foreign Language Department at Augustana College since 1991.

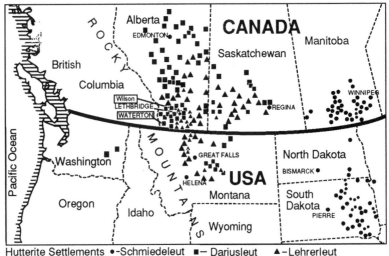

Hutterite Settlements •-Schmiedeleut ■— Dariusleut ▲-Lehrerleut

CONTENTS

Above: A 16th century illustration of a Hutterite family, its distinctive dress and building style. Below: A 17th century caricature of a Hutterite colony.

WINTER

Taking the Truck to God's Ark

Zwieback and bread are baked on Friday morning. Every third week, each woman has her "baking week duty," and every sixth week, she must work in the kitchen and milk the cows for seven days in a row.

A m I dreaming? Am I really sitting here in Sunday school, with a sanctimonious face, and rolling up spit-balls out of blotting paper? Am I sure these are my fellow students, the boys on the left side of the plain classroom, wearing black jackets which make them look like monks, their hair parted as if a ruler had been used, their laced shoes neat and shining? And on the right side the girls, a snowstorm of white-dotted kerchiefs, their pale faces are barely visible above the buttoned-up, high collars. I can see hardly anything but wide, floating garb — am I dreaming?

Yes, I am dreaming, but this dream is real! I am really sitting here wearing the standard jacket, with the part in my hair straight as a ruler line, with shining shoes, not any different from my neighbors, a stranger to myself for weeks already — a Hutterite.

A stranger to myself because, for weeks that seem like years to me, I have been living in the "Brudergemeinde Wilson," the brethren's community of Wilson, not far from the Rocky Mountains. Here, in the middle of the North American West, I am discovering a piece of living German past: the Hutterite people, long forgotten in Germany, followers of the anabaptist Jakob Hutter, who was burnt at the stake in Innsbruck in 1536, a people who have been on a sorrow-filled pilgrimage through the whole world for 450 years, "driven over the pasture like a herd of sheep," as the Hutterite chronicle recalls.

Throughout their history the Hutterites have been a thorn in the side of their fellow human beings mainly because they take the Bible at its word. The Ten Commandments are law to them, military service and adultery are horrors, and cursing and jealousy are the devil's work. To be able to love their neighbors as they love themselves, the Hutterites abolished private property 300 years before Karl Marx and have ever since lived according to the principle that "Everyone gives what he can and gets what he needs." In the empire of Charles V, this motto for life was just as provoking as it is today in the world of General Motors and McDonald's. The Hutterites, numbering more than 25,000, live in 200 small colonies that are called "brethren's communities" or "heavenly arks in the sea of earthly sin," far from the highways and widely scattered across the prairie. Two thirds of them are Canadians, and the others are citizens of the United States.

But first and foremost they consider themselves Hutterites, "God's holy people that He has chosen from all over the world and has called on of all peoples," as can be heard in a Hutterite children's prayer, "a thing for which we are despised, persecuted, and hated by all human beings."

As always at the beginning of Sunday school, we kneel down and say these words in prayer. The teacher Samuel Wurz, in front at the podium, is a stern man; with his pitch-black full beard, he makes an almost gloomy and threatening impression. He beats with his flat hand on the table whenever he feels it is time for a comma or a period, trying in vain to insert a little rhythm and emphasis into the mumbled murmur of our prayer: "We little and helpless children ask You from the bottom of our hearts, let us dwell in fear of You from childhood on, let us be brought up in Your obedience and in Your truth."

If I didn't have the words of the prayer before my eyes, I wouldn't be able to understand my own words. No matter with how much delay the teacher beats the rhythm, we still race through the 14 stanzas of the prayer at lightning speed in seven minutes, for the wooden floor is hard and our knees hurt. After a long-drawn-out "A-a-amen" which sounds like a relieved "Finally," we may sit down again. With a big gesture, teacher Samuel turns the pages of his worn-out bible. He looks for the reading that we heard this morning in the "Lehr" ("teaching"), the community's service. After he has found it, he looks straight at me from under his thick eyebrows. "Now, Miechel!" he shouts with strictness in his voice, and he really means me, "the Miechel who has come from Germany in order to get to know us Hutterites."

Yet it doesn't matter whether I come from Germany or from the moon. To the teacher I am, just like any other non-Hutterite, an "Englischa," a speaker of English, a "man of the world out there," baptized as a child and thus still not of age. Since the Hutterite anabaptists recognize baptism only if it is the conscious confession of faith by the adult Christian, I must attend Sunday school classes in spite of my being 31 years old — just like anyone who hasn't been baptized yet. Teacher Samuel is barely two years older than I, but the authority of his position as well as the apostolic dignity of his full beard make him appear to me almost like a father. "If you want to live here, you have to fit in," he tells me more than once a day. Therefore, he treats me as one of his 34 pupils and asks, "Well, Miechel, what did you hear today at the sermon?" I struggle to get up out of my bench, which is much too narrow and is way back in the last row, the spitballs still between my thumb and my index finger. Eighteen parted heads and sixteen kerchiefs turn around at me. I am as nervous as a little boy before confirmation. This morning the preacher Johannes Wurz, teacher Samuel's silver-bearded grandfather and spiritual head of the brethren's community, preached about the first letter of John for two hours. As in every sermon, there was much talk about light and darkness, about heavenly peace and eternal damnation. I memorized verse 16: "For all that is in the world," I quote the Bible with my eyes cast down, "the lust of the flesh, and the lust of the eyes, and the pride of life, is not of the Father, but is of the world." The teacher nods. "Sit down," he says curtly and lets his glance jump back and forth between the boys' side and the girls' side without moving his head. "Miechel here, he knows what he's talking about, he comes from the world out there. Eating, drinking, whoring — that's going on in Germany just as it is in Canada."

I feel I'm being put on the spot, but the teacher really doesn't mean to do this. On the contrary, he is almost impressed by how such a "man of the world," who really can't be blamed for having been born into the world, can stand to stay with the Hutterites for weeks, within the confined holy community, on the strait, narrow way which leadeth unto life (Matthew 7:15) without lust of the flesh, lust of the eyes, and the pride of life.

Here, in the brethren's community of Wilson, 120 people in twelve families live so close to one another that it seems as if there weren't enough space on this endless prairie bordered only on the west by the barrier of the Rocky Mountains. From a distance, Wilson appears to combine the features of an Israeli kibbutz and the Friedland refugee camp in West Germany: first the six long, gray living barracks, put up in rows of two from north to south; in front of them, the communal kitchen; behind them, the school building; and, a little further away, the stables, the shops, and the barns.

Working, praying, eating, sleeping — that's Hutterite life. The inner structure of the colony is as simple and clear as the view from the outside. God is "master of heaven and earth" and thus also master of the Hutterites, who are His holy people. God's representative in Wilson is the elected preacher Johannes Wurz, who has as many grandchildren and great-grandchildren as his life has years: 77. He was put at the head of the community as a shepherd who "will feed you with knowledge and understanding" (Jeremiah 3:15). At his side are his 58-year-old son, Georg Wurz, as the second preacher, along with the four brethren of the court: the "Säckelmann" or "housekeeper" Jakob Wurz, who is the preacher's brother and only two years younger than he; his second-oldest son Johannes, who, as "Weinzierl" ("winekeeper"), is in charge of the organization of work; the schoolteacher Samuel; and last, but not least, Johannes Hofer, bread cutter by trade, who must make sure that everybody gets enough to eat during mealtime. The brethren of the court are elected by the "Stiebel" (from the German "Stube" — a room in a house), which is the congregation composed of all baptized men, and are accountable to it.

The women have little say, either in the colony, where "the women keep silence in the churches" (1st Corinthians 14:34) or in the family, where "the husband is the head of the wife" (Ephesians 5:23). It is no coincidence that Wilson considers itself a brethren's community and does not mention the sisters. Their task is mainly to have children, a few less than a dozen on the average. During the past hundred years, God's holy people has doubled every 15 to 25 years — "God make you fruitful and multiply you" (Genesis 22). It is thus no surprise that the children and adolescents in Wilson form a majority of almost two thirds, a majority that the school teacher keeps under rigid control with a strictness taken from the Old Testament.

When Sunday school is over, after all of us have recited our little passages, sung a pious hymn and knelt for prayer one more time, schoolteacher Samuel takes out of the drawer an arm-long leather belt on which the words "Die liabe Ruthen" ("The Dear Rod") are inscribed; this is an indestructible heirloom from grandfather Johannes. Then, with his index finger, he motions nine-year-old Paul and eight-year-old Christian to come to his desk. Big words are not needed.

We all know what's coming now. Yesterday Paul and Christian were caught ice skating, and this, too, is a form of lust of the flesh to the Hutterites. The penalty is twelve "Deitsche" ("Germans"). Without a sound, Paul, as the older one, lies down first across the teacher's footstool. A dozen far-lifted blows rain down on the tightly pulled pants covering his rear end. The boy writhes like a worm on a hook. With his bare hands he tries to soften the force of the "Germans," but it seems that this hurts even more. His friend Christian has tears in his eyes just from watching. When it is his turn, the schoolmaster starts to sweat so much that he quits after ten blows.

After the whipping we have "Schutenhonkelich," the Hutterite sugar bread. With both ice skating sinners on his hands as if nothing has happened, Samuel walks with us across the yard from the schoolhouse to the communal kitchen ("Kuchel") for "Lunschen," lunching. There the women have already put the golden-brown bread made of flour, honey and cinnamon on the shelves. Each child grabs one piece in passing, first the boys, then the girls, the older ones before the younger ones. Only after all have helped themselves does Samuel take the last piece. We all sit down around the polished aluminum tables, here as everywhere separated according to gender and arranged according to age.

Elisabeth Hofer, the bread cutter's wife and mother of eleven children thus far, pours the watery youth-hostel coffee out of colossal tin pitchers into greenish plastic cups for us. Together with her neighbor, Rachel, and as does every woman between 16 and 50, she has kitchen service, "Kuchwuch," once every six weeks; then she must cook the meals, keep the kitchen clean, and serve. All women in the colonies do the dishes together after each of the three main meals, just as together they bake bread, wash the floor in the

---

Opposite Page, Top: *After their daily prayer, the brethren and sisters of the colony get ready for dinner. According to strict hierarchy, the men walk in front of the women and the older people in front of the younger ones. In the background the leaders of the congregation, the "shepherds," keep a watchful eye over the "Holy People."*

Bottom: *Those who don't memorize their verses well receive a spanking by the teacher after class since Solomon says that "he who spares the rod hates his son."*

schoolhouse, pull weeds in the summer or shake sunflower seeds in the fall.

Hutterites are alone only on rare occasions; the "Gmahschoft" (Gemeinschaft), the community, is their principle of existence.

Lunch takes place between the big meals, not in the eating halls for adults and children, but in the kitchen next to the immaculately clean ovens and cauldrons. "Cleanliness is next to Godliness," the Hutterite women say. Now everybody has a cup of coffee, and so we fold our hands. Paul prays out loud: "We ask You, Lord God, heavenly father, bless all these gifts of Yours that we take through Your rich gentleness and grace and have received through Jesum Christum. Amen." We nibble on our "Schutenhonkelich" in silence. To the Hutterites, eating is a sacred act; each cracker and each coffee bean is God's gift that is acknowledged in silence.

Those who want another cup briefly utter "coffee," and Elisabeth or Rachel comes and refills the cups. There aren't any real table manners. Maria, Rebecca and Ruth, at the age of six the smallest "Dindla" (girls) back at the end of the table, fish the soaked crackers out of the coffee cups with their hands without interference from the teacher. The main point is that everything goes down the throat as quickly as possible and without much enjoyment. For enjoyment gives birth to sin, and there is a straight line from sin to purgatory. "Live this life in joy and laughter, / There is only pain in death; / But a life that's filled with sorrow, / Gives you joy in your last breath." Thus go the words in one of the schoolmaster's favorite hymns. He and his brethren in faith strive to make life in the community as "lustless" as possible, which is not always an easy task, "for," as Samuel admits, "we Hutterites are made of blood and flesh like others."

Since "sin comes from a woman" (Sirach 25:32), Hutterite women and girls are required to hide everything that could be a source of lust for men's eyes. Every Saturday, after the weekend bath in the washhouse, the uncut and often knee-length hair is put into pigtails, squeezed together into a firm ball with strings and barrettes, and hidden under a double head-covering called "Mitz" ("cap") and the dotted "Tiechl," the kerchief. The women's dark-colored black, green, gray or blue-checkered skirts must have a minimum length: three inches above the ankle. A shorter skirt would be devil's work, in the teacher's view the beginning of a mini-skirt. The men's clothing is particularly simple: hats with a wide rim, jackets with hooks and eyes, pants held by wide suspenders that are called "Latrn," solid shoes — everything is black and humble ("demiatig").

The area of the Wilson colony includes 8,000 acres, yet I have been unable to find a single flower that was planted there; in the living quarters there is nothing that could entice the eye, no colored wallpaper, no pictures on the walls, no knickknack souvenirs from Miami Beach on the shelves and certainly no TV in the corner. Instead, there are only rooms painted white; solid chairs, tables and beds produced by the colony's own carpentry shop; hand-knit rag-rugs on the floor; and one naked light bulb in the exact center of every room's ceiling. Such simplicity and clarity actually have a liberating effect compared with the over-stuffed consumers' palaces of the world from which I come. I can't help but think of the paintings by old Dutch masters when I look into such a room in passing and see a woman bent over the sewing machine with her kerchief on, surrounded only by white walls.

And what a warm feeling it is to sit together at night in the shelter and security of an extended Hutterite family, for instance that of housekeeper Jakob, who sits on the wooden bench as the central figure, with white hair, as dignified as an apostle, surrounded by his sons Samuel, Georg, Joseph, and Heinrich. Behind the stove the "womenfolk" whisper, wife Susanne with sisters-in-law and female cousins, whirling knitting needles in their hands; on the floor, nothing but children, one or two dozen of the 54 Jakobean grandchildren or great-grandchildren, but also the sons and daughters of visitors from other colonies. We sit together like this almost every night, between 30 and 40 Hutterites in a room that is not really big, and we are satisfied with having each other. Whether the Chinese are now allowed to drink Coca-Cola, with whom Madame Trudeau is having an affair, what will become of Persia after the Shah's fall — all of this concerns nobody here, not even me, who used to read three different newspapers every day and was after news like the devil after a poor soul.

The news that moves us will soon be half a millennium old. It is passed on in four thick, black, leather-bound volumes, three old chronicles and a hymn book in which the ancestors wrote down their sufferings for the latter-born in lyrics and prose on a total of 3,404 pages. The hymn "From the Bottom of My Heart," for example, tells us what happened to the former monk Michael Sattler from Württemberg, one of the Hutterites' ancestors, "in the year of the Lord 1527, on the twenty-first day of the month of May" in Rottenburg on the Neckar River:

> "He was taken by the hangman, / And led straight to the town square. / There his tongue, it was cut out / As the tyrants thought was fair. / To a carriage was he tied, /But they were not satisfied. / Fiery tongs were the advice, / They embraced his body twice. Still this was not enough, / They led him then to die; /When they had left the town, / The godless crowd, oh why? / Remained there and stood still. / 'Twas Satan's work and will. / Three times they held him with the tongs, / It was their wish to kill. For more they thirsted still, / More than what's told us here; / They took him from this earth, / He died and had no fear. / They burnt him down to ashes, / And this is how

he died. / Oh God, have mercy on us all: /
The godless are such tyrants."

With a guttural voice, the housekeeper Jakob Wurz reads
out loud each line out of the 900-page "Hymn Book of the
Hutterite Brethren," and all those who are present in the
room re-chant his words, express their concern through
shrill lamenting, and scream out their fear of the devilish
world, a fear that seems to be just as great today as it was
during the times of Michael Sattler. I sit in the middle of
these screaming Hutterite hearts, every night deeply moved
again by these people's serious outlook on life. The scene
makes me think of African chants in the Kraal, the mystic
charming of ghosts; and again the question: Am I dreaming?

The martyr Michael Sattler belonged to a small, radical
group of Christians whose members dared not to give obedience to either the pope or the emperor, obeying only the
Bible and their conscience. The impulse of this anti-author-
itarian movement was given by the church reformers Martin
Luther and Ulrich Zwingli, both of whom the Hutterites
acknowledge to be the first to openly criticize the power of
the Catholic church. We read in the Hutterite chronicle, "In
the year 1519, they began to teach and to write: Martin
Luther, an Augustine monk at Wittenberg in Saxony, as well
as Ulrich Zwingli at Zurich in Switzerland, and they did so
against the evil horrors of the whores of Babylon, did so to
uncover and reveal all their cunning, drunkenness, and misdeeds; it was like blows of thunder that were used to strike
everything down."

According to the Hutterites, however, the protestant reformation came to a standstill at the very beginning because it
resulted in making arrangements with the political powers:
"Soon they clung to the worldly power and authority...
through which nothing better can be achieved... but through
which man relies more upon the help of man rather than
upon the help that comes from God." However, the rebels in
faith did not want to have anything to do with this world

anymore. "The Christian churches must consist of a holy and pure people, separated from the evils of the world; one must entirely give oneself to God in Christo, to sacrifice oneself, to give oneself and to part from the world," the old scripture quotes the ancestors' demands. In practice, this meant the negation of the Corpus Christianum, the unity of church and state which existed in Europe since the year 380, when the Roman emperor Theodosius raised Christianity to the status of the official religion. Through questioning this unity, the rebels threatened a main pillar of the basis of social order in the Hapsburg empire.

But the heretics went even further: They rattled at the foundations of the state and of the church itself. In "Seven Articles to Which Michael Sattler Gave Testimony With His Own Blood at Rottenburg on The Neckar River" are written down some of the principles that still today determine life at the Wilson colony. One such principle is the confession of absolute pacifism: "One shall not resist, even if the Turks invade the country, for it is written that thou shalt not kill. We shall not fight the Turks nor the ill-minded Christians but ask God in strict prayer that He supply resistance." Although the Old Testament required "an eye for an eye, a tooth for a tooth, a hand for a hand, a foot for a foot" (Exodus 21:24), new standards are set by the prince of peace, Jesus Christ: Whosoever shall smite thee on thy right cheek," says the son of God, "turn to him the other also" (Matthew 5:38). Thus the worldly authority that "beareth not the sword in vain" (Romans 13:4) cannot be composed of Christians. Therefore, a Christian cannot hold any worldly offices — an idea which led to the apolitical position of the brethren, who still today refuse to participate in general elections or other political events. It doesn't matter to them who governs the country, for their kingdom is not of this world. To them it is not the prime minister or the provincial governor who has true power, but God alone, and their commandments and prohibitions can be found in no legal code book other than Holy Scripture. "For in the division of the nations of the whole earth he set a ruler over every people; but Israel is the Lord's portion," we read in Sirach 17. The government, therefore, is an authority in charge of the order that God has given only to the heathens, and thus the chosen ones obey the worldly powers only if doing so does not make them sinners in the eyes of God: "We ought to obey God rather than men" (Acts 5:29), Peter admonishes. Even swearing an oath is not permitted to the believers, as Michael Sattler argues in his sixth chapter: "We believe that one must not swear an oath of loyalty to the authorities, for the Lord says in Matthew 5, thou shalt not forswear thyself; let your communication be Yea, yea; Nay, nay: for whatsoever is more than these cometh of evil."

In the ex-monk Sattler's opinion, what the churches — the Protestant church as well as the Catholic church — had done to the apostolic community of faith of early Christianity also came from evil. He maintained that the holy apostles had still been modest and upright men who endured persecution for their faith's sake, who lived in poverty and who did not convert their fellow human beings with the sword but with the word of God; all of this had now changed in a fundamental way. The pope, the so-called successor Petri and God's representative on earth, did not live in Christian poverty as had the son of God; rather, he lived in pompous wealth, and his churches resembled precious palaces rather than places of prayer and spiritual reflection.

Thus, the "heretics" wanted to return to the original Christianity. They joyfully accepted torture and exile, and images of Christ and statues of Mary were heathen masquerade. They even did without church buildings and held their prayers in living rooms, in hidden caves, or in the middle of the forest. "Where two or three are gathered in my name, I am amongst them," Christ says; of what use, then, are the "babylonic idol houses" of the Catholic church? Still today, the Hutterites do without pompous places of prayer and instead use the simple schoolroom or the eating hall; if, during field work, the way back to the colony is too far, they simply kneel down next to the tractor and fold their hands.

Splendor and material glitter are to the brethren and sisters the expression of the spiritual doom of the church, but it was not enough that the holy altars were stormed and that the images were torn from the church walls. It was Christian faith itself that had to be fundamentally renewed. Those things that the Bible did not command, Michael Sattler thought, were forbidden. "The mother of God and the saints as mediators and advocates sent before God? The scripture says nothing about this...and thus we do not recognize it." Thus, in his fifth article, Sattler argues for the prohibition of any adoration of saints.

The holy sacraments of baptism and communion, as the other Christian churches understood and practiced them, were and still are today to Michael Sattler's fellows in faith pure "idolatry." According to their belief, these holy acts are only "signs of a holy thing," unless the believer is ready to receive God's mercy through them. For this reason Sattler writes in his third article, the one which probably resulted in his execution, "Pertaining to baptism we say that a child's baptism is not useful for salvation, for it is written that we live only through faith. Therefore: Only he who believes *and* is baptized will have salvation." Baptism, "the answer of a good conscience toward God," (Peter 3:21) "thus presupposes faith and can therefore not be performed for a child for it knows neither good nor bad."

In regard to Holy Communion, the baptists refer to Christ himself, who said during the "Holy Meal" as he was breaking the bread, "This do in remembrance of me" (1 Corinthians 11:24). Here, too, bread and wine are only symbols of the Savior's crucifixion and not his own flesh and blood, as the Protestant and Catholic "idol-eaters" believe. "For it is but a mere sign, it cannot be the truth, as the pope and Luther said, and made idols out of bread," the Hutterites sing. In his article, the great ancestor Sattler mentions a naïve but nevertheless convincing argument directed against the idea of reincarnation: "Thus we read in the Scripture, 'Christ has ascended into heaven,' and it follows that he is in heaven and not in the bread, and therefore his body cannot be eaten with the bread." These seven articles, authored by the former monk Michael Sattler, are considered the oldest written testimony of the baptist faith. Toward the end of the third decade of the 16th century they spread very rapidly from the southern German language region up into Holland. Only a few years had passed since the first protestants in Zurich, the origin of the "baptist movement," rose against Zwingli, who had just successfully resisted the Catholic clergy. Then the revolutionary became a guardian of order and the persecuted a persecutor. First Zwingli exiled from the town the inconvenient citizens, the so-called Swiss Brethren, who considered his reforms to be not far-reaching enough. When exile proved ineffective, he tried to eliminate the anabaptists by having them drowned in the river.

In spite of high rewards and short court procedures, the heretic ideas of children's baptism as a "mire bath," of Holy Communion as "bread idolatry," and of Christianity as pacifistic could still not be banished from the face of the earth. A growing number of people from the entire southern German language region were baptized into the new faith and thus consciously violated the edict which emperor Charles V had proclaimed during the imperial diet at Speyer in 1529; it was an "ordinance against the anabaptists" according to which, "under penalty of death, no person who once was baptized according to Christian law may be baptized repeatedly or for a second time...."

In the "History Book of the Hutterite Brethren" we can see with what cruelty this law was enforced: "Several of them were stretched so fiercely that the sun could have been seen through their bodies; many were burnt to ashes and powder as heretics; many were fried at pillars; many torn with glowing tongs; many locked into houses and burnt with them; many executed by sword, strangled, and cut into pieces; many gagged with their tongues tied so they could not speak or defend themselves, and so they were led to the butcher's block and murdered in the devil's way. Several women were thrown into the water, taken out again and asked whether they wanted to abjure. When they refrained from doing so, they were drowned and killed. To others the pastors promised great gifts and wealth if they would just abjure, much power and many offices, but when they did not agree to do so, they were put into deep holes with rats and insects, and when their feet rotted away, the mice used their teeth on their living bodies. 'For thy sake we are killed all the day long; we are accounted as sheep for the slaughter' (Romans 8:36)."

Apparently nothing could bring the brethren and sisters, as the baptists called themselves, away from their faith, and no worldly treasures could be as precious to them as that which they believed they would gain through bearing pain and torture: eternal life in heavenly peace at the feet of the Lord.

The Hutterite chronicle reports of "many who were led to death and to the execution site; they sang and praised their God just like grooms on their way to the wedding, and the air resounded with their singing. When the time had come that they had to go to the place of death, young maidens put on their best dresses as if in anticipation of a day of joy... We see what diligent God-lovers they were, and God's fire was burning inside them; they preferred to die the most bitter death over giving up the truth that they had recognized."

This movement spread across the country like a brushfire. The people who watched the public executions were impressed by the intensity of faith of the sentenced. Instead of convincing the citizens of the so-called heretics' erroneous faith, the baptist tribunals gained much sympathy and acknowledgment for that faith among the population. Those who accept death so piously and joyfully, many thought, cannot really be the devil's hosts. "With this, God's people was growing daily in spite of all the misery," the Hutterite history book tells us.

Looking at the "List of Martyrs," we realize how widely the baptist faith had spread within just a few years: "In many towns a large number of faithful gave testimony of the truth with their own blood through fire, water, and the sword." In Austria, more than 700 heretics were killed, 79 in Swabia, 8 in Württemberg, 78 in Bavaria, 350 in the Palatinate, 617 in Alsace; in Switzerland, 42 men and women lost their lives.

By 1530 more than 2,000 baptists had died as martyrs for their faith, but between 12,000 and 15,000 brethren and sisters managed to escape to Moravia, where the rich and relatively independent country nobility granted them protection against the central power of the House of Hapsburg. Here in the country of Czech rebel of faith Johannes Hus (1370-1415), who in the 15th century had already criticized the Catholic teaching of Eucharistics and demanded the return to the early Christian ideal of poverty — here there was, for those times, such an unusual religious tolerance that the baptists even called it "our promised land."

It was in Moravia that, in 1529, the hatmaker Jakob Hutter appeared; he came from the village of Moos near Bruneck in the Puster valley in southern Tyrol. On his travels as a journeyman, young Hutter had learned about the Swiss Brethren's ideas and had soon joined them with great enthusiasm. Together with some fellow-believers he was looking for protection against Emperor Ferdinand's henchmen. In Austerlitz in Moravia he found a group of like-minded people who — unlike the majority of the baptists — not only formed a community in a spiritual sense but also kept all of their material possessions "in common." They believed that this was the only way to follow the example set by the original apostolic church, in which "those who believed were of one heart and soul, and no one said that any of the things which he possessed was his own, but they had everything in common," as Luke says in Acts 4:32. In the second chapter, verse 22, he expresses the same idea as follows: "And all who believed were together and had all things common."

Still today, teacher Samuel Wurz makes sure that all school children at the Wilson colony memorize the Hutterite "Community Song," a song which praises the renewal of the old godly order:

> "Destroyed was the community / With all apostles gone; / Through dev'lish cunning, jealousy, / Oppressed, changed to the wrong. / But now our God, the Lord / Has from His mercy rich / Awakened His community. / What the apostles teach / Is similar in deed and word.
>
> Community, our Christian mother / Has lost many a son; / Not Jakob Hutter, our brother, / The love of God he won. / He was a pious, upright man, / An enemy of selfishness, / With him only a few true men; / God gave protection in darkness."

First the hatmaker from Tyrol put the community of Austerlitz into order. In the case of several brethren, he noticed a "relapse into evil selfishness." On one he found 24 Gilders "in his own purse," "four pounds of Bern six-coins" on another. Hutter also searched the homes for prohibited private property and confiscated stacks of underwear and "much food and drink" that the sisters had taken from the community's kitchen. This strict enforcement then went too far for many a baptist, and many left the community. Secession was reached. On October 12, 1533, the ones who were "firm in their faith" elected Jakob to be their preacher. Less than three years was given to him to unite the brethren and sisters, who had been driven away from so many lands, into one community; this community would then survive many a mighty persecutor for many centuries.

Hutter succeeded because of a combination of his missionary ability to convince people and a very pronounced talent for organization. The unity of the teaching and the way of life was his key to success. He preached to his community that the true Christian must not only pray according to the Bible but also live by it. Even though such a life leads to eternal bliss, it would be full of abstinence and hardship. Only those who "have crucified the flesh with the affections and lusts" (Galatians 5:24) could have a place in the community of the chosen ones who would one day inherit the kingdom of God in heaven. Impure and independent souls must be kept away from the only church leading to bliss by being banned, "so that the good dough will not turn sour."

Thus a piece of sausage from the community's pantry in a brother's pocket, some undershirts purchased privately, or a Gilder which was not handed over could turn a chosen one into a sinner. "He that is faithful in that which is least is faithful also in much," we read in Luke 16:10. Hutter made sure that the community leaders whom he entrusted with considerable power of office put Luke's words into practice. These "foremen," "shepherds," or "guardians," as the elected leaders were called, were supposed to "cut off" the evil within the brethren's farms by isolating them from the surrounding world, no matter whether this world looked favorably upon the brethren or not.

In this, too, Hutter and his followers differed from the majority of the anabaptists. To the Dutch Mennonites or the Swiss Brethren, for example, the distance between them and those of different faiths was primarily a theological and not a practical consideration. Because they looked at the community proclaimed by the apostles as a spiritual "community of love" and not, as Hutter did, as a very real community of possessions, the distance between them and the world was more a logical result of expulsion. The distance between oneself and others, however, was and is to a Hutterite a religious doctrine.

In the same year that the hatmaker Jakob was elected to preside over the community, militant anabaptists captured the town of Münster in Westphalia, chased the bishop away, expropriated the property of the wealthy citizens, and proclaimed the kingdom of God on earth. To the Hapsburg Emperor Ferdinand the events in Münster were a welcome opportunity to intensify the pressure on the loathed heretics in his own empire. During the Moravian provincial diet at Znaim, the upper ranks of society finally gave in to his demand "to not tolerate the anabaptists any longer, but to decide to drive them away. "

The chronicle notes, "So Jakob took his bundle on his back, and so did all brethren and sisters as well as their children, and couple after couple followed Jakob, their shepherd; they went through the band of godless and infamous robbers who were grinding their teeth for evil and who harbored a desire and lust to rob and crush them. So the small group of the just were driven over the pasture like a herd of sheep and were prevented from settling down in one place."

In deepest desperation, Hutter, in a letter to the Imperial Commander of Moravia, emphasized that, in contrast to the Münsterites, his people did not intend to expropriate anyone's property and certainly did not want to convert anyone to the right faith by violent means. "Before we use our hands to beat our greatest enemies, not to speak of spears, swords, or halberds (as the world uses them), we would rather die and let our lives be taken." But all pleas for mercy failed. The commander made the expulsion even harsher by putting a price on Hutter's head. Because the community members worried about Jakob's safety, they urged him to return to Southern Tyrol and to hide out in the mountains for a while. Grievingly, Hutter said good-bye to his people. On his way to his former homeland, Imperial soldiers caught him near Klausen in Etsch country and brought him to Innsbruck, where he died at the stake on the Friday before the first week of Lent in 1536. However, in the heart of his community he will continue to "live until the end of the world."

Persecution continued under the new preacher, the cloth-maker Hans Amon from Bavaria. For almost 20 years, God's holy people wandered through the forests without rest. Holes in the ground served as temporary shelters, berries and poison ivy often were the only nourishment, and new-born babies died because their exhausted mothers could not feed them anymore. The misery was so great that at Easter time, during Holy Communion in "remembrance of the Lord," the bark from trees was broken instead of bread. Over and over again, when the people around found out about the wandering "heretics," the Imperial henchmen were soon there with "murder and fire and rape — worse than the Turks." Those who managed to save their lives during such ambushes by the authorities counted their blessings. Some brethren who were hiding near the lower Austrian town of Steinabrunn were arrested and brought to Triest, where they began service as slaves on Hapsburgian galleys in the war against the Turks. None of them ever returned.

Then, in 1556, as the history book continues, "a big comet star with a very long broom appeared in the sky and was seen." According to the brethren, this was God's sign to warn the earthlings. After the comet sighting, the situation lost some of its tension. Because of heavy fighting against Emperor Charles V, King Ferdinand had other worries; therefore the Hutterites could settle in Moravia again.

During the following 70 years, called by the brethren "our good time" or "the golden years," the communities of the sorely tried baptists blossomed under the protection of the Moravian nobility, who had regained their power. It was mostly through their handicraft skills, soon to be known and widely recognized, even outside of Moravia, that the Hut-terites developed into indispensable subjects of the rulers. Among the Hutterites were coppersmiths, sickle smiths, scythe smiths, locksmiths, and knife smiths; cartmakers, shoemakers, hatmakers, harnessmakers, sievemakers, lampmakers, and toolmakers; also saddlers, ropemakers, weavers, tanners, glassmakers, brewers, bookbinders, and slaters for thatched roofs. There was hardly a trade that could not be found in the colonies.

The Hutterites have preserved this kind of dexterity up to the present time. Each one of my brethren here at the Wilson colony perfectly masters on the average a good dozen trades. Samuel Wurz is not only the schoolteacher but also the community's gardener and bookbinder, and, if need be, he also works in the smithy and in the pigsty. Some years ago, when the schoolhouse was newly built, he had professionally laid the bricks, put in the timber work, poured the foundation and laid the electric wiring together with other "menfolk."

His brother Georg, "Hog-George," was also actively involved in the construction of the building. He makes shoes, sews horse saddles, boils soap, and takes care of the 100 sows of the Hutterite community together with his cousin Andreas, who is a tractor driver, duckbreeder, butcher, and broombinder. In the past, the old preacher used to work in the broom-bindery as well. Today Johannes is too old and "shaky" for this work. If he weren't approaching his eighties, he would now, as he did before, shear the sheep, tan the leather, milk the cows, do the plumbing, stand in the smokehouse during hog-butchering and ride on the combine through oats, rape, and winter wheat from early in the morning until late at night. Aside from his difficult work as the spiritual shepherd of the 120 people of the Wilson community, these days he takes care of the 300 fattened geese, but only from May to October.

As far as his learned trade is concerned, every Hutterite preacher is an ordinary member of the community; in one area he is the boss and is responsible for all, and in another area of colony economics he is a simple "hand." "We Hutterites can do everything," the old man tells me, and those

Broombinder Johannes produces approximately 30 brooms on a win-
ter day. The majority of the brooms are then sold to other Hutterite
farms or are exchanged for leather, wine, and small livestock.

who have carefully looked around his dominion must admit
that he is right. It is not only shoes, brooms, and cauldrons
that the brethren themselves produce; they also build automatic dough mixers, potato cleaners, laundry dryers and
even washing machines. They carefully inspect and measure
with a yardstick the machines exhibited at industrial trade-
fairs; their products are then much cruder but more solid
and often last three times as long as the original models. In
order to produce such miracles, the chosen ones do not
need to attend vocational schools or universities: "Commit
thy way unto the Lord; trust also in him; and he shall bring
it to pass (Psalm 37:5)."

The duck beheading machine has even been developed
from a Hutterite patent which is said to have originated in
late ancestor Jakob's times: An old horse cartwheel is put
up like a turnable table with one of its axles as the only
table leg. Eight tin-plate funnels with a wide opening on top
and a narrow opening at the bottom, similar to bullhorns,
are pinched between the spokes. When the 1500 ducks (the
Hutterite Sunday roasts) and the 300 fattened geese are
slaughtered in the fall, one person must stick the animals
into the funnel, "their little heads down, their little bottoms
up," as the old German nursery rhyme has it, and another
person stands across from him with the sharpened axe,
grabs the heads which hang down from the funnel, and cuts
the necks. The only work a third person must perform is to
pull the bled-out fowl from the rotating scaffold and carry it
to the slaughterhouse for plucking and drawing. What could
be a more effective way than that?

There is one trade, however, the secrets of which the
brethren and sisters have almost completely forgotten: nurs-
ing. Since medical treatment has become so cheap because
of general health insurance, the community people have
been sending their sick to St. Michael's Hospital in the
neighboring town of Lethbridge, and it bothers nobody that
this clinic is fully supported by the abominable Catholic

church. Few midwives, few "Kneiper" (masseurs), and few "bonesetters" are left in the colonies, and instead of finding cures through proven medicinal herbs as they did before, the Hutterites more and more often reach for antibiotics and aspirin in a quite worldly manner.

Their skill in medical treatment was very different four centuries ago in Moravia during the "golden years": Hutterites were good doctors and barbers and were sometimes consulted even by their worst enemies. Emperor Rudolph II, for example, had the "brotherly chief doctor" Georg Zobel come to his castle in Prague "since he had been lying down with a dangerous condition for a long time and could not become any better although many famous doctors and healers from Hispania, Italy, and other countries were with him." According to the history book, brother Zobel made the ruler well after six months, and "many gentlemen at court believed that the Emperor would have died had it not been for Georg."

These Moravian years between 1556 and 1593 were golden years for the baptists, not only in an economic but also in a spiritual sense. They owed this success to Peter Riedemann, a shoemaker from Silesia, who was very knowledgeable of the Bible, and to the Tyrolian scissors-grinder Peter Walbot, both of them "true credits to the entire community." As newly-elected preachers they developed a system for the Hutterite principles of faith and translated the theological positions into concrete instructions to be followed; even after 450 years, these instructions have lost hardly any of their binding nature for the Hutterite people. Peter Riedemann wrote the "Justification of our Religion, Teaching, and Faith," established in 1565 by the Brethren, as the Hutterites are called. Peter Walbot authored many hymns, prayers, sermons, and rules.

Both Riedemann and Walbot, who had formerly spread their faith among the population as missionaries and had often escaped death only very narrowly, were engaged in extensive missionary work with Moravia as their homebase. They sent so-called "messengers" to southern Germany as far as the Main River, to Austria and to Switzerland, and many of the messengers never returned. However, knowledge about the Hutterite communities, in which there was supposedly neither poverty nor wealth because everything was owned by everybody, and where thus jealousy, hatred, and quarrels were foreign to the people, and where instead only brotherly love reigned in the hearts — such knowledge, as well as almost incredible stories, spread quickly among the poor and enslaved population. People came in many groups, risked their lives, left the little they owned behind, and went to Moravia to the promised land of the godly communities. The Hutterite settlements very quickly reached approximately 30,000 members during those times. More than 100 colonies were founded, the economy flourished, and the nobility could not get enough of the industrious, god-fearing people.

Then, however, the Turks came, and with them came war:

"The enemy would move and turn, / Would rob and kill and burn; / This is what all had learned.

Misdeeds they did so wild / To old, to young, to husband, wife, / And would not spare the womb with child.

Many small children, even babes, / They fastened to their horses / At front and rear, as were their ways.

And those who did not please / Were thrown over the fence; / No one could give relief.

The mothers they saw this / Happening before their eyes / Much weeping, crying, begging would arise."

The hordes of Sultan Suleiman II burnt down 16 of the brethren's farms, killed 87 baptists, and carried off 238, mostly children, to be used as slaves in Turkey. When, after 13 years, the sons of Mohammed were finally defeated, the Thirty Years War broke out — the Hutterites remained stricken. In 1622, the emperor, the Bohemian king Ferdinand II, ordered the Hutterites to convert to Catholicism or leave his land of Moravia within four weeks. "Thus we left like the children of Israel," the chronicle notes without other comment. Siebenbürgen, however, the next station on their pilgrimage, was not the land of milk and honey either, and the plague awaited the chosen ones; one third of the population was freed from the misery of earthly existence. During the 18th century, Empress Maria Theresa sent the Jesuits to the survivors, had their children baptized by force, had the sermon books burnt and issued the order to catholicize the adults by means of club beatings. Worn out by endless persecution, many baptists, "not without remorse and tears," succumbed to the worldly power.

After even the community of possessions was abandoned, God's chosen people seemed to be near their end. But again a comet appeared in the skies, and as early as October 1755, 270 Protestants from Carinthia, artisans and peasants, arrived in the Hungarian diaspora; they had been driven away from their homeland by the Catholic empress. Persecuted for their faith, they read the writings of Peter Riedemann and Peter Walbot and decided to join those few brethren and sisters who were willing to again live according to their ancestors' order. This decision, however, provoked new conflicts with the house of Hapsburg and the religious mafia of the Jesuits.

In order to free themselves from these powers, the Hutterites again packed their bundles and went across the Transylvanian Alps into the Romanian Walachy. In primitive sod houses, they vegetated outside of Bucharest for 3 1/2 years. The climate and the lack of drinking water made life hard for the newcomers. To make matters worse, they were again between the fronts of two hostile armies during the war between Russia and Turkey. Thus it was not surprising that they followed the seducing call of Tsarina Catharine II, who, in her manifesto of 1763, made promises to all foreigners willing to immigrate "if they desire so to come into our empire... in order to find a permanent home;" she further promised freedom of religion as well as the freedom to abstain from any military or civil service. First the Hutterites settled in the Ukraine near Kiev, then they moved to the region north of the Black Sea into an area which was populated mostly by Mennonites, who were persecuted baptists just as they were, but who were opposed to the strict sharing of possessions. From the Mennonites the Hutterites learned most of the modern techniques of large-scale farming which they later continued to develop in America.

The Mennonite influence became stronger and stronger in the community life of the chosen people. For the first time in their history, they were not persecuted by those around them but welcomed as brethren and sisters related in faith. As external pressure eased, internal problems began to increase. The younger generation had never personally experienced the "evil and sinful world." What the young people knew were songs and stories about persecution and expulsion, about pillagings and the carrying-away of their ancestors, but their life in Russia was not bad. "Thus the old died and a generation grew who did not walk in their fathers' footsteps nor could appreciate their sour sweat," the chronicle informs us. "They thirsted for freedom, and each one of them wanted to have things go his way, which cannot be in the community."

Following the Mennonite model, many young heads of families began to work for their own pockets. What had once been small, private gardens in front of houses now grew into large fields; saddlers and carpenters sold their products for their individual profit instead of turning the money over to the housekeeper. The community of possessions was dead and gone. Again, the Hutterite proverb that "good times do not make good Christians" had held true.

Almost 30 years had gone by when, in 1859, the blacksmith Michael Waldner, the preacher in Huttertal, which had become a community that was a "Brethren's farm" in name only, had a dream full of meaning: An angel appeared to Michael and led him to the heavenly kingdom in order to show him how the heavenly hosts "glorified, honored and praised" their Lord with "unspeakably beautiful songs." Then, however, the angel pointed downward right into the realm of hell. "An unspeakably terrible sight" was revealed to the blacksmith, a sight "which no mortal is capable of imagining." Then Waldner asked his guide which of the two would be his place after his earthly death, heaven or hell? "Can you tell me," the angel replied, "whether anybody survived the flood who was not in Noah's ark? The ark, however, is the community, and now you know where you will end." To "Miechel the smith" this dream was a sign from God which told him to reintroduce the community of possessions according to the apostles' teachings. From then on, those brethren and sisters following his advice and again keeping "all things in common" called themselves the "Schmiedeleut" ("Smith people"). Shortly thereafter, the "Darius people" under Darius Walter followed this example; Darius Walter was the preacher in another community, and the colonists of the Wilson farm claim to be his descendants.

In Russia, the Hutterites lived without external oppression for almost 100 years. Then a wave of nationalism swept the Tsarist empire. General conscription was introduced, and in spite of all the promises made by the late Catharine II, the baptist minority was to be subjected to it as well. The Hutterites immediately sent delegates to America in order to explore the country and its political conditions. Unlike the United States, Canada guaranteed complete freedom from military service, but the soil and the climate in the province of Manitoba seemed to be much less suitable for farming than the fertile lands of South Dakota. Thus the decision was made to settle in South Dakota in the hope of a lasting peace:

> "The time and hour have now come, / It's to America we're gone; / The horses are now hitched by hand,
>
> We're going to a foreign land:
>
> Now all be strong and none be shy, / Don't make it hard to say good-bye. / There wind is wind, and dust is dust,
>
> There God is, too, in whom we trust.
>
> And when the voyage is begun, / Then many a good song is sung; / We do not fear the ocean there / For our God is everywhere."

The Hapag steam sailboat "Harmonia" took the first 113 Smith people from Hamburg to New York in 1874. Adults paid 32 dollars for the crossing, children under 12 half, and infants three dollars. During the following three years, 18,000 Mennonites and between 400 and 700 Hutterites came to America; most of them, however, settled as farmers on the prairie outside of the communities. Today this group of "prairie people" is almost totally integrated into American society. According to Hutterite tradition, the remaining brethren built their communities and named them after towns in the area. The Smith people's colony was named "Bon Home" and the Darius people's "Wolf Creek." The last group that came was that of the "Teacher people" ("Lehrerleut") with their preacher Jakob Wipf, who was a teacher. They founded the brethren's community of "Old Elmspring."

Although the fundamentals of their faiths have remained identical, the three Hutterite groups developed their own ways of life over the years. In a purely physical way, the different "people" can be distinguished by the fact that, for example, the "Teacher people's" women make dresses out of colorful material and the men have no moustaches. The

Smith people do not worry much about their attire in general. Today, their boys occasionally wear jeans, and some girls "forget" to cover their heads in the house. It is the Darius people who care for the old order in the strictest way. To them, "the apple rots first on the outside, then on the inside." Therefore, the women's dresses must be "humble" and in dark colors, and the men's pants must not be "styled" (too tight), as they are in the group of the Teacher people. Since their arrival in America, contact between the three groups has not been very close at all. Mutual visits are paid very rarely, and it is only in exceptional cases that, for example, a Darius girl marries a Smith boy. If they meet at a cattle auction in the neighborhood, they exchange friendly greetings, ask how things are going, and then try not to bid on the same bull in order to keep the price down.

It was only because of the anti-German campaign during the First World War that the "Hutterite Huns," as they were called by patriotic Americans, temporarily became a little closer to one other. Frightened and upset by anti-German demonstrations, the eldest of all three branches of brethren's communities authored a petition sent "to the honorable Woodrow Wilson, President of the United States, Washington D.C." asking "in all humbleness that we may be permitted to live according to our principles of conscience... that is in the community of possessions and pacifism, now and in the future as we have in the past." But all requests were futile. The hysteria of war could no longer be controlled. First the semi-official "State Council for Defense" prohibited the use of the German language in schools and churches. As one of the results, high school students in Yankton, South Dakota, a town with neighboring Hutterite communities, threw all their German books into the Missouri river. Then the Hutterite cattle were driven off the pastures because the brethren refused to buy "Liberty Bonds," i.e. war bonds. Finally, the military police of the U.S. Army deported able-bodied "Kaiser supporters" from the colonies to military camps. There they were stung with bayonets as if they were hogs being transported. They were hung by their feet, spat at, whipped and thrown into wet and cold cells where two of the Teacher people, Josef and Michael Hofer, died as a result of the abuse. This event made most of the Hutterites decide to settle in Canada immediately after the war. The forefathers of the Wilson colony, too, came from South Dakota in 1918 and settled in southern Alberta, 30 miles north of the border with the United States.

Only through a knowledge of the Hutterite's past am I able to understand their present. Through the singing meetings that take place in Jakob Wurz' crowded room every night, their story has become alive and contemporary to such an extent that I can hardly distinguish between yesterday and today, or between "Moravia Land" and Canada. As if I sat in a time machine, the centuries blend one into the other, and the times of the burning stakes and Turkish wars become a reality while the film "Saturday Night Fever" is probably in its 15th week in the neighboring town of Lethbridge, not even 30 miles from Wilson. To the people with whom I live here, the world has remained as strange and hostile as ever before, and what doesn't originate in the community is from "out there" and can mean only bad things.

Therefore I am not surprised at the frosty reception I received here at the brethren's settlement of Wilson, when, on a snowy and windy day in January, a truck filled with frozen meat took me to the colony's cow barn. There I was, the man of the world, a freezing stranger at 30 degrees below with no human soul in sight; the only living things I could see were the quietly goggling Holstein dairy cattle. The wind was driving grey smoke out of the chimneys of the houses into the god-forsaken, wintry desert made of ice and snow. Nothing stirred. The village seemed to play dead, yet I felt suspicious stares out of every darkened window. I was embarrassed and tried to act as naturally as possible, fumbled at my shoelaces which did not need tightening, watched the cows with great interest, and thus introduced myself to the invisible observers. After what seemed an eternity, the gate of the cow barn opened just a crack and a hand motioned me to approach. This was winekeeper Johannes' hand; he had been working on a broken waterpipe together with a dirty bunch of figures dressed in black. When I entered the barn with my two trunks, I was greeted by ice-cold silence. After a while, Johannes melted a little bit. "Well, you're from Germany," he asked, "how then did you get permission from the Catholics to come here?" I explained that the churches, even the Catholic church, were no longer as powerful as during Jakob Hutter's times, and that at least nobody was tortured or burnt alive for defending the faith any longer.

"And who taught you to speak German?" That the German language, their "holy tongue," is spoken in Germany as well was something the men in the cow barn could hardly comprehend.

To the Hutterites, language and faith are closely related to each other, and both make Hutterites different from those around them. The sermon during the service is delivered in the antiquated "High German" of the Hutterite "Books of Teachings" which have been copied by the preachers in painstakingly clear, old German handwriting during the long winter nights since the 16th and 17th centuries; slight linguistic corrections are made now and then under the influence of more recent Bible translations. About the creation of man on the sixth day — "so God created man in his own image" (Genesis 1:27) — we read in the "teaching" which was presumably written by the ancestor Peter Riedemann in the 16th century: "This means that He, according to all of the existing heavenly images, puts all faithful, pious, and just souls above everything and orders them to be in command, but that they cannot choose out of their own will but out of Godly order and spirit, but as we, too, just like He put everything in its right order, must profess His work toward the world in the right order, and must at all times be ready to show according to His instructions that our hands be offered to others so that we, too, are led on the road to perfection."

Just as complicated as the long-winded, tape-worm-like sentences of the written Hutterite language is the way they converse every day. The basis of the spoken language is a mixture of different upper German dialects, mostly Carinthian Tyrolese and Bavarian; however, linguistic traces of Hessian and Silesian can be detected as well. Thus still today, after almost half a millennium, we can determine from their language the geographical origins of the Hutterites whom Jakob Hutter united in his brethren's communities. The "Godly people's" subsequent way of the cross can also be easily reconstructed by noting the loan words from the old and from the more recent host countries; the Hutterite language is full of them: "Gasa" the Hutterites say in Romanian for potato soup, "Gugurutz" is Turkish for "corn," and the Russian words "Tchaikele," "Tchainikel," and "Tchabadan" mean seagull, tea kettle, and suitcase.

Naturally, most of the words that have been "hutterized" over the past one hundred years are English words: "Stamps" or "Matchstankele" (match sticks). When, for example, the Hutterites go shopping, they go to the "store." Sometimes the community must spend lots of "dollar" for a new machine, and if little Andreas doesn't do as he is supposed to, grandfather Jakob admonishes him, "Behaf di" (behave yourself). If a Hutterite is plagued by many worries, he has "plenty trouble." The everlasting cow barn inquisition conducted by winekeeper Johannes and his black bunch for my welcome was performed in a Bavarian-Austrian-English mixture. "What is your faith? Are your parents well? Do you have a TV at home? Are you baptized? What is your occupation? Do you have brothers and sisters? Do you smoke tobacco? Did you serve in the military? Did you come on the airship? At what airport did your airship land?"

This questioning lasted for hours, and the men dressed in black were particularly interested in the question "What has brought you here and what do you want?" This was a very embarrassing question for me. How could I explain to these shy and suspicious people what had brought me to them and what I wanted? How could I tell them that it had been purely by coincidence that I had read a remark about the Hutterites in one of the books by Erich Fromm, the well-known American psychoanalyst; in his book *To Have or to Be?*, he calls them a "religious community" which, in his opinion, coincides with the kibbutzim movement in Israel, the French *Communeautées de Travail*, and the thinking of such radical humanists as R. W. Emerson, Albert Schweitzer, Ernst Bloch, Ivan Illich, and Erhard Keppler in the following points (though the concepts are sometimes completely contradictory):

- that production must serve the real needs of the people, not the demands of the economic system;
- that a new relation must be established between people and nature, one of cooperation not of exploitation;
- that mutual antagonism must be replaced by solidarity;
- that the aim of all social arrangements must be human well-being and the prevention of ill-being;
- that not maximum consumption but sane consumption that furthers well-being must be striven for;
- that the individual must be an active, not a passive, participant in social life.

Up to that point, I had never heard about the "Hutteriten," as Fromm's German translator calls the Hutterites. I became curious and then found a library book from 1927 entitled *The Communism of the Moravian Anabaptists*. In this book, the author, the late Lydia Müller, states that today the Hutterites are still living in North America and that their secluded way of life has not changed fundamentally since the 16th century.

At the time when I read this book, there was already much talk about an "alternative lifestyle," and I, too, was sick of the society of consumption and tired of wealth. After my university education, attracted by possessions and success, I was proud to have gotten a secure job as a reporter for the well-respected magazine *Die Zeit* and was not ashamed of my fat bank account. Personal crises (for example, difficulties with my girlfriend or never-to-be-resolved problems with my mother) I suppressed through hard work, and I became more and more like my father, who took his life at age 65 after a lifetime of hard work. Afraid to go on living as before, I went to my boss and gave notice (but in a cowardly fashion making sure I would be rehired at a later date). I wanted to try to break away into a world with totally different values, different goals, and different hopes, but still a world which, in its origin, seemed to be somewhat related to my own person. Having gotten rid of my apartment, I flew to western Canada five days after New Year's Eve to the area in which the Hutterites must have their settlements, according to my vague knowledge. At the town hall of Lethbridge, a small, provincial town 200 miles south of Calgary, I asked about the anabaptists and was given the address of the Wilson colony.

Thus it had happened, but how could I explain all that to the Hutterites themselves? Presumably, Erich Fromm wouldn't mean anything to them, and I didn't want to start talking about fears related to my career or about my problems with women. Nobody would have understood. I decided to say that I had simply come in order to learn more about Hutterite life, that I had taken a year off, and that I was willing to integrate myself totally into the community, to share in the work, the prayers, the songs — in short, to experience everything first-hand in order to some day maybe write a book about my experiences.

Winekeeper Johannes didn't like this at all: "What do you want to write that book for?" he asked skeptically. "Do you want to use us to make money?" The idea that someone from "the world out there" would come and make a business out of God's chosen people for his own profit obviously disgusted him and the other brethren. I tried to explain to them that money was not so important to me and that back home in Germany I could earn more by holding a steady and high-paying job. No, I told them, the things that were important to me were the personal experience of getting to know this small, almost forgotten people and the hope that I might learn much which I couldn't learn in the world. "We send no willing man away," Johannes said to me after having hesitated for a long time, "and we are going to discuss the matter with the preacher." With this said, the men turned back to their leaking waterpipe and continued their repair work, which they had been neglecting during our conversation. I sat down on one of my trunks and watched them. Just as in a surgery room, everybody here seemed to know exactly when he had to do what, so before I got a chance to become impatient, the water main was fixed.

Now the winekeeper took me to his grandfather, the old and honorable Johannes Wurz, called "cousin Johannes," head of all Darius colonies, a patriarch with a long, white beard. Johannes received me sitting on a rough-carpeted wooden bench right next to a rustling gas oven. His feet were covered by thick felt slippers, and his hands were holding a heavy bible. Here, as in the cow barn, there was neither handshake nor greeting of welcome, but only silence and skeptical glances. The whole questioning started again, and the women in the adjoining room, the door of which stood wide open, perked up their ears. The preacher wanted to know everything in much greater detail than had the men in the cow barn, and some of these details surprised me. For example, he asked how many people fit into the "airship" that had carried me to Canada, whether it was only women who waited on the passengers or also men, and how many pilots it took to steer the "airship." Only at the end did we talk about my "request" to live in Wilson. Johannes said that if I could keep the strict community rules, which would be found out very soon, he wouldn't be opposed to giving it a try — "for God's sake." After the old man had finally given his holy okay, I could have shouted with joy. Although with reservation, I was nevertheless accepted by God's chosen people. The long trip had not been taken for nothing. However, ominous anguish was mixed with this joy: one year in God's ark, one year without lust of the eyes, without lust of the flesh, and without living in pride — wouldn't this be too much for a sinful man of the world like myself? It was good that the preacher Johannes did not know my thoughts at that moment.

In the Hutterite language, which was, at the time, incomprehensible to me, he gave some quick orders to the men in the room as well as to the women in the next room. Then several young fellows showed me the way to a small, shingle-covered wooden barracks, the "bookbinder's house," at the edge of the colony, where I was to have my quarters next to paper presses and glue cans.

They furnished me with a wide double bed, a newly bound bible as reading material, and washing utensils with a towel and home-cooked soap; a table, a chair, and a trunk for clothes had already been in my room. A Hutterite doesn't need more. A path leading to the outhouse was shovelled through a huge snowdrift. In case I might have problems with my bowel movements at minus 20 or 30 Canadian degrees, the landlord Jakob promised me prunes as a laxative.

So that I wouldn't set a bad example for the colony's unbaptized adolescents, shepherd Samuel, the treasurer's son, came before the evening service in order to cut my hair down to standard length. As he cut my hair around the ears and down the neck very quickly, not in steps but in a square, Prussian-like military style, he quoted from First Corinthians 11:14: "Doeth not even nature itself teach you, that, if man have long hair, it is a shame unto him?" The women joined us, between ten and fifteen in a group, mainly out of curiosity ("Do you already have a girlfriend?"), but also to take measurements for my hand-tailored Hutterite wardrobe.

As soon as my measurements had been taken in inches and yards, a piercing cry came from outside: "Praaayyyer!" At once, the men left my little house, and I followed them. We stepped into a long, marching row of silent Hutterites led by the community's shepherd, the preacher Johannes. The procession went through a narrow ditch in the snow to the daily service in the schoolhouse. An icy wind had started to blow, and the girls' wide skirts fluttered like flags. The men turned their heads against the wind and held their hats with their hands.

According to my age, I was assigned a seat on the second-to-last bench between the 30-year-old smith Benjamin and Georg, who was three years older, a shoemaker and hog-boss by trade. As if in a state of trance, I experienced my first evening prayer in the sweet and stuffy smell of a poorly ventilated classroom. I listened to the screeching singing dominated by the shrill women's voices on the left and the children's from up front. I saw the staring glances of the full-bearded brethren of the court, who were sitting at the head of the room turned toward the faithful — biblical figures — and who were barely distinguishable from one another. I listened to the conjuring sermon delivered by the dignified Johannes without understanding a word of it, but his admonishing right index finger pointing over and over again to the ceiling made me realize what the sermon was about. Together with the others, I fell down on my knees for the prayer of nine long stanzas and hardly noticed that my knees hurt.

Only then did I fully realize that this trip of 7,000 miles from Germany had brought me not only to a foreign country but also to a different time. Here, in the brethren's community of Wilson, the clock had been stopped centuries ago, had been stopped by a "Godly order" in spite of emperors, sultans, tsars, popes, and presidents. I felt consternation and familiarity at the same time, like a very old man who, after centuries, returns to the long-forgotten places of his childhood. On the blackboard behind the preacher there was something written in beautiful, old-German style, the way I had learned it as a first-grader and had soon afterwards forgotten. And the women's kerchiefs reminded me of my Silesian grandmother, who had never walked in the street without her "little cloth," not even during the hot summers after the war. Here, in "God's Ark," I was somehow to find the way back to myself, back to my origins.

This feeling became even stronger immediately after the prayer, when I sat down for supper at one of the three long men's tables, hemmed in between the smith and the hog-keeper. On my plastic plate there were three glassy-eyed, boiled duck heads which were supposed to be eaten with a hearty potato soup and semi-sweet zwieback. First I ate the soup while watching my neighbors in order to find out how they would handle the duck heads. With their forks they scooped the cheek meat out of the skull, nibbled on the necks until the vertebrae were bare, and then, as if it were a nut, crushed the top of the skull with their molar teeth. Since all of them, men and women alike, started to bite at approximately the same time, there was a noise as if the trees of an entire oak forest were being cut down. I lost my appetite, but I knew what was at stake. In order not to create a bad first impression, I also cracked a skull and sucked out the brain for which I would have paid a lot of money in a specialty restaurant — here I tasted only soft-boiled cartilage from a foot. Fortunately, there was no time left for me to start on the remaining duck heads as we already folded our hands and treasurer Jakob (as the oldest man in the dining hall) spoke the final prayer: "Fame, praise, and thank for meat and drink. God's grace has nurtured us physically, Lord, nurture us spiritually as well through Jesum Christum. Amen."

While I was still under shock from the duck meal, they led me to the preacher Johannes, who, as usual, did not eat with the community but at home with his son Jerg, his deputy. (As I found out later, these private meals are the only privilege that a Hutterite preacher has. The food itself is the same as that of the other community members.) Johannes had one very specific question regarding my place of residence in Germany. Gnawing on his last duck head, the old man wanted to know where in Hamburg the "hole" was, and whether I had heard about or even seen it. At first, I didn't understand anything. What hole? "Well, the hole into which the bad daughter went," the preacher said. "Which bad daughter?" I asked and wondered whether the old man had all his marbles. Instead of answering, Johannes and his entire family sang a song to me, the song of "the bad daughter":

"I will tell you of a city, / In Hesse land it's found,

The name of it is Hamburg, / It's well known all around.

A good and righteous man lived there, / Wheel casting was his trade, / This man was rich and fair.

His name, it was Jerg Schneider, / All knew him by this name. / He found a wife and married / When he was thirty-four. / A good, god-fearing man was he, / And with his wife he had a girl, / An only little child was she."

This little daughter, the song tells us in 19 long-winded stanzas, became disobedient to her parents. She did not want to be "bent," "ran through all the boys' streets, and was full of sin and shame." When the girl wanted to marry a young street actor against her parents' will, then happened what had to happen:

> "The daughter began to tremble / And, by my words, to shake, / A frightening noise then came / And everything fell down. / A smoke appeared so thick and warm / Through which the young girl sank / In misery, up to her arms.
>
> Then she burned like sulphur, / And sulphur was the smell, / Her father, he came to her, / Fearful was he of hell. / A goat jumped at the girl so young, / He was surrounded by hot flames / And licked her with his tongue.
>
> And then the daughter disappeared, / Went down with the burning goat, / The fearful people could not see
>
> Anything but that hole / Into which the daughter sank;
>
> One heard her screaming miserably, / She cried out once and again."

Just two days earlier, I had eaten breakfast in Hamburg, a city which lies on the river Elbe and not in Hesse, as the Hutterites are surprised to learn. Now I found out not only that this city is the gateway to the world but that the gate of hell must be there as well. That evening nobody could believe that I had never heard nor seen nor smelled that sulfuric Hanseatic gate of hell. (I decided not to mention the Reeperbahn, Hamburg's famous amusement and red light district.) The preacher Johannes looked at me with a skeptical, almost confused expression. His view of the world seemed to be a little shaken for the moment. Overall, we had all been a little much for one another, the Hutterites for me and I for them. We needed a break in order to digest all the new impressions, and thus, on that snowy January evening, the chosen colonists went to bed even earlier than usual.

At nine o'clock I was lying in my feather bed after I had run over to the kitchen building to get a pail of water for washing; that building and the cow barn are the only places in the village with running water. First I had wanted to write down my first impressions in my diary, but then I was too tired. The low rustling of the gas oven accompanied me into a deep sleep. It was just like sinking into the night, like a long fall into the darkness of a bottomless well. The deeper I fell, the more pressing the blackness around me became, and the faster I fell. I felt massive and heavy objects fly by me without seeing them. In order to avoid a collision, I took my legs into my arms so that I could be as small as possible; I wanted to hide in this darkness. I started to become hot in my confined position. Sweat ran into my eyes, drops which blinded me like headlights on a country road at night. Blindly I fell through glistening light and dead darkness and was stunned by this extraordinarily rapid fall and paralyzed by fear of striking the ground, which, though not there, seemed close and inevitable. Instead, I suddenly heard the incessant ringing of a distant bell.

When I opened my eyes, I was surrounded by darkness just as in my dream. The gas oven was still rustling. The luminous dials of my watch indicated that it was seven o'clock — the beginning of breakfast. I must have slept through the wake-up ringing half an hour earlier. As I entered the kitchen only minutes later without having washed and with the sleep still in my eyes, the community members were already leaving the dining hall. But Rachel Wurz, the haggard kitchen mistress and mother of nine, had seen that coming and had put a plate and a cup, zwieback and jam for me on the buffet next to the oven. "Have to get used to it" were the words with which she excused my tardiness.

While I was having breakfast, the women did the dishes. Forming a circle around a big aluminum tub, they stood there shoulder to shoulder, some in rubber boots, all under snowflake-kerchiefs, whispering and laughing as if they had been drinking. Maybe, so my thoughts went, my presence was somehow humorous. After the uneasy impressions of the previous day, this cheerfulness felt good. I ate masses of the soft zwieback slices, and they tasted better than the duck heads. Rachel noticed this and nodded with satisfaction. "You had to be hungry in Germany?" she asked me and was moved. "Here with us, you don't need to worry; there's meat every day." Her motherliness gave me a warm feeling. There cannot be too many places in the world, so I said to myself, where you can just come in as a total stranger without notice and, after not even a day, have your own roof over your head; where there's a warm bed; where somebody is working on your tailored clothes; and where in the morning the breakfast is kept warm on the kitchen table for those who sleep in.

The Hutterites had even thought of a steady work place for me. While I was still chewing my zwieback, winekeeper Johannes entered the kitchen in order to tell me that I should help in the cow barn until further notice. For this work he gave me felt-lined boots which were wider than they were long, coarse working gloves from a neighboring colony's leather shop, and a black racketeer's cap with a visor and ear flops (called "Katuss" in Hutterite-Russian) in which I felt like a Berlin paper boy during the twenties. The boots and gloves fit well; the cap was at first a little tight around my skull, but Johannes said that the sweat would stretch it eventually.

Full of optimism, I used my new footgear to trudge through the blowing snow to the cow barn and was determined to prove myself in the service of the community. The north wind bit my face so sharply that my eyes were watering, but for this short distance the temperature of 30 to 40 degrees below was actually fun. I enjoyed how the icy air made the inside of my nostrils freeze for seconds when I was breathing in. That's better than the Hanseatic winter with its sleet and rain, I thought to myself.

In the cow barn, three fellows between boyhood and manhood, as strong as bears, received me grinning skeptically. They were tall Heinrich and his two cousins Samuel and Andreas, who were wearing the same kind of felt boots, gloves, and racketeer's caps as I. I rubbed my cold nose and, slightly embarrassed, said hello. Instead of responding with a greeting, Heinrich handed me a dirty manure scraper and asked rhetorically, "Can you work?" That I, the man from the world, a big city boy on top of it, would be able to work and be useful to this heavenly ark was something none of the three really believed, and my first futile attempt at scraping the frozen cow pies off the wooden planks and pushing them through the cracks of the floor seemed to prove them right: First I slipped and landed on my elbows in the dirt. Put to shame, I lay there, but my colleagues were patient with me. Eagerly they showed me how the cow pies must be loosened from the floor with the right grip and the right thrust, and they obviously enjoyed their rustic Hutterite superiority. Even without my helping, the barn floor was cleaned within 15 minutes. Heinrich opened the tall barn door and whistled for his dog. "Bring'em in, Berry!" he shouted at the black and white spotted mixed-breed. With short and quick leaps, the dog flew through the powder snow in a wide arch toward the thirty cows standing a little forlornly at the colony's entrance, their rear ends turned toward the cold wind. When the cattle heard Berry's hoarse barking, they slowly accelerated their heavy bodies and hurried with swinging udders past the cow barn toward a fenced-in area where there was a towering haystack. I thought it strange that the animals had to be chased even to the place where they were fed, but maybe even the appetite freezes at these arctic temperatures.

With Samuel and Andreas I climbed up to the top of the
haystack, dug the bales out of the fresh snow, and threw
them down, directly into the crib. Heinrich stood there, cut
the hemp strings with which the hay was tied together, and
evenly distributed the bales into the troughs. Then we put a
load of hay on the trailer of a tractor and drove out of the
colony through the blinding white of the winter prairie to the
brown meat cattle that hibernated somewhere in the cold.
Their warm bodies snuggled tightly together, the 130 "Her-
forts" welcomed us with steaming noses — a small, dark
oasis of muscular flesh and hairy winter coat in the middle
of the snowy Canadian desert. To me it seemed to be almost
unbelievable that those creatures could survive out there
without shelter and at nightly temperatures of minus 50
degrees. But the boys thought that it was good for the animals, that it would make them "tough."

And being "tough," being hardy and resistant — that was
also my companions' goal. In a very provoking manner, they
left their ear flops folded up on this trip out to the cattle,
just as if they were going out for spring planting. I myself, on
the other hand, had to repeatedly rub some warmth into my
nose or it would have miserably frozen before our return to
the colony. The boys saw that and smiled complacently.
They seemed determined to demonstrate to me that their
fathers' claim to be chosen applied to them as well, not only
in heaven, but already here on earth. They wanted to prove
this to themselves and to me by being better at scratching
off the cow manure, by not letting the frosty wind bite them,
and finally by lifting two hay bales from the trailer at the
same time while I had quite a few problems lifting one.

My presence must have been a tremendously provoking
challenge for the three since, even after six weeks of barn-
cleaning and feeding, the daily competition in work between
the team of the chosen ones and me, the ordinary person,
had lost nothing of its intensity. On the contrary, once the
morning chores were over, it was mainly Heinrich, the tough

egg, who suggested comparing strengths by way of finger-pulling, throwing snowballs, or performing pull-ups. If they ran out of ideas, one cried out all of a sudden, "Who'll be first at the bell, you or we?" And up we jumped and started running, and he who first touched the bell in front of the kitchen was the winner. If it was one of my competitors, he had won as a representative of all Hutterites; if I was the winner, a point was given to the world. Naturally, the black collective had a sky-high lead over me, the single soldier.

Every morning around 8:30 there is "lunch" in the kitchen. As always, we meet Hog-Jerg with his two adolescent apprentices Samuel and Martin. When one is around them, one can all too distinctly smell where they have just come from. Next to them sits Georg, a colossus of 180 pounds who could easily match his strength with any of his 300 fattening bulls. My personal barber, the shepherd Samuel, is also there with his dog and his helpers, and Jakob announces as talkatively as ever the exact laying results of his 2850 hens.

After the short zwieback snack, the farmers very quickly turn into artisans. Georg binds brooms, Martin sews saddles, Samuel and Hog-Jerg make shoes, and Jakob fixes the generator of a gigantic tractor in the smithy. After my job as a cowfeeder, I am transformed into a shoemaker's apprentice. During the first two weeks of my training, I rolled fine hempstrings into tear-proof sewing yarn with my flat hand on my upper thigh, all under the shepherd's patient supervision. Then I had to thoroughly rub the string with impregnating beeswax before I could give it the Hutterite color with a piece of cobbler's wax. These strings are approximately four meters long, and are used to sew the shaft and sole together.

After having learned to master light cobbling tasks during those early weeks, I now, six weeks after my arrival, make my first pair of children's shoes, half-high laced boots, size I — size 28 in German standard. "The kids are not so picky," the shepherd says; the children don't mind if I don't always sew a straight line. The main thing is that the heels, made of old tires, be of equal height, "for otherwise they will walk themselves into cripples."

Working conditions here in the "cobbler's house" are excellent. Pressure to produce can hardly be felt. It is true that every year one pair of shoes per colony inhabitant must be manufactured and just as many old ones must be repaired, but the Canadian winter is long, and Jerg, the "boss" in charge, his assistant Samuel, as well as the three apprentices have much time for chatting, for napping from twelve to one, and, of course, for "lunching" in between in the kitchen with coffee and zwieback and "Schutenhonke-lich." We never work for more than 2 1/2 hours at a time.

With the authority of their knowledge, Jerg and Samuel teach the three apprentices. I rarely hear a sharp word, not even when the boys come late or sit in a corner being silly for a change. Yet, or maybe as a result, they learn their trade faster here than they would out in the world. A Hutterite job training usually lasts from fall, after the harvest has been stored in the barns, until the planting season in the spring. Thereafter the apprentice knows how to make shoes for even the very "picky" women, work for which each millimeter counts.

I glue, sew, and nail on my children's shoes for three days until they are finished. Then Samuel gets his four-year-old son Martin from the "Little School," the kindergarten, for the fitting. The size is right, the tire heels have almost exactly equal height, and Martin will not walk himself into a cripple in his new Sunday shoes. I cannot recall a moment at which I was as proud of my work as when I saw the little fellow walk through the shop in my shoes. His father has taught me to make use of my hands, and I have acquired dexterity and am thus useful. In the past, I could hardly pound a nail into a wall, and now I am a shoemaker!

Martin's new Sunday shoes have also helped to decrease the distance that can still be felt between the Hutterites and myself. In a physical sense, all differences have long disappeared since I have been wearing my tailored Hutterite costume including the suspenders, the jacket, and the wide-rimmed hat over my parted hair day after day. I have even grown a thin beard although normally only married men do this. Considering my age, however, the preacher Johannes suggested the beard, because what Hutterite will get married after he is older than 30? The inner distance to my surroundings, however, has seemed insurmountable for a long time. Even though I am constantly among people, I often feel terribly lonely and forsaken, cut off from the outside world, my world, like a man shipwrecked on a raft. Nobody here is able to understand that I once lived with a woman "like husband and wife" but am not married. All heard with disbelief that I hadn't been to church for years and that I had even officially left it when I was 20. It was a big surprise when I told them that my father had killed as a soldier and that my parents are divorced. In the heavenly ark of Wilson, these things become hard for me to believe. When we are feeding the cows, the boys tell me over and over again about the terrible rumors about my person that are spread in the colony: that I am a marriage swindler who has left wife and children in Germany, a bank robber who is hiding from the law, even a spy sent by the Vatican. One night the preacher asked me bluntly whether I kept a shotgun in my suitcase, and he justified his worry: "You have to know we have widows and orphans in our community."

Those who know a Hutterite's view of the world understand his mistrust: "For without are the dogs, and sorcerors, and whoremongers, and murderers, and idolaters, and whosoever loveth and maketh a lie" (Revelation of John 22:15). And now here comes "a man, an English one" from the bad world, from Hamburg of all places — a man who totally subjects himself to the divine order just to write a

book about it afterwards, a man who diligently feeds the
cows every day, who is never absent during the prayer and
who can now even make shoes "just like a Hutterite." Every
community service is a religious service, and thus the shoes
that I made for Martin are, in everybody's eyes, a good deed
which seems to counter all evil rumors. In spite of the centuries which separate us, we thus get a little closer.

On Sundays, the older classmates from Sunday school
even visit me in the book-binder's hut. Heinrich, Samuel,
and Andreas are almost always among the first, but here
they act differently than in the morning, scraping manure
and feeding the cattle: Here at my place, they don't act
tough but more like curious children. Everything I brought
from the world in my suitcase is of burning interest to them:
my hiking boots with the red laces, the plastic forks and
knives from the "airship," my diary, my deodorant stick.
They touch everything, they sniff everything, they try everything out. Within a short period of time, my aftershave bottle
is empty, and on Sunday my bookbinder's house often
smells like a Turkish bath. Heinrich loves to put on my
woolen Swedish gloves and to practice shadow-boxing. To
me, the boys seem like wild Indians, and I play Columbus.
That this perception of them as equivalent to "redskins," foreign to all civilization, cannot be entirely correct is something I notice only after Heinrich and others like him have
dropped some of their prejudices toward me and when I hear
from them about behavior of theirs which the strict
schoolteacher would be likely to punish with several dozens
of rod blows.

For example, Heinrich brags to me that he secretly owns
an old transistor radio. At night, when all are asleep, he listens to the sporting news under his blanket. I now understand how he is fairly well-informed about the rankings of
the Canadian ice hockey league. He is a fan of the "Edmonton Oilers." As if he wants to prove his worldliness in front of
the sinful man of the world, he tells me under the seal of

secrecy how (as a Hutterite) you get hold of such works of the devil: around the colony, you put up fox traps and catch two or three animals in one winter. The precious skins are then brought to a community neighbor who is in on the secret; he sells them at a good price and makes his Hutterite supplier happy with a meager percentage of his profit. Instead of cash, the neighbor sometimes pays with old ice skates, with flashlights, or, as in Heinrich's case, with a used radio. The batteries, however, have now been dead for weeks. Only when the next fox steps into Heinrich's iron will he again be able to listen to the sporting news — and that may take a while.

The young Hutterites consider these little side transactions as excusable since they have not yet been baptized and are therefore not full members of the chosen people. "As long as we are young, we enjoy life," says Heinrich with a twinkling of his eye. It seems that not even his schoolteacher's leather belt has been able to save the 21-year-old from leading a sinful life. In principle, however, he is all for his community. "We Hutterites are all right," he says. "We are the greatest." This sounds a little like the way he talks about the "Edmonton Oilers." When I ask him "Why the greatest?," he answers spontaneously, "Why, we are a community." Being part of the community means to him not to live alone and work against one another but to live together and work for one another. That this is much better one can see just by looking at the fox hunt — foxes would never be hunted by an individual but always in a team that would then split the profit in a Christian manner. To the boys, this is the secret of why they are much more successful at hunting than any of their worldly neighbors. And what farmers of the surrounding area could afford such modern equipment — six combines, seven tractors, a smithy with all the necessary equipment, and a pigsty with an automatic feeding installation? Who else makes such solid shoes, such long-lasting brooms, such good leather? Who has the strongest oxen, and who harvests the most wheat? — "We Hutterites," Heinrich answers the questions he has asked himself, and his Sunday school companions nod in agreement. It was young kibbuzniks in Israel that I heard rave about their communes similarly to Heinrich. It is a minority's elitist pride that is showing here. I think it only good that schoolteacher Samuel or even the preacher Johannes cannot hear what Heinrich has just been saying. Solid shoes, strong tractors, and fat hogs are certainly no argument to them. To them, these are "temporaneous things," lowly, worldly, fleeting. Hutterite life, however, is based upon the "spiritual," upon faith, the eternal, heavenly — which is the opposite. Even if this way of life resulted in economic ruin, it would still be the only possible lifestyle for a true Hutterite Christian, just as it was in Hungary during the Thirty Years War when the colonists were always preferred victims of the pillaging soldiers, who could always get more out of the colonies than out of individual farms. Even the social advantages of the community — no unemployment, no crime, no old people left alone, and no mentally ill banned from the community — are to them things that go without saying, normal ways of dealing with other human beings that only appear remarkable to the outside world because, in that world, "the devil is loose."

During the shearing of the sheep, days later, I myself experience the contrast between the Hutterites and the surrounding society. It is the beginning of March; the sun glances into the bookbinder's house during wake-up and gives me a first taste of a spring which is still far away. After the usual breakfast, which is quick as lightning, and after the feeding of the cattle, all men and women gather in the sheep barn. Their wooly bodies huddled against one another, 300 animals stand there in fearful expectation. Winekeeper Johannes, the work supervisor, distributes the electric shearing blades to the young "menfolk." Those, in turn, form a row under the glaring neon light. Each one grabs an animal out of the steaming woolen bunch, and presses it between his legs, and the clippers cut their way through the shaggy fur. With the patience of sheep, the animals let their wool be cut from their skin in long strips, on the belly first, then on the back, and at the end on the throat, the nose, and the ears. As soon as a sheep is bald and naked, and runs outside while still bleeding a little in some places, one of the girls picks up the wool from the floor. It looks almost like Irish sweaters already. On long, wooden tables, other women form pumpkin-size balls out of the greasy tufts by tying them together with strings of hemp. Then Rachel, breadcutter Johannes' third daughter, throws the bales with much verve into the giant jute sack which hangs on a wooden scaffold about five feet above the floor. I am standing up there under the brown beams of the roof and catch whatever the pretty sixteen-year-old throws at me, and I stomp the wool so tight that I'm sure at least 150 pounds will fit in the sack.

We cut, bind, and stomp all day long so that the sweat drips from us. From my elevated place I watch with the terror of a city boy as Samuel takes the female animals that, after the shearing, can easily be identified as not being pregnant and, with a pocket knife, cuts off one of their ears in order to mark them for the butcher. I can also see the "Little School Ankela," the kindergarten teacher, walk in with her 15 students, little "men" and girls, all between 2 1/2 and 6 years old, with red cheeks and big eyes, holding one another's hands. To me, those little ones in their Hutterite costumes that they already wear as "Duttelbobele," as babies, always look as if they were copying the adult world, as if they were playing mother, father, and child. They watch the activities around the shearing of the sheep with astonishment. To them, this is live social science. Soon the children will be allowed to help as eagerly as their older brothers and sisters, who during recess come running in order to catch stray sheep or to gather scattered wool — first probationary tests for the adolescents who then, after the eighth grade

and at 15 join the "people" as full workers. However, they
will become brethren and sisters only after their baptism.

When lunchtime has finally arrived, the old housekeeper
and treasurer Jakob makes his appearance, holding in both
of his hands two gallons of "flower wine," which is home-
made wine made from dandelion blossoms. He is the only
person in the colony who has a key to the wine cellar below
the kitchen and is therefore the second most important man
on the farm after his brother Johannes, the preacher. Along
with the flower wine we are having "cheese pie," a sinfully
sweet cheese cake with vanilla ice cream. This borders
almost on lust of the flesh. For our meal, we sit on my tightly packed sacks, here the men, there the women, and the little ones somewhere in between. Everybody is in a good
mood. Outside the sun shines down from the wide and open
prairie sky on the snow-capped Rockies on the horizon. Little Martin, exhausted from all the different impressions, has
fallen asleep on his mother's soft lap. Jakob personally gives
each one of us a piece of cake. The wine tastes "hellishly
good." How could people have a better life! When lunch is
over, Jakob rises, takes his hat off, and says grace with the
85th psalm of the sons of Korah: "I will hear what God the
Lord will speak: for he will speak peace unto his people, and
to his saints: but let them not turn again to folly. Surely his
salvation is nigh them that fear him; that glory may dwell in
our land. Mercy and truth are met together; righteousness
and peace have kissed each other...The Lord shall give that
which is good; and our land shall yield her increase. Amen."

Hutterite existence is always aware of its heavenly mission. Life and death are always connected to each other; one
reflects the other. And the community is the link between
heaven and earth. "We live in the outer courtyard of Paradise," Jakob keeps saying, and if one looks around in this
barn where everybody has a cake and Martin his soft sleep,
where "righteousness and peace kiss each other," then one
does not doubt his words. The brethren's community of Wil-

son — it really is the "new Jerusalem," "the tabernacle of
God with men" (Revelation 21:2,3). Who in this sheep barn
could question it?

I wonder why the people here are so satisfied with themselves and their fellow human beings — in spite of their biblical fear of guilt and punishment, in spite of this world
which to them is a valley of sorrow, a place of painful privation, and in spite of a life in which "humility is before honor"
(Proverbs 15:33). What is the reason? The answer sounds
paradoxical: It is not in spite but because of the fears, the
sorrow and the pain that the Hutterites are happier than
many an earthling on the outside who chases after happiness all his life, who is allowed to do everything and owns
many things, but who, in the end, lives in poverty and desperation. The brethren and sisters believe that salvation in
heaven can be obtained only through patiently-borne sufferings on earth; in the past, during times of bloody religious
persecutions, of torture and hunger, suffering of course was
more common than it is today, when some have stomach
aches because of ice cream and cheesecake. "Today we live
next to the bacon," the winekeeper laments. But because it
is written in Matthew 7:14 that only those will reach paradise who take the narrow and rocky way of renunciation,
the Hutterites throw their own rocks onto the path of their
lives in order to make sure it is a path of suffering. Thus we
kneel on the bare floor after we have gotten up in the morning, at night during the service, and before going to bed, and
we pray "until we feel it in our backs." Many times the
women tie their hair so tightly that I have seen young girls
cry for pain when they did their pigtails, and the renunciation of the pleasure of ice skating, of a long and enjoyable
meal or colorful flowers in the living room is perceived as an
almost lustful torment.

What makes me suffer the most, however, are the inade-
quate sanitary installations and the lack of running water in
the house. The colonists could have afforded baths and

water toilets long ago, since their community has enough money for more expensive milking machines and combines. Still, they keep the communal wash house and, (in front of each house) the little wooden outhouse with a low seat for the children and a higher one for the adults — "the evil flesh must suffer."

Never have I endured more physical suffering than when I had to trudge through snowdrifts to the unheated outhouse during a stormy night and let my pants down at arctic temperatures that make water freeze within minutes — never before in my entire life. The vulgar German expression referring to the "pole of water" of which one disposes becomes almost a daily reality at 30 below — and I don't want to mention more sizeable jobs. Without Jakob's dried prunes as a laxative, some night I certainly would have simply frozen to the seat. The medieval monks of the flagellant movement couldn't have suffered more when they whipped themselves with thorny lashes, crying out the words, "Rise up in torture's purest light, and stay away from sinful plight!" The Hutterites, too, know this little "saying."

So that the soul can rise on some judgment day, the "evil flesh" must suffer and be kept "low." Body and soul are in constant fight, and physical self-control is supposed to help to avoid the frightful hellish punishment which the sinful man of pleasure would undoubtedly have to suffer in the afterlife. On the other hand, the joys that await the true Christian in heaven are unimaginably great: "If now a man could be there for a single hour," one Riedemann sermon has it, "he would leave all the debauchery and lust of this world quite willingly in order to become part of this heavenly bliss. One day above the stars will be better than thousand times thousand here in this valley of sorrow. Because there will be no more night, and no one will need the sun because the Lord himself will be the light."

We see that the suffering is worth it. Willingly, the chosen ones do without those things that, to their worldly neighbors, make life worth living. For example, television or quick trips to Las Vegas or Miami, the pleasure of anticipation of life after death is experienced in a much more beautiful way at the heavenly outer courtyard of Wilson than are all false joys of the world of consumption put together. As I myself experience this here in the sheep barn in a very concrete way, my rejection of some areas of Hutterite life, such as the punishment of the children and the discrimination against women, diminishes. Besides, I am here not to admonishingly lift my critical index finger but to experience and understand.

As only a few trembling sheep are waiting for the shearing toward evening, something very harmless happens, but still I will never forget it. It is Rachel, the beauty with the softly curved lips, Rachel, who has been throwing the wool bales at me all day long, who all of a sudden looks at me longer than before, smiles and looks into my eyes — can one imagine that! For two or three seconds she looks up at me and smiles, almost much too long for a saint. For a moment I forget to tread in my wool sack and hug the bundle she has just thrown. Am I in heaven?

It is this look, forever to me uniquely Rachel's, that will keep me alive at Wilson from now on; it makes me happy in my dreams...

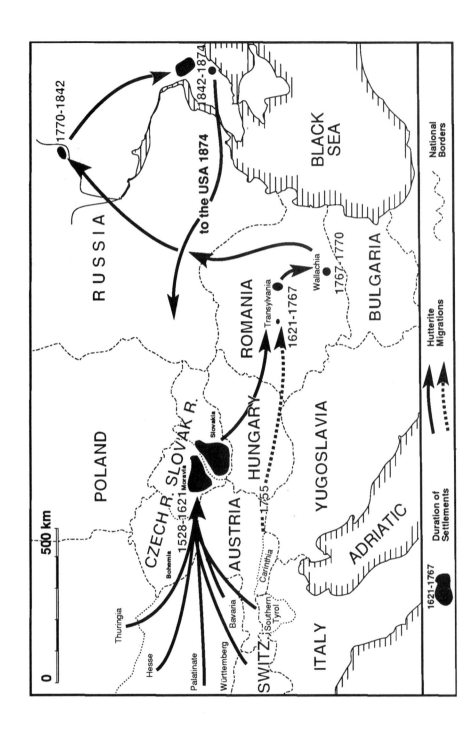

0   500 km

POLAND

RUSSIA

1770-1842

1842-1874

to the USA 1874

BLACK
SEA

BULGARIA

Wallachia
1767-1770

Transylvania
1621-1767

ROMANIA

HUNGARY

Slovakia

CZECH R.
Bohemia

SLOVAK R.
1528-1621 Moravia

AUSTRIA

Carinthia ...1755

YUGOSLAVIA

ADRIATIC

Thuringia

Hesse

Palatinate

Württemberg

Bavaria

SWITZ.

Southern
Tyrol

ITALY

Hutterite
Migrations

Duration of
Settlements

1621-1767

National
Borders

SPRING

Carnival of the Chosen People

The first messenger of spring came to us while there was still ice and snow at the Wilson colony. Right after wake-up, I found him crouched in a corner of my toilet; he was quite ruffled from the stormy weather, but otherwise seemed to be in quite good health: It was a blackbird that had probably preceded the flock and was now waiting for better days. I fed the bird left-over bread that bread-cutter Johannes slipped to me, and, for the time being, I used the outhouse that belonged to my neighbor Georg, the second preacher. But then the fat, black and gray cat from the barn must have found out about it, for one morning there were only a few bloody feathers instead of my blackbird. And spring failed to come.

Only as the April sun is becoming quite strong does it start to melt the feet-high snow under which the land has been hibernating for six months. The mighty organ pipes of icicles sweat in the glaring mid-day light and turn into tiny glass warts only to grow big again during the frosty night. Streams of melted ice gather in every depression in the ground and form puddles, ponds, and even sizable lakes. From an airplane the prairie must now look like Finnish lake country. Our colony almost disappears, sinking into water and mud. When we feed the cattle, the mud runs into our knee-high rubber boots, the cows wade up to the udder

Opposite Page, Top: Hutterites learn pious songs about heavenly bliss and hellish damnation when they are small children and sing them throughout their lives.

Bottom: Hutterites walk to their barren schoolhouse for prayer approximately 450 times a year. The sermons are hand-written texts dating back to the 16th and 17th centuries.

in their own manure, and even the four-wheel drive tractors with their great horsepower get hopelessly stuck. High tide at God's ark. But as always, the chaos follows a certain order. In this great country, every kind of weather has dramatic characteristics, in particular such a change of the seasons.

As soon as the first snow-free islands, pale and bleached from the long winter's night, spread on the wide pastures around the colony, the school boys leave the community's confines. Right after the afternoon lessons are over, they get their freshly greased iron traps, saddle the small, hardy prairie ponies, and, with two or three on one horse, they ride out hunting gophers. According to the German zoologist Brehm, gophers are "pouch rats," a north American cross between mole and weasel. The boys go after these harmful rodents that eat up tons of grain in the fall. Carefully the boys put up their irons in front of the gopher holes and tightly peg them down with chains into the freshly melted ground. Dried grass is sprinkled over the traps for camouflage, and then it's already time to return, for the preacher won't delay his sermon.

The excitement comes the next day. Who has caught what? The first one to have hunter's luck is 12-year-old Joschua. A fat brown and gray striped gopher's front legs are caught between the sharp iron bars. Surrounded by his classmates, Joschua pulls the peg out of the ground and with it hits the screeching gopher's neck two or three times. The animal is dead; "it's finished," as the boys say. But before they check the traps of the others, Joschua removes the thin, slightly bushy tail from his victim with his bare hands. He stuffs the torn-out tail into an empty preserves jar, for the Hutterite offspring get a piece of gum from the school teacher for each vermin killed. "One tail, one gum," Joschua calculates. He remembers having averaged approximately three gums per week last spring; that was the general average, he says.

The teacher, then, does not consider this gum-reward a contradiction to the adjuration of Paul, who says, "Look not every man on his own things, but every man also on the things of others" (Philippians 2:4). In an almost apologetic way, he explains to me that "kids are kids" and that they first have to be educated out of being egotistical and instinct-driven creatures and into becoming "righteous Christians," i.e. Hutterites. The gum is supposed only to sweeten a little the first works for the common good — no more. As soon as the 15-year-old boys leave school, join the "people" and become integrated into the community's work force, individual rewards are a thing of the past. Then the old Hutterite motto is enforced: "Everybody gives what he can and gets what he needs."

But until that point is reached, teacher Samuel Wurz and his wife Sarah, the school mistress, have to do a great deal of work with their students. Their pedagogical guidelines are old and have proven themselves over the centuries. The forefathers Peter Riedemann and Peter Walbot wrote down the regulations that Samuel and Sarah adhere to even today. In Walbot's "School Regulations" from 1568 we read in the preamble: "Herein are listed several necessary points demonstrating how the assigned brethren and sisters including their assistants should keep the order in schools pertaining to discipline and education of the young. First of all they must remember why they are placed in charge of the children by the Lord and His people. Both school master and school mistress must work together peacefully and with confidence in each other since this reflects a good portion of the school's order; they must give advice and keep strict and constant order in leading the young since being industrious and peace-loving makes good order — the lack of harmony and industriousness creates disorder." When the scissorgrinder Walbot wrote these lines, the Hutterites were the only people in Europe to practice the commonly mandatory school attendance for boys and girls — 200 years before

"Old Fritz," King Frederick of Prussia. Today they are the last ones in Canada to keep their own, one-room small schools in order to avoid sending their children to the public schools.

School life for a young Hutterite begins at an early age. It is true that, today, Hutterites no longer follow the explicit instructions in the book "On Child Education": "As soon as the mother takes the child from her breasts, she sends him to school." But right after the completion of their third year, the colony's children enter kindergarten, the "Little School."

Every morning, shortly after seven o'clock, eight girls and four boys assemble here at the Wilson colony in their small school and have breakfast in the little house right next to the duck cages. They sit around a long, wooden table to which the chairs are glued. The snow-white, synthetic tiles with which the walls of the entire room are covered give it the appearance of a sterile waiting-room in a hospital; only the magazines are missing. The preacher's wife, Sarah Wurz, who is round like a ball and herself a mother of sixteen grown-ups, sits at the head of the table as on a throne — a giant among dwarfs. She is one of the three "Little School Ankela," kindergarten teachers who take turns every day in watching the offspring. Just like Sarah, all kindergarten teachers are about 60 years old. "Child-rearing" is to them a retirement job when baking and cooking become too hard over the years. The children's seating order, the prayer, their sing-song intonation, the boys' suspenders, the girls' kerchiefs — everything here is like the adult world, just a few sizes smaller. Hutterite puppet theater.

After the over-easy eggs with zwieback and preserves, songs are sung according to the curriculum which is listed in painstaking German letters on a little board on the wall. Since today is Wednesday, they sing the "Wednesday-song":

> "Devil, dragon, here they tower, / I can
> laugh about their power; / On the cross He
> had to suffer, / He's alive, our God and

father. Death shows me its bitter teeth / In
this world that's far beneath, / Both to me
their wrath they send, / God in heaven is my
friend. Let the poor world scream and shout;
/ If it wants to cast me out, / I will say then
to its face: / God alone will judge my case. If
the world drives me away, / Up in heaven I
will stay; Heaven if I come to see, / This will
be enough for me. World, I leave you, it is
late, / What you love is what I hate. / You
can love the earthly mire, / It is God whom I
admire. Lord, if only you are mine, / I
renounce all worldly kind; / Let them lay me
in my grave, / When I am with you I'm
saved."

The children joyfully sing these lines as if they belonged to
a cheerful song to welcome spring. "Devil," "Dragon," "Earthly Mire" — such words come very merrily from their lips, and
all have more fun with the sounds than with the meaning.
"Bitter Teeth!" the entire room bawls, and I look into twelve
wide-open kids' mouths with gaps between their first teeth.
After the Wednesday-song, a seemingly endless Easter song
is practiced. Teacher Sarah takes the lead, and the children
screechingly repeat after her. They all sit upright and
straight, with their little hands obediently folded. Under the
table, however, their short little legs swing wildly back and
forth, thus making up for the discipline above the table. It is
Hutterite ritual, namely the ability to patiently sit for a long
time, that is probably the most important thing that the "little men" and girls are taught in kindergarten. And they will
need that ability soon, for a Hutterite spends approximately
450 hours per year on the hard benches during the service:
on weekdays, one hour; on Sundays, three; and on high
church holidays, up to six. Corporal punishment is practically non-existent in the "Little School" — it is enough for
Sarah to take the "Dear Rod" from the hook in a threatening
manner and to shout "Be quiet, or else!" and then the little

ones are quiet for the next five minutes in order not to find out what "or else" refers to.

The reward for one hour's worth of singing consists of two hours of play in the yard — joy follows suffering. In the warm spring air, the children have fun on see-saws, swings, and slides, but the real fun starts when the teacher gets lunch from the kitchen at around 11 o'clock. Then they are without supervision and control during the most precious ten minutes of the day. Shepherd Samuel's Martin is, as always, the first to drop his pants as soon as Sarah has disappeared behind the corner. Full of pride, he pulls his little "birdie" out of the turquoise-colored underpants and pees from the terrace of the kindergarten down onto the pasture, forming a beautiful golden arch. He squeaks out of pleasure; he is the youngest among his group, but nobody can pee as he can. Salomon, Samuel, and Joschua stand right next to him and follow suit. But it's not only the "little men" who show what they can do. In a squatting position, Sarah too lustily lets the waters run, and Martha, who I am sure would prefer to have been born a boy, even shows to the slightly shy Heinrich how one must arch his back to make sure something will come trickling out. Only on rare occasions have I seen the children so happy yet focused as during that activity. Freud would have loved this. As soon as the supervisor comes back with the pot full of food, the flies are quickly pulled up and the skirts pulled down. Again, the children play on the swings and see-saws as if nothing has happened. However, the quiet triumph over the adult world can still be seen in their glowing faces during lunch hour.

In the Little School, nap time starts at noon and lasts for an hour and a half. The children lie down next to one another in two rows on covered foam mattresses, the boys prudently separated from the girls. Each has a cushion; blankets are not needed since the room is still heated. On an extra bed, old Sarah sleeps like a drone with her ears open.

Who knows what would go on here if the young were left in their beds without supervision? It can hardly be imagined!

At night, Hutterite children rarely sleep alone. In wine-keeper Johannes' family, for example, mother Maria packs her "dozen" into four wide beds. Miriam, 14 years old, sleeps next to her eleven- and twelve-year-old sisters, and Martha, 8, Maria, 6, and Katharina, 5, share another bed. In the next room, the oldest son, Elias, holds his one-year-old baby brother David in his arms as he would a stuffed pet, and ten-year-old Johannes holds the two-year-old Andreas. Once the thirteenth offspring is born, it will sleep in a crib in the parents' bedroom while Maria breast-feeds it for a full year.

Now I understand why I have a big double bed in the book-binder's house even though I am by myself. The single person, back home in Germany more and more the rule, is still an exception in the colony's society. I also see why the carpenter shop doesn't produce any single beds, the "death-bed" excepted. With so many children, it would be a waste of space to give everybody a separate bed. Besides, we all know that it is warmer when two or three people sleep in one bed.

After three years in the Little School the Hutterite child knows what's important in life: The girls obey the boys, the young obey the old, the students obey the teacher, the teacher obeys the preacher, and the preacher obeys God. A small, "headstrong" child, spoiled by everybody, now turns into a human being who begins to feel a member of the group, a miniature member who still doesn't know how to do much other than pray, repeat religious phrases, and pee golden arches, but who is eager some-day, like the grown-ups, to drive the tractor, bake bread, or shear the sheep.

The children of the Little School don't see much of teacher Samuel during school hours. Although he is officially responsible for their education as well, he leaves the daily work mainly up to the three old women and only occasionally peeks in through the door in order to see whether things are all right. His entire worry and energy is devoted to the German school for the boys and girls aged six to fifteen. What the teacher must do there is clearly spelled out in ancestor Walbot's "School Regulation": "The schoolmaster must make the boys and girls learn because they are our great treasure entrusted to us by God. He must ask them questions and teach them how to write and to read. In particular, he must teach them the Ten Commandments and the Bible, so that they know and understand how God loves the righteous and blesses them, how He hates evil men and punishes them with eternal fire."

Samuel has divided his 28 students into two groups: The "big" students who already know the German alphabet, and the "little" students who still need to learn it. After the usual prayers and songs whose words are only slightly different from those in the Little School, first the little illiterates, three little men and three girls, step in front of Samuel's podium. All six children hold their reading books in their hands. Chorally, they first read according to syllables: "E-u, eu, r-e, re — eure (your). E-l, el, t-e-r-n, tern — Eltern (parents). S-i-n-d, sind (are). G-u-t, gut (good). Eure Eltern sind gut" — Your parents are good. After the sentence has been split up and divided according to letters, syllables, and words, the teacher asks about the meaning of the sentence that has just been read: "What does this mean?" Blank stares. Here standard German is the first foreign language, and thus Samuel must translate everything back into Hutterite German: "Enkra Eltern sein guet" — "Eure Eltern sind gut" in standard German. Now each child has understood. "'Parents', that means father and mother," six-year-old Paul says with comprehension. "Yes, that's what it means," the teacher confirms and strokes his hair in praise. During the reading exercise the older students sit on their benches in the back of the room and copy Hutterite songs in old German handwriting. After 30 minutes, each student must·show at least five completed stanzas. Samuel makes spotchecks and watches carefully for the general writing style. It must look "nice" and "clean" since the content cannot be changed anyway. Beginning student Paul raises his hand and says, "Outhouse!" — He must go to the bathroom. Samuel lets him go, for the school regulations specify: "A schoolmaster must let the boys satisfy their pressing needs once in the morning, in the evening, and so at noon and must see that it is done. In between those times, he must still let them leave the room if their bodies' needs require it. For there should be no law governing these natural needs because it is harmful to suppress them. The same applies to girls and should be watched with equal care." This time, the schoolmaster does without the "see that it is done." Instead, he checks what the older students memorized as their homework assignment: pages and pages of Bible prose, recited in the tiresome and to me hardly intelligible Hutter-sing-song, without periods or commas: "Asobedientchildrendonotactasbeforewhenyouwerelivinginlustandignorance." This kind of Bible study thus consists mainly of monotonous copying and memorizing of the Holy Scripture. If, once in a while, knowledge is required, for example about the Fall of Man, the questions and answers are always the same: Teacher: "Who picked the apples, Martha?" Martha: "Why, that was Eve." Teacher: "Who told her to pick the apples, Sarah?" Sarah: "The snake told her to." Teacher: "And who told her not to, Judith?" Judith: "The heavenly father." Teacher: "And what would happen if they still picked them, Greta?" Greta: "They would die." Teacher: "Did Adam and Eve obey, Susanna?" Susanna: "No, they didn't." Teacher: "Why didn't they obey, Theresa?" Theresa: "Because they wanted to be smart and know what is good and what is evil."

It is no coincidence that Samuel asks only the girls about the Fall; meanwhile, the boys roll their blotting-paper balls without being disturbed. For it was Eve with her desire to be smart who caused our earthly misery. And nobody is supposed to become smarter through Samuel's teaching, God forbid, not smarter but more devout. This happens only through the word of God and, if necessary, through the rod, "for if the Lord's vineyard should bear good fruit, it must be cultivated!" The 400-year-old regulation specifies exactly how that must be done: "The schoolmaster must avoid their punishment through warnings and threats as much as he can — if that has no effect, he must use the rod without anger and must not hit their heads either with the rod or his fist, and in particular must not beat for the sake of mere pain but on the appropriate place with the humility of the rod...Disciplining must happen in the fear of the Lord and must be different for the old ones, the cunning, the liars, the thieves, and the fornicators, and must be performed with seriousness and according to the gravity of their deeds; that must not be done in hidden secrecy but in the open before all children so that they learn to fear it." Thus Samuel reaches for the worn-out leather belt at least once a day after Bible study or after the meals and hands out his hard blows in the fear of God. I must add, however, that cruel child abuse, which is committed a thousand times in my world, does not exist here in spite of all strictness of faith.

The rearing of the children, "certainly one of the most important things that can be done in this world," is the community's Godly task, and the teacher in charge of this task is chosen by the colony's community council. The parents play only a minor role in child rearing, and the fathers reach for the leather belt only rarely, rather choosing to report to the teacher when their children do not behave. Still, Samuel Wurz does not hold the only position of power in education at the Wilson colony. There is yet another person, a short and rather chubby Miss Thompson, who walks around without a kerchief and without the long skirt but rather with a permanent and a tight blouse and jeans. She is a state-certified teacher and head of the "English School" in the middle of the colony; that school is a thorn in the eye of her colleague Samuel Wurz. After the First World War, the Hutterites were granted permission to immigrate to Canada under the condition that they subject themselves to the mandatory schooling laws of the country. Gnashing their teeth, they agreed to the establishment of a "worldly" school in their colony so that they didn't have to send their children to public schools in neighboring towns. Every weekday morning, Miss Thompson comes in her fire-engine red Chevy 30 miles from Lethbridge and relieves Samuel of his duties at 8:30 sharp. Then Samuel's face turns sour like the face of a gardener who watches a cow trample down his tulips but can't do anything about it. With a grouchy greeting he opens the classroom door for her and, for five hours, leaves his grapevine to his pedagogical counterpart and thus to "the worldly wisdom, art and exercise which does not know much about our religion."

As soon as Samuel has closed the door behind him, the school comes alive. First the children make a lot of noise by pushing their benches around the classroom so that they sit down according to their age instead of their sex. In front of the blackboard the teacher places a globe, "our good old world," and hangs up colorful pictures of Canada on the walls, despite the fact that the Bible prescribes, "Ye shall make no idols nor graven image" (Leviticus 26:1).

In fact, pictures are strictly taboo for the Canadian Hutterites. The order is taken so seriously that they don't have regular driver's licenses in order not to have to be photographed. To be allowed to drive, they carry a temporary license that must be renewed every three months, requiring a troublesome procedure. When they visit relatives in the United States (there the Hutterite communities are not as strict in regard to passport pictures), the customs official gets to see not a regular passport but only the birth certificate which contains no photograph.

That pictures are not allowed, my friend the photographer Timm Rautert experienced when he visited me at the colony in the spring, and, later, in the fall. Timm wanted to take pictures for the planned book about my life in the community of the chosen ones, but more than two weeks passed before he dared even to take the camera out of his suitcase. A long-winded discussion with the brethren about whether or not it was a sin to take pictures had preceded. It wasn't enough just to write about the community, the photographer argued; words on paper, even big words, may not be enough. Therefore, he said, the book needed illustrations so that the readers in Germany could see with their own eyes that the Hutterites still live according to the old faith, in spite of all persecution. The holy ones were intrigued by this worldly argument. The preacher thought that it was necessary so that "the people in Germany can see what a life in righteousness looks like." On the other hand, there was no explaining away of Moses' laws either. After heated debates in the community council, the brethren therefore agreed on a Solomonic compromise and decided neither to permit the taking of photographs nor to refuse permission. They wisely overlooked Timm Rautert when, with a black conscience, he once in a while pushed the release button; this didn't happen too often, because Timotheus, as the Hutterites called him in a biblical manner, had to work hard on the farm. "Fortunately," in their view, he would not have much time to snap pictures during the building of fences, the feeding of cows, and the castrating of piglets.

Physical changes such as the mixed seating order or pictures on the wall are not the only changes for Miss Thompson's English course. Just about everything is different after she takes over. The teacher maintains that the story of the Fall of Man is only a biblical legend because the ape is supposedly the origin of mankind. In her opinion, the earth is billions of years old, much older than Samuel and the Bible say — that is, 2000 years from creation to the destruction of Sodom and Gomorrha, another 2000 years until the birth of Christ, and then almost another 2000 years to our time, all of which adds up to a maximum of 6000 years. So now every rock outside is supposed to be a thousand times older than the biblical age of the world? For the children this is hard to believe! And then, says Miss Thompson, the sun does not revolve around the earth, although Solomon, the son of David, announces specifically, "The sun also ariseth and the sun goeth down, and hasteth to his place where he arose" (Ecclesiastes 1:5). No, that's all wrong; the earth turns, the sun stands still, and the children are confused. Who, they ask, is telling the truth, and who is the liar?

The short break between the German and the English school is to them a daily change of times, a switch between centuries, from pre-enlightenment to our present age, from medieval times to the atomic age. There was only one way and one view of the world before 8:30, but now, after the break, there are seemingly countless possibilities; whereas before the world was synonymous with evil itself, it is now a good and beautiful world worthy of living in — for success, for honor, for wealth, and for worldly happiness, each of these items pure deadly sins according to Hutterite beliefs. Now there is hardly any more talk about the baptists' reward of life or of heavenly bliss.

After having been a guest-observer of both Samuel's and his colleague's teaching two or three times, I wonder what it must look like in the children's minds — what confusion, what contradictions in those little heads! Every day a foreign world breaks into the strict yet comprehensible and clearly ordered holy community, and the waves of a sinful ocean splash into the ark. Save yourselves if you can! However, the children do not take the young woman in jeans ("The woman shall not wear that which pertaineth unto a man," Deuteronomy 22:5) very seriously. She doesn't even know how to speak or write "real German." She smokes during recess, goes dancing at the evil "inn" on some weekends, is a passionate ice-skater, and plays "wanton" country songs on her harmonica. All such behavior would bring her students eternal damnation. This is why the teacher herself does not believe she really belongs there. "If I fulfill my assignment," she tells me during recess, "and educate these children to become critical thinkers and curious, open-minded human beings, I inevitably create a conflict between them and their surroundings." Critical thinking, curiosity, openmindedness — they simply do not belong to the narrowness of the brethren's communities, where there is room only for the fear of God and for pious modesty. The children have just heard repeatedly that it was curiosity which drove Eve to pilfer from the tree of knowledge, and that, when the Jews disregarded the Lord's laws on Mount Sinai, the punishment was fire raining from the sky.

The Hutterites have learned from these mistakes made by preceding chosen people. This is why Samuel sets the threshold of conflict with his colleague at a very low level, as shown by the case of "Jessy": Jessy, the teacher's dog, one day gave birth to puppies, and Miss Thompson reported the event to her students on the next day. In the afternoon, the children came home and spread the following all over the colony: "The Teacher's dog just had five little ones." Samuel heard that and, on the next day, asked this 28-year-old woman not to talk about "such things," contending that this was nothing for Hutterite children. The teacher argued that "such things" were common, everyday occurrences, especially in agriculture. "Maybe," Samuel replied, "but we don't talk about it, especially not with our children." Miss Thompson has many problems with earning the "kids'" respect even without the rod, since corporal punishment is in violation of Canadian educational laws. The students, however, are used to a violation of the rules resulting in the "Germans." First she tried simply to talk sensibly, then the sinners had to stand in a corner, and finally she even used scotchtape to shut the mouths of those that were real cheeky — it was no use. In her desperation she finally turned to teacher Samuel and reported the sinners. That worked. From then on, the classroom was under control.

I myself had some discipline problems with the Hutterite children. Very soon the school boys wanted to find out what kind of a guy I was and how far they could go with me. Because of my clumsiness in everyday farming life, they unfortunately did not have much respect for me. I didn't even know how to ride a horse. First the "little men" called me derogatory names such as "Tall Miechel" or "Old Hamburger," without suffering any consequences. When I even let their throwing potatoes at me go without immediate physical punishment and instead wanted to have a "serious talk" with the wrongdoers, those fellows thought I was completely crazy. This went on for several weeks until I made a decision; after yet another potato-attack, I took a branch freshly broken from a tree and, in front of the entire class, treated little Paul's rear end with such intensity that he wasn't able to sit still for days. I was so angry that I was beside myself. I was ashamed because my action had been directly opposed to my liberal principles of education. To make things even worse, the results of my action were surprisingly positive. Instead of hating me, Paul proudly told me the following night how many gophers he had caught. Today I am his friend. I had reacted in the way that he had learned to understand and adjust to. Only now were he and his classmates able to accept me, and the ditch that had separated us was filled in.

Seldom can the tension between the German and the English school be felt so intensely as on Friday, the day on which Drama is in the teacher's lesson plan. Then the desks are pushed against the walls, and all students sit in a circle on the floor. Miss Thompson announces the topic: "Today we imagine that we live on Mars." She must have just seen "Star Wars," for this drama begins with her marching into the circle with machine-like movements of her arms and legs and her self-introduction, "My name is R 1245. I am a robot." Now the children stand up and imitate the teacher, at first somewhat reluctantly, but then with increasing enthusiasm. Samuel is next to continue the story about Mars. "I am another robot and I'm flying to earth." After a while, all students run around the room with their arms spread out wide. What wonderful chaos! When everybody has calmed down, Elias says, "I have landed on earth and am walking on a street in the big city."

The city that Elias and his fellow students are looking at with wide-opened children's eyes is, needless to say, the prairie-town of Lethbridge, which to all colonists is a babylon and sodomite breeding ground of all evil. The Hutterites drive to town only when they must go to the doctor or when the community has business that must be taken care of; that means, for example, business with the feed company which provides the vitamin concentrate for the hogs, or with the grain storage co-op which buys the grain from Wilson. The children don't get to go to town very often, but when they do, they are all the more curious. They have no business being there, the parents and the teacher say, for the town is "the home of sinfulness."

But Joschua, the drama's next actor, sees no murderers, whores, or child molesters. No, but he does see a candy shop, which he and the others are now storming. And this is the beginning of an orgy of sweets: Martha grabs candy bars from the shelves, Elisabeth plunders the ice box, and Johannes makes a clean slate of the gum shelf. With their mouths and pockets filled, the class begins its return flight to the home planet of Mars, where there are lots of rocks but very few candy bars. They really seem to be different people as they are allowed to let their imaginations roam freely for an hour. Miss Thompson told me that at the beginning it had been very difficult to stimulate the children's creativity and spontaneity, since German class requires mostly sitting still, listening, and repeating. It certainly can't be easy to switch all of a sudden from the Fall of Man to a flight to Mars.

Although in a very different way, I myself experience a taste of that contrast with its problems every Sunday in Sunday school. Over the course of the 19 years that I spent in school, my teachers had tried to foster my individual abilities and talents, while Samuel's declared goal of education is to carve the children's personalities, while as yet independent and untouched, into "living stones" with which God's "spiritual house" (1 Peter 5) can be built. "If, at a very early age, the children are taught to deny and extinguish their own will, then it is a spiritual planting to turn such young twigs and lambs into Christian boys and girls through God's blessing." This is how the age-old "School Regulations" read. Therefore, the teacher doesn't ask me in Sunday school what I think of the sermon that I heard in the morning or even whether I have my own thoughts about it — God forbid! He only wants to know what "I heard during the service" and whether I listened carefully or fell asleep — nothing more. Yet this is quite a lot to me because I find it very difficult to decide on one "little passage" and then remember it through the two-hour service, the following duck meal, and the after-lunch nap in order to then cite it without error in spite of being as nervous as a candidate for confirmation.

What my fellow students can come up with is simply amazing. Like recording machines they whir entire sermon passages as if to do so were nothing. Hutterites do not forget very easily what they have heard only once. Beginning in Little School, their memories are trained well. But when was it that I had to memorize a poem or a song during my years in school back home? When she had reached a very old age, my grandmother still knew by heart a famous poem by Schiller from the first through the last stanza, but things have changed. When we sit together here at night singing songs, and people ask me to sing a song that is sung in Germany today, I can't get past the first lines of "O Tannenbaum" or "Evening's Quiet." Elvis Presley's "There Goes my Everything" or the Beatles' "Yellow Submarine" would certainly be easier for me, but such "hopping wanton songs" are not in demand here. Sometimes I feel terrible and miserable, poor and almost without culture, during those nights of song below the naked light bulb.

What is the source of energy and strength which allows these people to hold on to their history and spiritual identity in such a tenacious way? Isn't it a miracle that this small group of Hutterite people didn't dissolve in the North American "melting pot" long ago and wasn't consumed by the all-devouring American Way of Life which has influenced the original Hutterite homeland across the ocean more than the brethren's communities in the American West? The thing that fascinates me so much is the way in which time has stood still in the brethren's and sisters' spiritual lives, and this is a fascination in which both admiration and horror are mixed. In 1978, Michael Sattler's suffering narrated in the song sung at the Wilson colony is just as real as it was in 1527 in Rottenburg on the Neckar river. Throughout the years, the "School Regulations" have lost nothing of their validity and are still binding. On the contrary, the older a document is, the more meaningful and valid is its content. Time seems to stand still in God's hut even though the world outside its door revolves faster and faster and the ages come and go more and more rapidly, not to speak of fashions and fads.

Hutterland is the eye in the storm of world history — an oasis which, through persecution, kept changing its location but never lost its inner structure (with the exception of short interruptions, as in Russia, when the community was given up). The anabaptists' historical continuity becomes particularly visible when we read what Hans Jakob Christoph von Grimmelshausen writes, in his "Simplicissimus," about a Hutterite community in Hungary during the Thirty Years War. There he had encountered a society "composed both of married and single men and women who, in the manner of anabaptists, were striving to earn their livelihood through manual labor under a "sympathetic" supervisor, and who devoted the rest of the time to God's praise and service for their souls' salvation...They had at first great treasures and excessive food which, however, they did not let go to waste; no murmured curse or impatience could ever be heard in their company, and there was no unnecessary word spoken; I saw artisans work in their shops as if they were paid for it; their schoolmaster taught the young as if they were his own children; I never saw men and womenfolk mixed and together but everywhere do their particular work separated by sex; no man saw his wife except in their bedroom in which there was only a bed and a water pitcher and bowl for the hands so that he could go to bed and rise in the morning with his hands clean; moreover, they called one another sisters and brethren, but such honorable familiarity was no reason for unchastity. They had certain hours for eating, a certain hour for sleeping but not one minute for playing or walking around except for the young who, after the meal, take an hour-long walk with their leader for the sake of good health while they still have to pray and sing spiritual songs."

Here at the Wilson colony, Grimmelshausen, the man of the world, becomes my contemporary because of that report. 300 years ago, he described a present time that can't be changed, a timeless Hutterite existence with the exception of some few changes that the education of the children has undergone since the Thirty Years War: During those times, the children still slept in the schoolhouse under supervision of the schoolmaster, his wife, and the so-called female guardians that had to watch for a "child becoming restless because he is thirsty or itches or has the unclean habit of wetting his bed — then he must be taken out because not everything can be done with the rod." At that time, when the Hutterites still entertained an active mission for their cause, the monopoly of education was in the community's hands to a larger extent than today. Some parents had not been with the Hutterites for a long time, perhaps spoke a different dialect, were former Protestants, Catholics, Mennonites, or followers of Thomas Münzer. They themselves had yet to learn how the narrow path through Hutterite life is chosen, and the colony took care of their children night and day. This was done in such a strict way that parents who wanted to visit their sons or daughters were allowed to do so only "with the schoolmaster's knowledge and permission." Even breastfeeding mothers were kept at a distance from their babies. Grimmelshausen describes "rooms in which were only women in childbed with their children well-cared for by their fellow-sisters without their husbands being present; there were other strange rooms in which there were only many cribs with sucklings that were cleaned and fed by designated women so that their own mothers should not care for them with the exception of three times a day when they could come and offer their milk-rich breasts to them."

Nowadays, the babies and small children stay at home with their mothers until they become students at the Little School, and then they still sleep at home. Through the centuries, the family has become a little more important to Hutterite life, and this is a continuing development. Very similar processes can be observed within the Israeli Kibbutz movement, in which, with decreasing political tension, the collective loses importance in favor of the small group. At the end of his description of a Hutterite farm, Grimmelshausen asks a few questions that touch me strangely here in the bookbinder's house: "I, too," the Catholic writes, "would have liked to live such a blissful life as the anabaptists did...But soon I thought: Tomorrow, you will be different from today... today you embrace chastity, but tomorrow may bring burning desires."

Hardly ever have I enjoyed spring in a more chaste manner than here at the brethren's community of Wilson. Every morning, this spring impresses me over again when I leave my feather bed at the sound of the gong and push aside the white cloth curtains: I see an open landscape with clear lines and poplars straight as sticks at the edge of the colony in the middle of fresh, green colors; behind them, the blooming pastures and fields heavy with moisture. Even the sad-looking telegraph poles along the road past the colony do not bother me anymore. At this early morning hour, a swarm of blackbirds gathers on the wires in a sunlight which is as flat as if this were the beginning of autumn. I see this scenery every day and am happy with an intact world. "There was no wrath, no eagerness, no desire for revenge, no jealousy, no animosity, no worry about things temporary, no pride, no regrets! In summa, it was certainly a lovely harmonia." The way the soldier Grimmelshausen describes the Hungarian community is the way I feel in the morning at the open window in the undisturbed calm of a Hutterite spring.

With the change of the seasons, some things are different on the farm. After breakfast, my fellow-workers Samuel, Heinrich, and Andreas don't feed the cows with me anymore since the Holsteins are now out on pasture. In the morning and in the afternoon, cow-dog Berry chases them to the barn only for milking. Instead of charging us with feeding the cows, winekeeper Johannes sends us behind the smithy to the colony's machinery site. There, machines weighing tons are overhauled for spring planting: 35-foot-wide harrows, ploughs with 12 shares, and giant four-wheel drive tractors that seem to me too big to turn around even in the West German federal state of Saarland. The 30-year-old Benjamin, who is the boss of the mechanics' shop, tells us where old parts need to be replaced, and where greasing is needed and screws must be tightened. Soon the sun will have dried up the lakes of melting water in the fields, and by then everything must be ready for field work around the clock.

Inside the houses, the women whirl around with cleaning rags and scrubbers and turn everything inside out according to their motto "cleanliness is next to godliness." They kneel down in a row on the eating hall's linoleum floor, kerchief next to kerchief, and scrub and chatter endlessly. Before the windows are cleaned, their white frames are scraped with sandpaper, and fresh varnish is applied. The women do this every other year although, to my eyes, everything shines like new even before the "coloring." It wouldn't be necessary, either, to polish the shining pots, pans, and silverware for days, but what do I, a man of the world, understand about women's work and the salvation of the soul!

After school, teacher Samuel and his students pick up from the driveway all kinds of trash that could not be seen because of the snow cover during the long winter. Old paper and scraps of wood are burnt in old oil barrels that are used as trash cans here. Old tires and scrap metal are thrown on the garbage pile behind the barn.

The drive for cleanliness and order, however, is more than a worldly spring cleaning. The great cleaning here is connected with the two holy events that are now in store for us: Baptism and then Easter two weeks later, two highlights on the Hutterite calendar. "The dwelling of God with men" is supposed to look as immaculate and unstained as "a bride adorned for her husband" (Revelation 21:2,3) when the candidates for baptism are spiritually born anew and all brethren and sisters remember the Savior during the Easter communion.

This year, five candidates want to enter "the holy union with God": Martin Wurz, the widowed cook Rachel's son; Sarah and Maria Hofer, breadcutter Johannes' two oldest children; and Lydia and Sarah, the substitute preacher Georg's daughters. They have been preparing for this holy act for a long time. For six weeks, they have been returning straight to their rooms after supper in order to memorize pious vows and to copy endless poems in beautiful German handwriting, each stanza of which begins with a decoratively adorned capital letter. And, instead of participating in Sunday school, they appear before the brethren of the court, the preachers, the housekeeper, the winekeeper, and the bread-cutter in order to be "admonished" for hours about the nature of "the secret of baptism and about what they are supposed to know and do in Christum," as the preacher announces at the beginning of each admonishing session. The intense preparation corresponds to the gravity of the act, for there is only one other event in these five candidates' earthly existence that is as important and momentous as baptism, and that is their physical death.

Baptism itself, however, already is a kind of anticipated death. In order to make "the answer of a good conscience toward God" (1 Peter 3:21), man must overcome his "Adamite" birth, and he must "drown the old Adam" in order to be spiritually reborn. What that really means to a Hutterite is what preacher Johannes reads to the five candidates every Sunday from the "Beautiful and Merry Book Containing Several Main Articles of Our Christian Faith," which his predecessor Peter Walbot wrote back in the 16th century about the topic of "New Birth," and which has since been copied in handwriting by preacher after preacher throughout the centuries. "Dear brethren and sisters," he reads out loud with his thick glasses on his fleshy nose, "you know your innate nature for which you lust against the will of God. Nature makes you proud and haughty. Prove the new birth and be modest, humble, and obedient. Has nature made you greedy, then take what your heart loves, break the greed, and give it away. Are you jealous of nature, full of hate and animosity, then be friendly and do not let this dog's nature do its works. Has nature made you lustful and unchaste, and are your eyes often full of evil desire and your heart full of harmful lust and impure thoughts, then be chaste, honorable, and withdrawn and drive the harmful devil of unchastity away from you. Are you insatiable with food and drink, then be moderate unlike the he-goats and the swine. Has nature made you a lazy donkey that does not want to carry the sack, which is the cross of Christ, then be industrious and eager in the service of God, which is the service of the community. Then and from now on all sins and vices in your flesh shall be like dead, and the ash of the fear of God shall cover and keep hidden the fire of sin just like a dead man whose body may be made of flesh and blood but has no more life. Thus, your flesh must be killed, and Satan, who blows into the fire, must be aborted and chased away through the spirit of God."

These gruesome words are nothing but the strict interpretation of a biblical mission: "For as much then as Christ hath suffered for us in the flesh," Peter writes, "arm yourselves likewise with the same mind: for he that hath suffered in the flesh hath ceased from sin; that he no longer should live the rest of his time in the flesh to the lusts of men, but to the will of God" (1 Peter 4:1-2), and in Romans 6:3 and 4, we read, "Know ye not, that so many of us as were baptized into Christ Jesus were baptized into his death? Therefore we are buried with him by baptism into death."

The reward for this complete self-sacrifice by man, however, is as high as its price, for he who overcomes himself and kills his nature will be born again in the spirit of God and thus attain immortality, "being born again, not of corruptible seed, but of incorruptible, by the word of God, which liveth and abideth forever" (1 Peter 1:23). To a Hutterite, no travail is too hard if one thereby gains eternal life in heaven, which is the goal of every Christian. The individual, however, is too weak for such a degree of overcoming oneself. Man needs the community of all faithful, who "shall be together like the bees in their hive, the sheep in the barn, or the pigeons in their swarm so that the hellish wolf, the eternal tempter, may not harm them," Walbot writes.

With baptism, the human being becomes a member of the sheltering community, a "living stone in the temple of the Lord," symmetrically carved, one like the other, fitting into the whole without any faults. For this, Peter Walbot admonishes the candidates for baptism, "Whoever wants to give himself with body and soul and spirit to God and His community in baptism shall give himself as one who is no longer his own and who does not act according to his will any longer, but as one who has given himself to God and His community so that he can be used for the good of the community and can be used as one who has entered the state of serenity and given up his own free will."

Although it cannot be found in the Bible, the concept of serenity is of central importance in Hutterite life. A serene person has overcome his evil nature. Hatred, jealousy, envy, self-interest, lasciviousness, and, most of all, a free will are things foreign to him. Only by overcoming them can he be integrated into the holy flock's social organism.

"For as our body has many members but not all members have one purpose for it has eyes, ears, a mouth and a nose, hands and feet that keep the body in order. How could the body exist in its order if one of these members did not want to serenely serve the body? So it is in the spiritual sense, in the community and house of the Lord: The eyes as the supervisors and preachers must be used as God demands it of their offices. The ears are the next servants of the need, as there are the winekeeper, the treasurer and all the brethren of the court who must be obedient and do everything necessary to their office. The hands and feet as the subordinate members of the body of Christ must then carry honey, wax, and water like the diligent bees, that is, do sweet and sour things, and help build the body, which is the community, and feed the old, the sick, the widows, and the orphans. In short: Serving God requires the real death of the old Adam and the resurrection with Christ in a new life."

And what about the world and the Lutheran and Catholic "Christians of the mouth?" Do they live according to God's will rather than their own? Peter Walbot's regulations provide the answer: "In the morning they go to their splendid churches that cost up to 100,000 Thalers and gather in blindness and think they serve God. But what they say is not what they do. For during the day, they go to war, one faithful strangles and kills the other through shooting, stabbing, and burning. Then at night, they go to the inn for eating and drinking, and their lust is unharnessed like that of the wild boar and the stallion." In this regard, too, nothing has changed from the ancestors' days to ours, the preacher Johannes believes.

The five candidates for baptism are so excited that, for days, they have hardly been able to sleep. If they are asked later what their birth date is, they will not be able to give an exact answer. "In January," or "in spring" could then be their vague reply. The date of their baptism, however, is something they will remember exactly, even in their graves, "so that we can tell it to the heavenly father on Judgment Day," as the candidate David once entrusted to me.

For him and his four sisters in baptism, that day is the eighth day of April. Pale like the defendants in juvenile court, the five candidates sit at the very head of the classroom of the Wilson colony, eye to eye with the preachers and the brethren of the court, with the community at their backs, just as on the witness stand. The only item pointing to the special occasion is an aluminum milk jug filled with water on the prayer table, which is covered by the white Sunday cloth. First we abundantly sing and pray as at the beginning of each service. The sermon is about Matthew 28:19: "Go ye therefore and teach all nations, baptizing them in the name of the Father, and of the Son, and of the Holy Ghost." Johannes Wurz begins with trembling voice: "Now, dear brethren and sisters, you will know the reason of our gathering here; we are gathered here in all our simplicity in order to give specific instructions and help to these young souls who decided several weeks ago to enter a union with God and all righteous men." Then follows a long-winded summary of all the admonishings that the candidates have had to endure over the past six weeks. For two and a half hours the topic is again child baptism, the death of the flesh, and the service of the community, and we all feel the hard benches. The children in the front become more and more restless in spite of teacher Samuel's occasional strict glances. Johannes and my little friend Paul leave the room, one shortly after the other, since they had been picking their noses until they started to bleed; they don't come back. Picking your nose until it bleeds seems to be a trick to somewhat shorten the long service. At the moment, the teacher is powerless, but afterwards there will be six "Germans" for each of the two boys.

However, the candidates must remain. Before Johannes reaches for the milk jug, all say their baptismal verses, which begin as follows: "O Lord, my God, for mercy I pray, / For righteousness on Judgment Day; / Relieve me from my inborn sin / For the new life I now begin."

David gets stuck already in the first of the 27 verses. His face turned toward the floor, he stands there helplessly in his slightly over-sized candidate costume with the black, knee-long coat, the white shirt, and the usual Sunday trousers. Just two weeks earlier in the shoemaker's house he had bragged to me and said, "Why, getting baptized is to me like eating sausage." Now he fights his tears and stutters and mumbles the verses as if this were already Judgment Day and preacher Johannes were the Savior himself. Now he really seems to become aware of the fact that the "narrow path" which Matthew describes will become even more narrow and stony for him. The youthful sins that until now had been punished and forgiven through half a dozen blows or kneeling for several hours during service will now be punished and atoned for much more severely. In a letter to the preacher, he confessed all his sins: the regular hockey tournaments in the narrow hall of the pigsty for which David used gas pipes from the garbage pile as sticks, with electric tape wrapped around for a handle, and a piece of an old tire as a puck. Then he confessed the skating races on the frozen waste-water pond behind the cowbarn after lunch break when the grown-ups were sleeping from twelve to one.

Full of repentance and following the preacher's orders, he turned in his skates to teacher Samuel with a bleeding heart and had to watch the schoolmaster burn them after Sunday school.

He also had to reveal the well-kept secret of how he got the skates if he wanted to be baptized with a "clean conscience" and unstained hands. Last winter, when he accompanied a hog transport to the stockyards at Lethbridge, the treasurer gave him the usual "subsistence" of one dollar. Everybody has the right to get this dollar when leaving the home community for a few hours so as not to starve in a foreign environment. David, however, did not go to eat a hot dog at Burger King but went rather to the Salvation Army store and spent his subsistence on a pair of rather used ice skates that he managed to smuggle back to the colony in the toolbox of the community's truck. After supper, late at night, he then patched them together secretly in the shoemaker's house, and then professionally smoothed the rusty skids in the smithy. I know for certain that David is not the only wintersports athlete here at the Wilson colony. We can be sure that the gap in the chosen people's hockey team that his baptism now caused to open will soon be filled with young and unbaptized junior players.

"Do you regret your sins against God with your full heart," the preacher asks after David has finally finished stuttering his verses, "and do you wish to fear God from now on and to rather suffer death than to commit an evil deed against God?" In tears, the guilt-laden candidate mutters the answer, "Yes." "Do you then wish to give yourself to the Lord in heaven and sacrifice yourself with body and soul and everything you have and to enter into the obedience of Christ and His community?" "Yes." "Do you then wish to be baptized?" "Yes." Then the preacher puts his right hand on the kneeling David's head, pours the water out of the milk jug over his hair and says, "So I baptize you in the name of the Father, and the Son, and the Holy Spirit. The almighty God who has mercy on you through the death of Christ and the prayer of His community is asked to raise you up into the highest and write your name into the book of life everlasting and keep you righteous and faithful until death. This I wish for you through Jesum Christum. Amen."

At that moment, David is not the only one who weeps. All of the community members assembled here, including myself, have watery eyes. It is simply impossible to keep an inner distance in the middle of all these people, in the confined space of the classroom, wedged in between hog-keeper Georg and shepherd Samuel, whose tears run into their beards. I have never experienced anything like it. Something totally foreign to me, which would even disgust me if I only read or heard about it, all of a sudden becomes an experience which is very personal and almost overwhelms me. I am simply swept along by the Hutterite strength of faith and excited by the honest emotion of the men and women around me. Their tears are tears of grief and joy at the same time, for this is an occasion marking both death and new birth. With both hands, the old preacher helps the baptized up to his feet, saying, "Stand up, my brother. The grace of God be with you." Then he turns to the four girls in order to question and baptize them.

With his eyes reddened from weeping, David meanwhile joins his baptized brethren. Each one of them kisses him on the cheek, saying, "May God protect you." He also goes to the sisters, who, one after the other, shake hands with him, also saying, "May God protect you." Finally, the girls have been baptized as well and are welcomed into the community by the men with a handshake and the women with a kiss. After 3 1/2 hours the five have finally entered into the union with God. We all certainly deserve our Sunday duck. In order to celebrate the occasion, just as during the shearing of the sheep, we have cheesecake with vanilla ice cream for dessert.

During my long and deep nap after lunch I have a dream: I'm sitting in the theater, in the Hamburg Schauspielhaus. As the stage light comes on and the curtain lifts, I look into the faces of my Hutterite brethren and sisters up front in the first row, the women on the left, the men on the right side, the children further in the back in the second row. Only now do I realize what will be performed here: It is I on the stage, the decor is my old Hamburg appartment, and the Hutterites have come "in order to see how one lives in the world," as it is printed in the program. I bend over the glaring ramp and try to convince preacher Johannes that such a play is nothing but lust of the eyes and that he will commit a sin by watching it. But Johannes and the others just don't listen. They turn over the pages of their bibles and sway their upper bodies back and forth like Jews at the Wailing Wall. "Miechel, Miechel, Miechel," they hum, and then the curtain falls and I wake up.

A week later I experience the theater as reality here in the Wilson colony. It is the morning of Easter Sunday. Yesterday we sat for almost seven hours in the service — four hours in the morning and three hours in the afternoon — in order to listen to the exegesis of 1 Corinthians 10, verse 1 ("All our fathers were under the cloud, and all passed through the sea"). Preacher Johannes and his son Georg then make the analogy between the people of Israel and the Hutterites. The Jews, they say, were baptized as they went through the Red Sea, overcame evil, which was the "hellish Pharao," and, through the privation in the desert, grew together into a community in a land of milk and honey. But because they did not obey the Lord's commandments and worshipped a golden calf and later even crucified his son, they threw away their claim to be chosen and have since been cursed "unto the third and fourth generation" (Exodus 20:5). To the Hutterites, the pogroms of the middle ages and, yes, even Auschwitz, are the punishment for "this crime on the Mount of Olives." According to the godly instruction given by their ancestor Jakob Hutter, the brethren and sisters have thus taken it upon themselves to become the chosen people and are separated from evil not by the Red Sea but by the water out of the milk jug; heaven is their promised land, and the earth is the desert, the "valley of tears," in which they must remain not just for forty days but throughout their lives.

We who are not baptized do not need to attend the four-hour communion on Monday morning. Only those community members who have already had the "holy bath" of baptism gather in the schoolhouse at eight o'clock sharp. Andreas Ehrenpreis, from 1639 to 1662 preacher of the Hutterite brethren in Hungary, explains in his "message" why only baptized Christians may be present: "And just as the grain can become no bread unless it is ground and broken, those who wish to hold communion must first be ground and broken by the millstone of God's word (baptism) and must break their entire being and will and transform it into Christian obedience just as the kernels must mix and each one must give its abilities in order to form flour and bread. Those kernels that remain must not enter the bread but be cast out in unworthiness."

At the moment in which the baptized members of the community have disappeared into the schoolhouse single-file, the boys and girls, still unbroken, meet in the colony's kitchen. The Hutterite youth have been ardently awaiting this moment for a year, for the colony belongs to them for the next four hours; no grown-up will be permitted to leave the Lord's dinner company because the holy rule forbids it. During the last days I have often wondered how the "little men" and girls would be able to cope with this morning. How does a strictly guarded flock of young sheep react when both the dog and the shepherd are gone for a couple of hours? Will the animals continue their peaceful grazing, or will they run off into the forest where the wolf will devour all of them?

At first, it looks as though the whole thing won't be too
bad. Having great fun, the girls stand around the range and
make honey candy, and beautiful Rachel willingly tells me
the recipe: "Put some honey in the pan, then butter, then let
it boil until it's brown, and when it is brown, add some soda,
mix it, then you let it cool off and stretch them until they are
nice and golden." With both hands, we then stretch the
sticky, brown honey lumps as if we were working out on a
body-building apparatus and indeed the stuff turns into
sweet lumps of gold. Suddenly I notice that, with the exception of myself, there is no male human being in the kitchen.
"Where are the guys?" I ask a little uneasily. "How should I
know?" Rachel returns the question and pulls her shoulders
up, but her sisters' giggling tells me that they all know very
well where the boys are. Only a few minutes later I see
through the window their march toward the kitchen. Heinrich flaunts in the front, on his head a giant black cowboy
hat, tall as a chimney and wide as a flying saucer. They
storm into the kitchen, a bunch of freaked-out deputy sher-
iffs in mutiny; their lips are painted bright red, their finger-
nails painted silver, gold, and turquoise; they wear thick
shadow around their eyes and have glimmering make-up on
their cheeks in the manner of war-paint. Almost all of them
wear high-heeled cowboy boots that are strictly forbidden
here; under the jackets, their shirts are opened down to the
chest, and the rims of the hats are bent up toward the sky
— a parade of lust of the eye, lust of the flesh, and pride,
sneering at everything that is holy to the community and the
teacher, a babylonic revolt! Teacher Samuel can't move away
from the chosen people's holy communion; he sits there less
than 200 yards away while his flock goes crazy!

For the next 3 1/2 hours, square-faced Heinrich, as the
oldest of the unbaptized, seizes the ark's rudder. Everybody
now listens to his commands. He tells Samuel and Martin to
take a truck from the shop and to drive to Lethbridge to get
beer and liquor. There is still a little money left from the fox

hunt in the winter, and it will be just enough for two cases.
Until the two are back from town, one resorts to the flower
wine, which is taken out of the cellar in gallon jars. In his
excitement over the communion, the old treasurer Jakob
must have left the key to the wine cellar at home. Even without alcohol, the mood is almost exuberant. To be without
grown-ups once a year for four hours, unsupervised, free!
This feeling has a stronger effect than the hardest drug.
When, toward 10 o'clock, the wine begins to show its effect
and fresh supplies from town arrive with two completely
drunk delivery men, there is simply no stopping anymore.
The "Blueberry Liqueur" makes its round, there is a chaos of
screams and shouts, and honey lumps are thrown in the air;
Joschua, the first victim of alcohol, throws up into the sink.
In the corner, the members of some kind of band have taken
their places. Samuel (harmonica), Josef (washboard), Heinrich (cooking-pan percussions), and Martin (frying-pan
banjo) clatter and bawl, singing the same words over and
over again: "We get married in June, have a long honeymoon, and will never be apart." Heinrich has heard this
country song from his transistor radio at night under the
blanket, and now the boys dance and gyrate their hips to
the imaginary rhythm of the band, as if they were possessed
by the devil himself.

The girls huddle together at the range, sip reluctantly
from the blueberry liqueur, giggle and whisper. But I also
notice anxiety and fear in their eyes; this is not unadulterat-
ed joy to them. I can imagine their thoughts all too well,
since I am nervous, too. Again and again the fellows toast
with me, ask me for a dance and tell me that it won't make
any difference to a man of the world, for purgatory will be
my certain destiny since it is the fate "of the evil daughter."
Why not tickle the flesh for a little while? Why not drink and
dance?

How I would like to let loose now after more than three
months of voluntary asceticism and iron abstinence! From

the bottom of my heart, I would like to catch another
glimpse of Rachel's eyes and her softly curved lips. By God,
after two bottles of beer, the flesh really tempts me as never
before in the Hutterite colony. So far I have simply resigned
to the fact that I would live here at the Wilson monastery
regardless of the consequences. My fate could be compared
to that of a sailor who becomes very calm as soon as the
anchor is lifted. Just as on the high sea, there has been no
temptation on the ark. Therefore, it has not been difficult for
me to keep my flesh down, as they say here. But now there
is such a turned-on, almost ecstatic atmosphere that it is
hard for me to stand passively in the corner away from the
party as a quiet yet sympathizing observer. My reticence
makes Captain Heinrich a little skeptical. With a grand
gesture he motions me to come over to him. I play his game
and do as he orders. "You won't say a word to the old people," he warns me, and I promise to mention nothing that I
see here.

While the band continues to bawl "We get married in
June," I stick my head out of the window in order to breathe
a little fresh spring air. From the neighboring schoolhouse I
can hear the community's hymn: "Humility, this is the door
/ To our heav'nly hall, As Jesus Christ has said before, /
This path allows no fall."

Now I must really pinch my leg to make sure this is no
dream. This is true. The little kindergarten kids now gather
below the kitchen windows. They, too, are without adult
supervision today. Elisabeth, a girl of about twelve, brings
them their food and occasionally checks on them, but I'm
sure there has been plenty of time for extended peeing
games in celebration of the day. Little Martin at least is in
high spirits. He and the others now demand their share of
the Hutterite carnival. "Candy, candy, candy," they shout
until Heinrich the Great condescendingly throws a few sweet
lumps to them. Entrance to the kitchen, however, is not permitted to them, for the adolescents, too, care about having

an exclusive society. Only those students who already attend German school and are thus six years or older are allowed to carry on in this particular place.

Shortly before noon, the kitchen orgy reaches its climax although Heinrich, the hero of the day, has already abdicated and gone to bed with a green face. Completely drunk, Andreas pulls a picture of the "Playmate of the Month" out of his jacket pocket and shows his buddies the "evil flesh" as if it were a precious host. The girls have an idea of what it is that's making its rounds over there, and all of them hide their faces. This, after all, is too much lust of the eyes for them. Rachel and her sister Anna run outside and repentantly hide in their house. Even though the patriarchs of the church may not know anything about these sinful activities, they still fear that the heavenly father may see everything. Surely He must have seen the truck-theft in the shop, the drunken boys' crazy dance, and Samuel's harmonica, and even the little radio without batteries in Heinrich's pocket could not be hidden from His eyes. He has probably added these sins to His list on which certainly many a fox hunt in self-interest and many a merry ice skating round could be found. And woe, when, on the last day, "the judgment [is] set, and the books [are] opened" (Daniel 7:10), for then "there shall be weeping and gnashing of teeth" (Matthew 8:12).

Today, the Hutterite youth are going to experience a foretaste of Judgment Day. After communion, shortly after one o' clock, the grown-ups leave the schoolhouse with careworn faces. During bread and wine, they must have been sitting on hot coals, anticipating the worst. After all, they once were young and unbaptized themselves. I am told that such sinful outbreaks are a tradition reaching back to Jakob Hutter's days although they are not mentioned in the pious songs and chronicles. To be sure, the girls quickly eliminated the worst traces of the orgy in the kitchen shortly before it was "High Noon"; they hid the empty bottles, wiped the floor, and polished the range that had been sticky with honey, but during lunch the gaps in the rows of the boys who still show quite visible signs of make-up reveal the extent of the wicked activities. Heinrich, Samuel, Andreas, and Jakob are completely drunk and lie in their beds. Even three hours later during Sunday school, they are so fuddled that they don't really feel the force of Samuel's blows. Responding to the teacher's question, the boys meekly declare that, from now on, they will neither drink themselves silly nor paint their faces with left-over make-up. (Heinrich had found old cans and tubes in a municipal trash can next to a beauty shop.) Kneeling down, we then vow all together never to do anything like this morning again, for "not doing it again is the greatest repentance." The next communion, Heinrich whispers to me as we leave the room, is in exactly one year. Until then, he certainly will keep being reminded of a thing or two.

To me, the revolt of the young Hutterite flesh was a key experience. As I saw the rebelling boys with their colorfully painted faces dance in beautiful drunkenness, I felt somewhat relieved in spite of being worried about the threatening consequences. For the first time, I got an impressive confirmation of teacher Samuel's words "that we Hutterites, too, are made of flesh and blood." To me, the chosen people just became more human after I had seen their weaknesses. For months, the bright light of the righteous way of life had blinded me at work, during the meals, during prayer, and during the singing at night, but now I had finally seen some shadows. What a relief! Eventually it would have become weird to live together with saints rather than human beings.

The high moral standards from morning until night, the strict education of unselfishness, self-sacrifices, and serenity without a will of one's own — these could only result in tensions that the young had to discharge. Just as medieval people were able to laugh at the worldly and religious authorities by way of the carnival before the beginning of the time of abstinence during Lent, the Hutterite youth protested against everything that is holy to the old by way of the orgy during communion. Their Lent, which will last all through their adult lives, will begin early enough with baptism. The great God will certainly wink at this; "the Lord is merciful and gracious...for as the heaven is high above the earth...the Lord pitieth them that fear him," we read in the 103rd Psalm of King David, who, as we know, did not always walk on the path of virtue himself.

Much different from the medieval bishops of Cologne, Mainz, or Munich, the preacher Johannes Wurz at the Wilson colony must nowadays cope with conflicts that are carried into the community from a completely foreign and even contradictory environment. For in spite of their isolation from North American society and in spite of their withdrawn, hedgehog-like existence on the prairie away from the towns and major highways, it is increasingly difficult for the Hutterites to keep the "world" out. Even if the batteries in Heinrich's transistor radio are empty, the Hutterite youth from the Wilson farm are not completely cut off from the world around them. When, for example, the policeman and gentleman rancher Bill West comes from the neighboring farm and brings his defective tractor to the shop at the Wilson colony in order to have the generator repaired for little money, the boys listen up. There is a radio in the 100-horse-power tractor, and at night at 10 o'clock, when everybody is asleep, Radio CFCN — "Your friendly voice in the Rockies" — broadcasts live the decisive ice hockey game of the "Montreal Canadians" versus the "Boston Bruins." To Heinrich, who uses the radiant portrait of the national storm Ron Ellis as a bookmarker in his Bible, this is definitely worth a sound beating. Thus, with a couple of inductees, he slips out of his well-caring parents' house in order to listen to the program in front of the tractor's radio in the dark smithy.

Also, it happens often enough that Sergeant West requests a few Hutterite hands for snow shoveling, cleaning the barn, or haying. "Love your enemies" (Matthew 5:44) is Christ's commandment, and thus winekeeper Johannes usually can't say no when the officer calls. To the young, the job at the neighbor's is great fun. At noon they sit in the rancher's furniture-stuffed living room, eat "finger licking good" Kentucky Fried Chicken and gaze at the almighty Kojak on TV. However, an animated commercial for a detergent impresses them much more than the bald-head's heroic deeds. There you actually see an elephant with huge ears fly through the air as if it were a bird. If the world shows such "lies" on the screen, "how then are you supposed to know what's true and what isn't?" asks Heinrich. The landing on the moon, too, had been shown on TV, and a few brethren watched it at Bill West's home more than ten years ago. Believing their own eyes, however, was something they didn't do, for if God had wanted people to be on the moon, he would have created them right there just as he created Adam and Eve here on earth. And besides, what is really "true" in the world, what is "real"? The armour in the corner next to the plush-covered TV is made of plastic as are the flowers in the window and the rustic "wood" beams on the ceiling. The chicken on their plates does not come from Kentucky and is not exactly "finger licking good" but tough like a dog, and even the reddish shimmer of the artificial fire in the fireplace is cold and dead. Everything here is only make-believe.

The boys can feel that, but nevertheless they are fascinated by the blinding gleam of that world of consumption, and nowhere can this be noticed more than in the prairie town of Lethbridge northwest of the Wilson colony. When the sheep's wool is sold, I am allowed to come along to town for the first time in almost four months. First, of course, I must report to each of the five brethren of the court and state exactly the nature of my "business" in town. If I get lost in the evil world, they must know where to look for me, as Johannes explains the old rule. The sacks into which I had treaded the wool during the shearing of the sheep in February are in the back of the truck. Like black triplets, treasurer Jakob, shepherd Samuel and I sit in the front. Samuel drives and Jakob goes through a stack of bills. There is almost no traffic on Highway 4, which goes straight northwest. On both sides of this road, there are flat fields and pastures up to the horizon. No tree or bush prevents the eye from looking. If there weren't the snow-capped Rocky Mountains over in the west, the eye would find nothing to hold on to on these endless North American plains. The Hutterites need this empty space as a safe distance between themselves and the others, between the holy community and the vicious world. Had they remained in Moravia during Jakob Hutter's time, the over-population in Central Europe would have absorbed them long ago. Here in Alberta, however, there is space. And it's at least 30 miles to sinful Lethbridge, "where sin is no longer sin and shame no longer shame."

When I came here from Germany more than three months ago, this place looked to me like a typical Western town — faceless and dead: boring suburban homes on the outskirts, the typical motel strip, a few supermarkets, a few banks, the police station, and of course McDonald's, Kentucky Fried Chicken, and Burger King, united in their battle for total destruction of any kind of cultivated eating. Lethbridge was just dead boring — then.

Now, four months later, it seems as if hell has broken loose. The hectic pace of the people, the noise of the street, the screaming advertising, the smell of dust! Only now do I realize where I am: in 20th-century America, the Babylon of modern times. Jakob asks me whether Hamburg is as big as Lethbridge. I nod and don't mention that it is 40 times as big.

In a dark and gloomy factory yard we load our wool sacks on a scale. A man wearing red-checkered pants adds up 4,100 pounds. With Jakob and Samuel he disappears into the gray building. I must watch our truck. After half an hour my brethren return; they smell slightly of liquor and have a check for $2,200. The treasurer is in a very good mood and takes his leather wallet out of his jackèt. Samuel and I get one dollar each. "This is your subsistence so that you don't have to starve," the gray-beard tells me generously. This is the first time since my arrival that I have held a dollar bill in my hand. It is a strange feeling. Money, the center around which everything turns, has completely disappeared from my thoughts and simply plays no role anymore. In Wilson I have everything necessary for my "temporary needs" — food, work, clothing, and a roof over my head. There I am totally free of money and materialistically independent; "Mother Community" takes care of the future. And now there is the consumption money, the subsistence. I wonder what I should buy with that green paper — a hot dog, ice cream, a cup of coffee — or should I save it? These are strange thoughts.

This Thaler is the only legal cash owned by a Hutterite. On the average, the "menfolk" are in town on business twice a month, the women only about once every other month when they have to go to the doctor. Just as we have today, all Hutterites come to Lethbridge almost exclusively on Thursdays in order to sell eggs, hogs, grain, and, in the summer, fresh vegetables to the wholesale dealers. "Thursday is Hutterite Day," the local people say. They may be upset because gynecologists, optometrists, and dentists, in particular, are almost completely booked up on Hutterite Day, but every person living in town knows how important the "Black Birds" have become to the country's economy.

Although the colonies farm only between 1 and 2 percent of the land devoted to agriculture in the province of Alberta (which is almost three times as big as West Germany), their market share in the production of eggs is 30% and in hog production 25%; almost 10% of all frying chickens come from Hutterite barns. Between 1972 and 1975, milk production increased from 3.6% to 5% of the country's total, and the Hutterites have even had a monopoly of 100% in the production of duck and goose feathers. Market orientation is not the brethren's only concern. They also promote a wide range of employment at the colonies (unemployment in Canada is at 9% but at 0% among the Hutterites). They produce in a variety of sectors in order not to be hard-hit when prices fluctuate. If grain is cheap, the price of beef may be high; if eggs don't yield much profit, then sheep's wool may. This is how the treasurers keep their budgets stable, and the entire country's economic structure benefits. When, five years ago, the cost of hog feed doubled, many farmers got out of the "pig business," for it wasn't worth it anymore. The Hutterites remained in the business and today are said to be leading hog breeders.

The case is similar in duck production. Three years ago, the price for one pound of feathers was at $10; today it is a mere $3.50. To the Hutterites, the Sunday roast is more important, so they continue to fatten between 1,000 and 1,500 animals per colony annually. Besides, Georg, the broombinder at Wilson, must be occupied during the summer, and it makes no difference whether his work is profitable or not. Money is of only secondary importance. "We Hutterites, we don't work for the Thaler but for our community" is the economic motto here. However, it is the economic principle of distributed risk that is so successful, for it does not depend on supply and demand. Through their size, flexibility, and thriftiness, the brethren's communities widely surpass the ordinary family operation. The Hutterites have plenty of cheap workers, consume no profits, and can thus afford the latest technology, which, in turn, they can use optimally on their big farms.

The heavenly community established by Jakob Hutter 450 years ago proves to be an appropriate and modern economic model which reflects much more accurately the development of mass production in our times than does its "worldly" competition. Even though the brethren and sisters take advantage of the technical progress of the otherwise-hated world and run high risks in doing so, they do not forget old and trustworthy ways. The most expensive combines, which cost $25,000 each, are right next to the antediluvian broom-bindery at Wilson; women in 16th-century costume work brand-new milking machines, shepherd Samuel feeds his lambs the latest vitamin diet, and his wife makes the sauerkraut with the other women just as their great-grand-mothers did: "cut the cabbage, put it in a trough, add some salt, pour hot water over it, then close it and wait until it's good." Hutterland: the technicized Middle Ages.

Whether the pact between old and new will hold for much longer is a question many a worried preacher asks today. Only 50 years ago, there were heated debates among the principals about whether the automobile was devil's work or not. Arguing that everything that is useful for the community must be good, they decided in favor of progress and bought the first black Ford pickup truck. With that purchase, a piece of the voluntary isolation from the world was given up, for the 30 miles between Lethbridge and the Wilson colony had meant half a day's trip. Today it takes not quite 45 minutes, and if one is in a hurry as were the thirsty communion sinners on last Easter Monday, one can make it in 30 minutes. Besides, the automobile was not the only thing. Combines, power generators, electronic welding equipment, refrigerators, chicken farm equipment, artificial fertilizer were purchased — everything for the good of the community, to be sure. But with each technical novelty a piece of the evil world enters God's hut as well; relations between inside and outside become closer, and some of the contrasts begin to fade.

Just how intensified the worldly contact has become cannot be overlooked on this Thursday in Lethbridge. The streets around the little city park where the brethren gather are black with Hutterites. On every corner, there are the "town-goers" from the five dozen colonies around Lethbridge who put their beards together, whispering about the latest news — presenting a picture of what might be the Jewish section of old Antwerp. The women, too, have much to talk about, although they prefer to meet in the trucks and vans. They dare to venture in the streets only in order to quickly spend their subsistence on something sweet or to cast a curious and bewildered glance at the full supermarket shelves. This is a foreign world which must cause much confusion in their heads. This is in particular true for the young Hutterites, such as Heinrich and his followers, who came to town today with the egg transport from Wilson. I meet them at "Wolco," the biggest department store in town. In the electronics department, they stand motionless in front of a wall of dozens of television sets and watch six or seven channels simultaneously. Even for somebody like myself who is more than used to watching TV, it is difficult to watch a Western, a musical, commercials, and children's programs all at the same time without being able to hear anything because there is no sound. How confusing these optical fireworks must be for the boys from Wilson! And they don't watch by themselves: Thirty or forty "black" boys stand breathless and bedazzled in front of the television wall with their mouths wide open. They don't know where to look and are chased from the flying detergent elephant to war in the burning steppe, from the cowboy at sunset to the mathematical formula of the educational programming — from one light stimulus to the other. If I knew at this moment where the fuse box was in this store, I would turn off the electricity instantly. How in the world do the adolescents cope with such city impressions? The conflict between the inner and the outer world that can't be experienced more intensely than here in front of that mountain of televisions — must it not lead, in the long run, to the self-destruction of the brethren's communities?

No wonder then that many a boy freaks out when he comes to town. It is not overly unusual for some adolescents to use the visit in town to simply run away. Then they make quick money working as cowboys on a ranch or drilling for oil in the extreme north. They always find jobs, for the "Huts" are known and wanted as cheap and hard workers. They can earn around one thousand dollars on the oil rigs — an astronomical sum for somebody who used to get a subsistence of two Thalers per month. It is surprising, however, that sooner or later almost all runaways contritely return to the colonies. No matter how many sins they have committed out there, — those who confess and repent are forgiven.

Thirty-year-old Johannes Hofer from the Kily colony in the neighboring province of Saskatchewan was out in the world for 15 years. He drilled for oil from Alaska to Saudi-Arabia and hopped on a plane to see the Munich October-fest. "I've been all across the ocean, I've been to the end of the world, and it couldn't go any more badly," the athletically built man says. Fortunately, he was still unbaptized, and thus the punishment was quite mild: For four weeks, he had to kneel down during the two-hour service every Sunday. In addition, he was not permitted to go into town for six months. Today, he is the hog-boss and, as he says, more content than ever even though the oil company "Santa Fe" in Texas still sends its ex-driller Hofer express letters containing job offers ("Our offer: $4,100/month") to the colony. Johannes is not tempted anymore, for he has had enough of the world. "I believed that being a Hutterite could be forgotten with passing time," but he admits, "for fifteen years I tried to silence my conscience with liquor and with women. But what's inside of you is something you can't get out. A Hutterite belongs to his community; anywhere else he is eaten by the wolves."

Every Thursday in Lethbridge I realize how right Johannes is. Without protection, the Hutterites are confronted with glistening wealth. Just like the impoverished Indians from the Blackfoot reservation nearby, some of them ashamedly go through trash cans and garbage containers of the city, looking for things for which the world has no more use. It even happens that they reach out in the supermarkets and department stores and shoplift the forbidden fruits of consumption despite the Seventh Commandment. The apple tree in paradise wasn't worth a tired glance compared with the sweet praline boxes or the colorful stickers with the pictures of ice hockey heroes. Yet Young Heinrich doesn't think that all is so terrible. "You have to have fun," he merrily says in front of the television sets, "and as long as you're young and not baptized, that can't hurt."

I, myself, have some problems in town as well. My fingers start to itch, for example, when I sneak along a newspaper and magazine stand with almost the same kind of inconspicuous and gliding walk as my brethren; then I cast a quick glance at the colorful magazines, and I can feel them trying to grab me, trying to take all my time with all the sensations of the worldly theater. "Carter's Crisis," "Revolt in Nicaragua," "Muhammed Ali Defeated" — these headlines make me really nervous. I feel like an alcoholic who has been dry for four months and now enters a liquor store in order to get change for the phone. I promised myself not to read any newspapers as long as I was with the Hutterites. And now the headlines scream at me in such a way that I can't help but simply turn the pages of *Newsweek* and *Time*. Well, I am made of blood and flesh, too.

All of a sudden, however, just as I want to reach for *Playboy*, an older Hutterite comes from the candy aisle in the supermarket, looks at me, stops short, and comes at me. "I've never seen you, cousin. What community do you belong to?" I explain to him that I've been at the Wilson colony for four months but that I actually come from Germany. "What, you've been at Wilson four months," the black-bearded man says, "and you've already learned to speak German?" He, too, is one of those who can't really believe that I learned and spoke German in Germany and that all people there learn to speak that language when they are little children and speak it as the chosen people do, just in a different dialect. The Hutterite with the broad shoulders is Elias Wurz, the preacher of the Waterton colony, which is a community 60 miles west directly in the foothills of the Rocky Mountains. The people at Waterton are closely related to those at Wilson. Twenty years ago, they "said good-bye" to one another when it became too crowded in the brethren's community of Wilson. Four families remained on the old farm, and four moved to the new one. The Waterton colony split up again three years ago. Now there are 80 people remaining there, and, because most of them are children, there is a lack of workers in preacher Elias's community — particularly now during harvesting time.

"Why don't you come and help us? The people at Wilson have enough workers — and we need every hand we can get!" Elias says. On the same Thursday, he asks preacher Johannes (who is his uncle) on the street next to the city park "whether the German can't work at our place?" The old man has nothing against it. "You can have him," he says; I am at his disposal. Although nobody asked me, this is just fine with me. I would like for once to experience a different colony, and the Rockies tempt me, too, for I can see them wave at me every morning when I look out the window of the bookbinder's house.

Thus I pack my things and yet find it difficult to leave Wilson. I have spent four months in this colony; according to my diary, the gas oven's low rustling has accompanied my sleep and many a dream in the bookbinder's hut during 115 nights. On the last evening in the circle of the community, treasurer Jakob gives me a newly bound songbook containing all the martyrs' ballads that we sang together. "Don't forget us and come back," the old man says. His wife Sarah, too, has a farewell present for me: hand-knitted woolen socks, for up in my new Hutterite home in the mountains of Waterton, it is still cold at the end of April. Through their self-evident cordiality, they have become particularly dear to me. I will miss them both. I also hate to leave Heinrich and his accomplices. Now the fellows must find a new partner for their contests, and I think they don't like the thought very much. They have really had their fun with me, the man of the world who sometimes acts so wonderfully stupid. Now they will be left to themselves again.

With the eggs from the 2,835 colony hens, we drive into town the next morning. Near the park, the brethren's gathering point, preacher Elias from the Waterton community is already waiting for me in his hog truck. After a brief hello we are on our way westward 60 miles toward the mountains. The land becomes rolling only very gradually and, with almost no transition, we leave the endless plains of the prairie and rise up into the foothills. Our road leads us through the reservation of the Blackfoot Indians; every 200 yards, there is a run-down shack that almost can't be seen because of big junked cars. Some half-tame horses graze on scanty pastures. Much land here is not used. The "Yellow ones," as the Hutterites call their red-skinned neighbors, "are bad farmers," Elias says slightly contemptuously. "They only know how to drink; that's all they know." That the Indians are uprooted and desperate refugees is something he knows as well, but he doesn't understand their lethargy. "Why can't they work like we do?" is his only comment.

Five miles down the road I find a different world: ploughed fields, huge herds of cattle, freshly painted grain bins, and finally, across an iron bridge, the Waterton colony. My arrival at preacher Elias's community is very different from that at the brethren's farm at Wilson. Whereas there I stood alone and forsaken on the farm for an eternity and was suspiciously watched from dark windows, here I get a big welcome. As soon as Elias has stopped the truck in front of the kitchen, the people come running with children and grandchildren; it seems that the teacher has cancelled class for my arrival.

But the questions I have to answer I know almost by heart already: "Are you Miechel from Germany? Are your parents in good health? Have you been baptized yet? Do you have a TV at home? Were you in the military? What is your profession? Do you have a girlfriend? Did you come on the airship?" Of course, the people here at Waterton already know all the answers. Word goes around quickly from colony to colony, and nothing remains secret in Hutterland. But still they want to hear me say these things: that I was baptized when I was eight years old, that I have a TV at home, that I never was a soldier, that I have problems with my girlfriend, that I am a professional writer, and that I flew across the ocean in an airplane big enough to hold the population of three or four Hutterite colonies, which constitutes a number of people that almost can't be imagined. "Siberian" is the word that is whispered in the rows in front of the kitchen and probably meaning something like "gigantic" or "of Siberian proportions." My arrival here is different from my arrival at the Wilson community in that I do not feel like a stranger at Waterton at all. I am familiar with many things, and I can orient myself right away. At first glance I recognize the long, drawn-out living quarters, the cow barn, the kitchen, the school, and the bookbinder's house, and, of course, this is where I am going to live. During my time at the Wilson colony I have also gotten used to getting up in the middle of the night, to eating duck heads for breakfast, and to the long praying. I have adapted to Sunday school and obediently recite my "verses" when the teacher at Waterton, Paul Hofer, looks at me with the same stern look used by his colleague Samuel Wurz from the Wilson community and asks, "Well, Miechel, what did you hear at the service?" Mother colony and daughter colony resemble each other like identical twins.

Only the landscape is very different. Whereas Wilson is situated on prairie that is flat as a pancake, Waterton is surrounded by foothills of the Rocky Mountains. Sheep, cows, and horses graze on the slopes around the colony, and a herd of pigs wallow in the mire of a sand pit. Behind the stables, the Waterton River thunders down into the valley, a wide and wild river; the melted water of spring has made it rise over its banks. To the east, I see the high and dammed-up Waterton Lake, and to the west, the mountains threaten: a wall of black and gray rock with the mountain tops still covered with snow. Jakob Hutter, the Tyrolese ancestor from Weiler Moos in the Puster valley, would have felt at home here.

Because the spring rain runs off faster in hilly Waterton than out on the plains, housekeeper Johannes Wurz can start to work in the dried fields earlier than can his cousin with the same name down at Wilson. And so, for the first time in my life, I found myself on a tractor (the Hutterites call it "engine") the morning after my arrival. With short and precise words, the 40-year-old Johannes explains to me how this monster with the power of 80 horses is handled, when each of the 16 gears is used, where the clutch is and where the hydraulics are.

After 10 minutes of theoretical driving lessons I creep across a sea of fertile and brown mother soil, pulling a 30-yard-wide harrow behind me. It is a wonderful feeling to sit up here in the soft-cushioned driver's seat with my hand relaxed on the power-steering wheel and the field at my feet. The flat morning light molds graceful forms out of the gentle hills and the wide valleys around me. No power lines and certainly no asphalt cut through the vastness; here the eye can still roam freely. Now I would like to slow down and just shut off the thundering engine, climb down from the driver's cabin, and just stretch out below the rejoicing larks in the blue western sky... But God knows there's no time for daydreaming. Nearly 1,500 acres must be finished in the next few weeks; to me, the European, this immense area seems to be larger than half of West Germany. (The remaining

1,500 acres farmed by the colony have been planted with winter wheat in the fall.)

From morning to night, I harrow three miles per hour, row after row, uphill, downhill, field after field. From Monday to Wednesday it is oats, from Thursday to Saturday barley, and rape during the entire week that follows. Soon nothing is left of the initial romantic view of the city person. The dust comes in through the smallest cracks, and the supposedly sound-proof cabin of the tractor resounds and vibrates hellishly. At times, I develop claustrophobic anxieties in this glass cage.

Fortunately, I am not alone out in the country. As always, the community is everywhere. There are three other community tractors that are out with me; they are driven by Christian, Andreas, and Georg, the sons of the preacher, the treasurer, and the chicken keeper. Twenty-four-year-old Christian pulls the 12-share plough; his uncle Andreas, who is about the same age, cuts through the soil with the disk; and Georg, at 20 the youngest of us, fills the field with kernels using a gigantic planter; then I rake the field with my 30-yard harrow into a finely woven Barbary rug. Other men, smith Jacob, shepherd Georg, and hog keeper Johannes, drive their trucks back and forth between the colony's bins and the fields and bring new grain seed. During recess three times a day, schoolteacher Paul comes to bring us lunch. Winekeeper Johannes busily drives around in his white station wagon, called the "white horse" by the children, so that nothing can go wrong. If, once in a while, my harrow breaks because I make a turn that is too sharp and drive over my own rope or if one of the axles cannot stand this permanent stress, then the "white horse" is right there with spare parts and welding equipment, and my harrow is ready to go again after minutes of feverishly hastened work.

Everything must go quickly now; time is pressing, for at 900 meters above sea level, the growth period is very short: This is the middle of May, and the first frost may come as early as September and ruin the crops. Nothing may be left to chance, but chance doesn't really exist for the God-fearing Hutterites anyway. The shearing of the sheep at the Wilson colony has already given me a taste of the precision and smoothness with which the heavenly community handles its big common projects. As there, the community here reminds me of an industrious anthill or a busy beehive in which everybody works into the other's hands and, for the common good, is responsible and immensely diligent. Nobody cares about how many days the work goes on from morning to night; nobody figures out the number of hours worked, and nobody works a little less hard just because the winekeeper happens to be gone for a while. The more sweat runs down the back under the warm midday sun, the better: "In the sweat of the face shalt thou eat bread" (Genesis 3:19), and none of us sweat "for his own Thaler" but for "our land," for "our holy community" in short, for ourselves.

At this work, at this religious service, there are no hierarchies, neither those who command nor those who obey. To be sure, Johannes, as winekeeper, is responsible for planning and coordinating, but before the day's work begins, he discusses with his men in front of the kitchen after breakfast which field must be ploughed first or who will get a spare part from town. This way, each person knows what the others are doing, and there are few misunderstandings and little waste of time. The preacher doesn't consider himself too good to fix a clogged water pipe in between his other jobs; because of the current shortage of workers, his father, treasurer Elias, still reaches for his hammer to straighten out bent bolts in spite of his 72 years. The Hutterite beehive hums with righteous activity, and the women prepare extra rations of steak and lamb meat for us hungry "menfolk" out in the fields.

The worldly farmers in the neighborhood cannot compete with this kind of community awareness. The Waterton colony is almost always the first farm in the entire area to be finished with planting. The neighbor Walter Meyer, for instance, whose ancestors immigrated from Germany, owns a typical family operation of 700 acres of grazing and farming land with 30 cattle and three horses. Long ago, he gave up trying to keep up with the "black competition" and sold his outdated machinery. When the men from Waterton have finished planting, they drive over to Meyer's land and cultivate his fields. Hiring them is cheaper for him and saves the work. His son doesn't feel like taking over his father's farm anyway. Thus Meyer will sell his acres to the colony in a few years and retire to Florida's sunshine.

After exactly 20 days, all fields are finally cultivated. Blissfully, I lie in the "bathing trough", a bathtub in the communal wash house. There are six stalls next to one another; each contains a trough which is similar to the miners' pithead baths in West Germany's industrial Ruhr area. Today is Saturday, and I enjoy my weekend-bath even though the water turns into a pitch-black broth as soon as I have sat down. Every itching and pinching of a long work week on the tractor is rewarded with ten lust-filled minutes. Afterwards, I feel as if I have been born anew. Of course, it is not only we dirty tractor drivers who clean up before the holy Sunday. At noon, the women and girls were in the tubs. After 4 o'clock, genders are switched and the men and boys form lines outside the doors of the stalls.

This morning, the women polished the floor in the schoolhouse so that the planks shimmer with brilliance, and they took the Sunday roasts, the ducks, out of the freezer and piled them into the kitchen sink to thaw. The mothers now comb and make pigtails in their freshly washed little daughters' hair, using fat full milk so that the hairdo will keep for an entire week. The braiding and twisting hurts Susanna, who is not even four years old; as on every Saturday, her mother Katharina, schoolteacher Paul's massive wife, comforts her daughter by telling her a fairy tale that even I know: "Once upon a time, there were a father and a mother who had two little children. One was a boy and one was a girl, and their names were Hansel and Gretel...."

After lunch, preacher Elias retreats into his room in order to prepare for the prayer for the upcoming "Holy Eve" and for the service tomorrow morning. The stocky man with the broad face around which the black full beard begins to show some gray sits at his "Alma," the bookshelf-desk in which the precious sermons are locked and guarded like a treasure since they constitute the Hutterites' spiritual foundation. These are old, well-thumbed volumes with Roman numerals on their backs. Some of them were written in German script by great-grandfather in Russia. Most of them, however, Elias had to copy himself in the light of the naked bulb during many long winter nights after he was elected preacher ten years ago. Although many scriptures disappeared during the century-long persecutions and were either burned by Jesuits or simply lost, there are still 600 sermons and introductions that the brethren use on a daily basis today. The titles refer to the contents: "The Sermon About Humility," "The Sermon About Punishment," "The Sermon for Women," "The Sermon for Weddings," "The Sermon for Funerals."

For the evening prayer, he has chosen the 104th Psalm: "O Lord my God, thou art very great...He sendeth the springs into the valleys, which run among the hills. They give drink to every beast of the field: the wild asses quench their thirst...He watereth the hills from his chambers: the earth is satisfied with the fruit of thy works. He causes the grass to grow for the cattle, and herbs for the service of man that he may bring forth food out of the earth...These wait all upon thee, that thou mayest give them their meat in due season."

What will now become of our seeds that start to grow in the Hutterite soil? Whether they will give the community the bread from the earth — this is now for almighty God to decide. With sweat and work alone, the preacher says, a good harvest can't be forced. "We did what was in our power. Now we must pray and wait and see whether it will be good and God will bless us with good fruit." All summer long we will have to be patient; in the fall, we will then see whether God has shown mercy on his people by granting the right amounts of sunshine and rainfall or whether he will want to try them with drought and scarce results. Whatever may happen, Elias knows, "What God does is done well."

SUMMER

The Song of Songs
for My Rachel

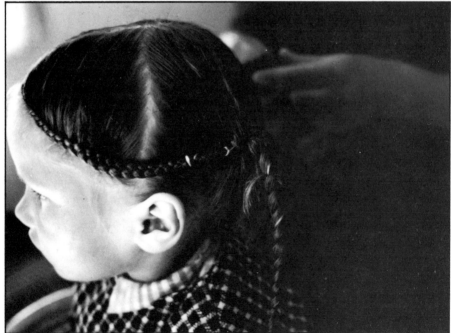

In Hutterland, the summer turns the schoolteacher into a gardener. The taller the weeds grow under the increasingly hot sun, the more often Paul Hofer must transfer the afternoon "German School" to the communal garden. At three o'clock sharp he doesn't wait with his bible under his arm as usual but stands next to a little red tractor; he is impatient and waits for his pedagogical adversary, the English teacher, to finally come to the end of her Mars stories, her theory about the origin of the species, and other "worldly wisdom" so that he can load the 28 students entrusted to him on the wooden trailer. Today, again, the children won't get much time to play, for they must go from their desks directly into the vegetables at the edge of the colony to weed. "Life is work," Paul quotes some Bible passage, "and those who work do not sin." Hutterite children must get used to that idea from early on.

And there is enough to do in his garden. On an area of three acres, the plants grow in long and straight rows, but before I can understand what grows where, I must first broaden my knowledge of the Hutterite tongue. The Russian words "Kratsawitz" and "Bageliana" are used for cucumbers and tomatoes; just as in the south of Germany, sunflowers are "Sunnarosn," carrots "Mädl," and sweet peas "Zuckerstrankl." But instead of the good old Bavarian or Carinthian dialect words "Kirbis" (pumpkin) or "Radi" (radish), the English words are used. The gardener doesn't even know the German word for vegetable anymore. In the best beautiful Hutterite gibberish he calls everything that the Heavenly Father lets thrive in his garden simply "garden stuff."

The fruits in this garden also include potatoes, head lettuce, garlic, onions, and red beets, and the community's annual turnover through sales to individual neighbors and to wholesale dealers in Lethbridge amounts to more than $20,000. Paul, however, naturally believes in the garden's spiritual and educational significance.

Between pumpkins and kohlrabi he shows his children that the bad weeds must be kept low through constant hoeing so that the good fruit can grow. "The same is true for human beings," he teaches his little ones, "for those whom the rod doesn't keep away from evil from early on will never turn into good people."

Thus evil has little chance for survival in the Lord's garden: In the morning, the women hoe, and in the afternoon the children come with their rakes and comb the plant beds in long rows, the "little men" on one side, the girls on the other. The offspring work eagerly in the garden. It seems to me that this work outside is just more fun to the children than Bible cramming in the confined classroom. So that the older students don't get too far ahead, the teacher helps the little ones, in particular Georg and Elisabeth, who just started school and can't keep up with the others yet.

It doesn't matter what kind of job it is with which the community charges brother Paul, whether it be his work as a teacher, gardener, goose breeder, bookbinder, or as a food courier during planting — the short, tenacious man with the thin black beard completes each task with the same amount of dedication. Even after he has served the evening meal to his students in the dining hall at night and "has given, handed out, and distributed not according to who it is but according to need" as the school regulations prescribe, Paul's job is far from being done. First, he goes down to the river, where his 1,500 geese enjoy their brief lives in a fenced-in area until they are slaughtered in the fall; he pours five big buckets of barley into their crib. Then, after the communal prayer for the night, he usually stops by the bookbinder's house in order to glue some torn spelling books or to rebind the text of a sermon that is falling apart. While there, he often likes to chat with me and asks, "Well, Miechel, what does it look like in Germany?" "Siberian," he then says in astonishment when I tell him that, in the port of Hamburg, there are ships larger than the colony's cow barn. Finally, Paul never goes to bed without checking his garden one more time in order to see whether the bull has run away again and stands on the peas or whether the plastic bags that are supposed to protect the tender tomato plants against possible night frost have been blown off. "The garden," Paul says, "is my realm, and I take care of it so that everything will turn out right."

Just as at the Wilson colony, all adults in Waterton have an area for which the community has charged them with the sole responsibility. Paul's younger brother Georg, called "Chicken-George," is in charge of the henhouse; his brother-in-law Johannes takes care of the pigs; his sister-in-law Katharina is the head of the kitchen, his cousin Jakob has the say in the smithy, and, in the fall, he is the fisherman who takes the fat lake trout out of the reservoir. Their direct supervisor is winekeeper Johannes, who, in turn, is the "helper" of the "servant of need," housekeeper and treasurer Elias. Their duties and responsibilities are spelled out in the "Community Rules," which were written by the elders between 1651 and 1873. Similar to the "School Regulations," this book specifies all the duties of the respective persons so that nothing is left to the cursed individual will and initiative.

The cook "shall not use an extensive amount of fat and shall see to it that the food is clean and useful as well as nutritious and good as it is appropriate. The sick in particular shall be given what they need. The dishes shall be handled with attention and care so that they will not break and be thrown away. Not everybody shall be allowed into the kitchen, for this leads to disorder and grumbling; few people shall be responsible in case of complaints."

The bread-cutter "shall perform his duties with care and serve the people in the dining hall well and in good faith; he shall serve bread, drink, salt, and food from the kitchen and shall under no circumstances do other work in his own interest but remain in the dining hall so that he can be found at all times. He shall cut the bread into small pieces and cover them well so that no mouse turd or spiders can fall in. He shall also watch the baker, who shall not bake too much, particularly in the summer, so that the bread will not mold." Bread-cutter Johannes, who also has to fatten more than 100 sows here in Waterton, makes painstakingly sure that the amount of bread on the dining hall tables does not exceed his brethren's and sisters' capacity to eat. Anyone who is hungrier than usual must request each additional slice of bread from the bread-cutter by raising a hand, and if, unexpectedly, there is bread left, Johannes carefully saves it in a plastic bag. Like any kind of food, bread is sacred to the Hutterites.

In the shops, there is order as well: "There the supervisor shall see to it that there is harmony and politeness and shall prevent the workers from treating one another with resistance, bitterness, wrath, and animosity, encouraging rather familiarity, friendliness, and good advice. During the summer, on Sundays, on holidays, or during the noon hour nobody shall wander around aimlessly or lie down in the garden under the fruit trees and the like. The young apprentices must be watched carefully so that they learn to work with diligence and produce work of good quality. If they are disobedient, they shall not be watched for a long time but shall be reported to the schoolmaster."

The brethren of the court — that is, the community council — are called to order in a particularly strict way: "The winekeeper, who is the housekeeper's helper, shall hand out the work to the people and shall see to it that it proceeds and is performed with faithful diligence.

He shall also make sure everything such as hoes, rakes, and sickles is in its place so that nothing is lost and so that it will be found when it is needed. A winekeeper shall not go to bed and sleep before he has discussed the next morning's work with the housekeeper."

Not quite according to the rule, here in the colony this discussion takes place not before bedtime, but rather after breakfast in front of the kitchen. There every morning the menfolk get together with their hands buried deep in their pockets; everybody is still a little grouchy from getting up early, and housekeeper Elias briefly asks, "What'll it be today?" Winekeeper Johannes then gives a brief overview of the day's projects; he says, for example, that cement is needed for the new cow barn, which is supposed to be built yet this year, that eggs must be brought to town, that a tractor tire must be patched, and that the first hay needs to be cut. The jobs are distributed, and, if there are no other comments, the daily plan has been decided upon. As silently as they got together, they all now go to work.

At some time in the morning, the housekeeper Elias himself usually inspects the shops, looks into the cow barn and pigsty and checks the fields in order to make sure that everything is going all right, for, according to the rules, "he shall look around everywhere in the house in order to see that all things proceed orderly and also shall see to it that all needs will be filled on time and that those things that the community needs will be purchased for the welfare of all. Daily he shall look into the stables, also at night, to see how the cattle are fed and how hay and straw are treated. He shall look into the shops, the wash house, and the bakery to see whether candles can be saved by having people sit closer to each other. At times, a housekeeper himself shall enter the kitchen, try the food and make sure that everything is done for the sick, the children, the old, and the healthy. With the sisters, cooks and others, he shall not joke, for this often starts with sitting together and unnecessary talking and may then lead to the unchaste touching of the neck and other parts."

It is hard to imagine the white-bearded, 72-year-old Elias hanging around on a wooden bench in the kitchen with a glass of sweet wine in his hand and the cook Katharina (his own sister!) in his arms. During his regular daily work, the pious old man is obliged to follow the commandment of chastity ("Purify your hearts," James 4:8) as well as the biblical orders to be thrifty ("Gather up the fragments that remain, that nothing be lost," John 6:12), to be obedient ("Thou shalt therefore obey the voice of the Lord," Deuteronomy 27:10), and to love his fellow human beings ("Thou shalt love thy neighbor as thyself," Leviticus 19:18). To him, these are obvious Hutterite rules specifying the regulations only so that they are clear once and for all.

The Hutterites' greatest need is that of clarity and continuity. Those two things have given and still give them the inner security which enables them to stand up against the outside world "in which sin is no longer sin and shame no longer shame." Whether in Moravia after the reformation, in Hungary during the Thirty Years War, in Tsarina Catherine II's Russia, or nowadays in sodomite North America, the Hutterites have their rules and regulations to which they can hold on, and there is hardly an area of life for which an ancestor did not find an adjunction in the Bible. In his "Justification," the Silesian shoemaker Peter Riedemann not only expresses what must be thought of the "mire-bath" of child baptism, of Holy communion, and of military service but also explains in which way a righteous Christian prays, sings, celebrates, and drinks, with whom he can use the

handshake as a greeting, and why the community of possessions is so important.

Naturally, only spiritual songs may be sung in the
colonies "so that they cause and move man to heavenly
blissfulness. But those who sing for lust of the flesh or for
the pleasing sound or listen for the sound wrongfully turn
them into songs of the flesh and of the world and do not sing
in the spirit but according to letters and thus commit a sin
against God every time they do so because they use the
word of God for the lust of the flesh and for great sin."
Therefore, the Hutterites ardently press the songs out of
their throats and, according to my worldly ear, do not really
sing but rather lament and caw. Because nothing must entice the ear, all musical instruments are strictly forbidden
here on earth. In heaven, however, and this is something the
scripture-versed Hutterites know for certain, their acoustical
asceticism will be rewarded with trombones, harps, and
other heavenly instruments.

Neither may the "flesh be given reason or opportunity for
sinning" through "greeting, shaking of the hands, or em-
bracing," Riedemann writes. "The greeting is a gesture of
peace and dear and godly unity so that we prove in the
church that we are of one being, one heart, and one soul.
For in the way we put our hands into one anothers', we also
show how our hearts are entwined. Gamblers, drunkards,
and the like" may not even receive a "hint of a greeting."
When they are in town, the Hutterites are glad they don't
have to shake hands with the "English," for which "English"
doesn't belong to the group of gamblers, whorers, or drunkards?

"Toasting to one another, however, is the cause of all evil
and breaking God's commandments," the ancestor writes,
"for toasting to one another leads to drunkenness, through
which man wastes and ruins soul and body; therefore, it
cannot be permitted among ourselves. Such toasting
through which one wants to please the other causes man to

omit God's order, to forget the creator and, with it, man himself, and everybody wants to be a rooster in the field. 'Woe to those who run after strong drink,' Isaiah warns us." When Hutterites drink a glass of wine, they do it for health reasons. Teacher Paul, for example, maintains that a little glass before going to bed calms his nerves and leads to better sleep. During sheep-shearing or planting, housekeeper Elias, too, hands out his home-brewed stuff like sweet medicine "because it's good for the blood and for the soul." Alcohol per se is nothing bad, the Hutterites say, for, after all, the son of God himself made wine at Canaan; it is only evil in the hands of the "men of the world."

The commandment of the community of goods is a fundamental pillar of Hutterite order. Riedemann writes, "Because all of God's gifts, not only spiritual but worldly gifts as well, have been given to man so that he should not own them himself but share them with his comrades, be it established within the holy community that no one shall live in affluence and another in need but that all shall be equal."

The shoemaker argues for mandatory community of possessions by saying that love for fellow human beings and the unity of the community are possible only where private property and thus self-interest have been abolished. "For what causes war and bloodshed, what causes quarrels and fights, what causes much jealousy and hatred, and what causes disagreement and separation? Private property and private living cause all of these things. For the words 'mine' and 'yours' have caused many wars and still cause them today. For those who succumb to 'mine' and 'yours' — that is, private property — are friends with greed and his two daughters that are the bloodsuckers of the shameful worm of greed, and their two names are 'Give me.'"

The kinds of personal belongings which the community people require for "worldly needs" have been specified exactly for each moment of life and down to the last ounce in the "Rule of Sharing" since the times of Jakob Hutter and Peter

Riedemann. When a woman expects her first child, she receives 10 pounds of eiderdown for "cushions and blankets," bedding with a length of two yards and eleven inches and a width of two yards and nine inches, six yards of diaper material, and a crib from the carpenter. After giving birth, "the new mother shall receive a beverage and eggs fried in lard every morning during the first week; nutmeg shall be added. For two weeks, she will eat tender chicken meat; each shall have a quarter of wheat flour and then two loaves of bread made of cooking flour. On the side, she shall have a special bread for her health for four weeks. The other two weeks she shall also have soup every morning. She shall not be asked to eat sour things or to stuff herself with all kinds of food which can be harmful to her youth; she shall particularly avoid drinking cold water." In addition to all these extras, there are 165 eggs, 12 pounds of sugar, and 4 pounds of prunes, as well as an extra ration of "flower wine" for the faithful husband.

Once the "Bobela," the "baby-doll," has grown into a student at the Little School after three years, a boy can "now claim two yards of trouser material, two yards of jacket material, two yards of inside lining, half a yard of pocket material, and two yards of handkerchief material; for the vest, 18 inches for the front, 18 inches for the back, and one yard 18 inches of inside lining. This shall happen every year until the child is six years old." Of course, the amount of material grows with the boy. For the warm long johns for the winter, a three-year-old gets 2 1/4 yards of cotton material, those who are older than six get 2 1/2 yards, and those ten years and older exactly 3 yards. Once a boy has finished his schooling at age 15 and joins the men, the housekeeper gives him according to the rule "a knife, a fork, a spoon, a wrench box, a butcher knife, gloves, boots, grease traps, and every third year a hat." Instead of the toolbox, the grease trap, and the hat, the girls get a pair of scissors, a rolling pin, and 32 inches of material for the kerchief. The milking stool is omitted from the list since the colony owns automatic milking equipment. Since progress has been spreading over the heavenly arks, the thick fur sacks for the horse buggies and the spinning wheels have been stricken from the partial rule without substitution.

Twice a year, the clothing material is handed out in the kitchen. Then all women sit around a big table, and the cook, Katharina, has the say and the scissors. She has a long list of names and ages of all community members. The bales of material are stacked on the floor. The black bales are for the men's costume, the dark-blue or green ones for the women's. The snowstorm kerchiefs are made of the material with the white polka dots, and the warm underwear for both men and women out of the turquoise-pink and bright green cotton rolls — an exceptional joy of color where it can't entice the eye.

Cook Katharina cuts the "stuff" for each brother and sister. Every mother receives her family's "packet"; the more children she has, the bigger is her stack. Newly wed, childless Johanna can carry the things for her and her Christian easily under her arm, while the chubby teacher's wife, Katharina, with her nine children, must make two trips with the handcart. And, since one in addition to the nine doesn't make any difference anymore, my own clothing ration is on her cart as well: "Four yards of trouser material, four yards of jacket material, three yards of inside lining, 32 inches of vest material, five yards of shirts, and five yards of sweatshirt material."

As a matter that goes without saying, the cook didn't forget me during the distribution, for "everybody gets what is needed." This Hutterite principle goes for me, too. Long ago, I received a pair of rubber boots from the housekeeper as well as new gloves and a beautiful Hutter-hat for the holidays. Like every grownup over fifteen, I receive a quarter of a gallon of the yellowish house wine at the beginning of the month; Elias, with his slightly reddish nose, taps it for me

out of one of the big-bellied barrels in the wine cellar below
the kitchen and fills my hand-soldered mug. "Only for your
health," he warns me repeatedly, as though he knew from
his own experience how a person can get used to the drink.

There is no aspect of Hutterite life that fascinates me as
much as the condemnation of private property; this constitutes the greatest contrast between the colonies and the rest
of the world. While the communist nations have written
equality and brotherhood on their banners, people in the
East as in the West live in the hope that, with material
wealth, life's happiness and fulfillment may be obtained.
One dreams of a Mercedes, the other of an East German
Trabant — that is the difference, but it is no alternative. In
the Hutterites' case, the alternative is offered by cloth-cutter
Peter Walbot, who writes about the "community of goods" in
his "Article Book" in 1577: "The more people own, the
greater their needs. For those who seek much will lack
much and those who desire many things will lack much
more." Property, then, does not liberate people but enslaves
them. "For where your treasure is, there will your heart be
also" (Matthew 6:21); therefore, man "cannot serve God and
mammon" (Matthew 6:24). Private property and wealth that
are the actual goal in life around the world are to Peter Walbot "a disease and evil sickness" the cause of which is man's
egotism and self-interest. Only serenity is the right medicine
that will cure this evil of "academic nature." "If we cannot
render our hearts free and serene and cannot keep our
hands free of greed and self-interest, then we cannot become
healthy." Thus, the ego must first be overcome through baptism so that man can find his true self. As Jesus says, "For
whosoever would save his life shall lose it: but whosoever
will lose his life for my sake, the same shall have it" (Luke
9:24).

Referring to Erich Fromm, one must conclude that the
Hutterites clearly decided for "being" and against "having."
They reverse the old German commonplace "If you have

something, you are somebody" and say, "Only those who have nothing can have a good life." To the brethren and sisters at Waterton, as Fromm would state it, "not having is the basis of being."

It is the spirit of unselfishness that I, as an affluent person, have been experiencing daily for half a year already that so surprisingly facilitates my life here at the colony. Looking at the distribution of goods, at the work, at the meals, and at the brethren's and sisters' gathering every night, I, like Grimmelshausen 300 years ago, can detect no "envy, fighting, and no jealousy." The community people live their earthly lives with great serenity, as if they took a valium pill every morning. Eighty-six people, most related to each other furthermore, live here together along the Waterton River in six houses very close to each other, yet I rarely observe any disagreement. Physical conflict among adults is simply unimaginable, and if there happens to be a difference of opinion, very rarely does one hear an insulting word. The women radiate an immense calm as they walk in their dark costumes across the yard, garden hoes gracefully across their shoulders; it is as if they floated across the pasture. It is so wonderfully relaxing to watch teacher Paul bind his books with loving accuracy and unlimited patience; in his halting way of speaking, he then likes to read pages to me just for the joy of the pious word.

When I had a slight fever and had to stay in bed shortly after planting, I physically experienced Hutterite serenity. Early in the evening, I had fallen asleep for a while; when I woke up, I saw that the entire colony had silently gathered in the little bookbinder's house. Old Elias with his six sons, the women with their knitting, the Little School tricklers — all had come and nobody said a word. They just looked at me and took part in my suffering as if I were dying. However, the gravity of my illness mattered to nobody. The main thing was that I wasn't alone; to a Hutterite, the state of being alone is unthinkable and hurts more than the worst pain.

Thus, my Waterton brethren and sisters sat silently around my bed without even a trace of obtrusion or penetrating curiosity. Nobody was in a hurry, and nobody became impatient, not even the children. As I slowly turned my head to look around me, I could see a big, dark oil painting of silent people from another time in the twilight of the evening. I enjoyed their sympathy and pretended to be a little sicker than I actually was. Those who are not well at the Hutterites' colony can count on the others' particular solidarity. This alone is different from the outside world, in which only the strong count. I'm sure they included me in their prayers right away, for I was up and well again the next day.

Summer has kept us waiting for a long time here in Waterton, but since the seeds in the fields and the garden have started to grow, the sun shines down on the land with such heat that it is hard for me to imagine that only $2^1/_2$ months ago there was more than 7 feet of snow! Now Paul and his students must water the plant beds with a big tanker every evening, and automatic irrigation pipes with a length of up to 1200 feet roll across the fields on huge wheels so that the grass won't burn to straw during the day. Fortunately, the Waterton reservoir is still filled up to the brim with the last snow water from the mountains so that the plants lack neither moisture nor warmth.

Unfortunately, here at the colony there is no lack of pesticides and fertilizers either. Like all of the country's farmers and ranchers, the Hutterites spray the chemical insect killers, weed killers, and vitamin treatments over hill and dale by the cubic foot. To winekeeper Johannes, protection of the environment means as much as to his neighbors. The earth is a valley of sorrows anyway, a place which will soon be "burned up with all the works that are therein" (2 Peter 3:10). Why then protect it? The only exception the Hutterites make in their willingness to use modern farming technology is the artificial insemination of the cattle. Such progress, Johannes feels, is "against nature," and thus the colony's two strong bulls have a good life in Waterton. But that keeping the chickens in hundreds of small cages could be just as unnatural doesn't occur to Johannes. Here the often-heard motto applies again: What is good for the community justifies the means.

"Replenish the earth, and subdue it," says Moses (Genesis 1:28), and the Hutterites follow this advice as radically and relentlessly as the rest of the world. Teacher Paul thinks nothing of strewing poisonous bird feed around the sunflower field so that the starlings are killed when they come in great flocks in the evening. He finds my suggestion of putting up a scarecrow too "old-fashioned." What a word out of the mouth of a Hutterite whose greatest pride is his 450-year-old tradition of faith and life!

These contradictions in their existence have affected the Hutterites' minds; the longer I live with them, the more clearly I can see these effects. There are, for example, women who tell me that it is actually "uncivilized" to live without a water toilet, and I hear the bread-cutter rave about an electric bread knife, the purchase of which has thus far fortunately met with the thrifty treasurer's steadfast resistance. In all its ugliness, the world takes on an increasingly attractive air even for the Hutter-people, and it is this contrast which could cause the arks to capsize within a short time. When the first cars were purchased by the chosen ones, the world got a foot in their door; the "separation" from the sinful world around, a fundamental principle of Hutter-ite life, has been increasingly reduced to a physical distance which can be overcome all too easily. In their hearts, already many Hutterites secretly live more in town than in their community.

When this thought occurs to me, I always clearly remember Holy Communion day at the Wilson colony, the almost orgiastic creation of that kitchen mess of honey candy and blueberry-liqueur while the pious partook of bread and wine in the Lord's remembrance next door. Then, Heinrich and his followers kept squalling one song over and over again: "We get married in June, have a long honeymoon." I have to think of these lines especially now as there is a rumor in the colony: Paul's niece Sarah, his oldest brother Johannes's daughter, has a boyfriend; that's the exciting news that the women whisper to each other. The young man, whose name is supposedly Josef Gross, had come last summer from the neighboring province of Saskatchewan to visit his aunt. But that was only the excuse all Hutterites use when they are ready to get married and they go looking for a bride. Actually, Josef Gross had come only to "hunt for girls."

Whenever such a wooer shows up in the community, all of the older adolescents get together after supper in a backroom that is a little out of the way; it is rare to be among their own for two hours, although they all know that the grown-ups within reach sharpen their ears in order to prevent any communion-day excesses. Like the adults, the adolescents sit "in the round" and play with naive devotion the game called "I see what you can't see." It is likely that it was last year during that game that Josef fell in love with the slim, black-haired Sarah and she with him. Before his return to his home colony of Kyle, 600 miles away, he probably put his arm around her and may have "hugged and kissed her a little." Certainly nothing more than that happened. A little hugging and kissing is then the absolutely greatest affection Hutterites show before they marry. For more than a very long year, the two of them have been writing each other longing but well-behaved love letters; these letters, were written in English since words like "sweetheart," "darling," and "never-ending love" don't look good in old German handwriting.

To clearly express his devotion, Josef had used his subsistence savings and bought a nice and colorful gift packet full of sweets in the form of a giant red heart; he gave it to Sarah for her baptism last Easter. The sweet token of love now lies well-protected in Sarah's trunk ("Kischtl"), which is the only private place a Hutterite has. All colonists get such a rough-cut trunk when they join the "people" at age 15; the trunk holds the few personal things that are needed daily — the "earthly needs." Since all trunks can be locked, the more recent models even with a safety bolt, there is something mysterious about them. And it is not only the pants, shirts, skirts, or toothpaste that are hidden in them. Often the wooden boxes contain color photographs of "boyfriends" or "girlfriends" next to aftershave, lipsticks, nail polish, and perfume such as the popular brand "Evening in Paris." All of these things can be used only for the Holy Communion's carnival, if they can be used at all. Here the girls keep forbidden bras and the boys their secretly obtained cowboy boots, or, very rarely, maybe a "Playmate of the Month." Everything that is otherwise outlawed can be stored in the trunk. If one asks about the reason for such unexpected tolerance, one gets the indifferent reply, "It's always been this way; it's what the rule says." The ancestors may have well known that even a Hutterheart is made of "flesh and blood" and needs its hidden space for living.

Since Sarah locked Josef's heart in her trunk, the matter has become serious; everybody is already talking about the wedding's taking place before long. First, however, the juicy hay must be taken from the fields; the 50-pound bales need to be piled in blocks as high as houses around the cow and sheep barn, the stock needed for the long Canadian winter. We average between 50,000 and 60,000 bales with the first cut, a good result which my arms can feel days after the work is done. Anyway, this year's harvest promises to be a good one. In the spring there was abundant rain so that the fields, which are now green and wave in the wind over the hilly area, carry heavy and full heads. In Paul's garden, too, the sunflowers are in full blossom, the corn grows quickly, and the pumpkins swell up; the schoolteacher has good reason to hope that even the tomatoes will catch enough sun to ripen.

Now that the hay has been stacked and there is not much more to do in the garden but to weed, the groom may come. On a hot afternoon in July, the angry barking of the community dogs announces the arrival of the important guest. Josef comes with his father, Johannes, and his two oldest brothers in a big, two-ton vehicle. He is a short and somewhat stocky young man whose receding blond hairline indicates the ripe old age of 28. Hutterites usually marry between the ages of 20 and 25, but Josef took his time hunting girls. Maybe he was also a little nervous about the straining marriage procedure, for Hutterite weddings are anything but pure joy. In this complicated act, the future spouse's wish to be married is of little importance. Before the parents are asked, the couple's community council members decide whether the two will be married or not. This is because every baptized Christian has lost his right to self-determination in becoming a community member, "one who is no longer himself and cannot behave and act according to his own will," as the baptismal order, the "Incorporation," spells out very clearly.

Therefore, Josef must first see Sarah's preacher for the purpose of "proposing." In his newly tailored Sunday best he takes his father and goes to see Elias; there, he stammers his "wedding passage" in his best "standard German": "My dear brother, I have a strong desire to enter into Christian matrimony and want to ask you to help me with it, with the help of God. Amen." The preacher rises from his wooden bench. He shakes hands with father and son and replies momentously, "I'll discuss it with the brethren." The next evening, all the community's baptized men remain in the schoolhouse after prayer and discuss the case. Afterwards, the preacher Johannes announces the result to the couple: "We've decided it'll work. You can have your wedding next week." But before the wedding can take place the following

week, the groom must still formally propose in a meeting
with Sarah's parents, which is an evening-long transaction
with an almost oriental back-and-forth.

Almost the entire colony is gathered in the house of the
bride's father. The next-of-kin and the community's older
citizens sit on chairs and benches in the living room with
their backs to the bare walls. The younger folk, in the next
room, push and shove for the best positions near the open
door. The school children are outside and flatten their noses
on the windows.

Josef gets up first; beads of sweat on his forehead, he addresses the future parents-in-law, "Johannes, Elisabeth — I
want Sarah and will care for her as I care for my right
hand."

Embarrassed silence. Finally, the bride's father replies,
"Josef, what you want is something unspeakably great; she's
my oldest."

Again, there is an anxious, silent pause.

Then the groom's father makes a reluctant comment:
"What can you do? What God has started should not be opposed by us men."

Naturally, the couple's parents assume that Josef and
Sarah found one another through heavenly guidance without the "will of the flesh," without "reasons of a beautiful
body or whatever the flesh desires" having played any role.
That would be against the rules as written down by Peter
Riedemann and, of course, against the Bible, in which we
read, "Listen to what I tell you... Those who enter into matrimony and do not look at God in their heart but only do this
so that they can satisfy the will of the flesh like the asses
and horses... Yes, over these the devil has power" (Tobit
6:16-17).

To the Hutterite elders, the ideal role model comes from
the Old Testament: Abraham, who went into a foreign country in order to wed Sara without having seen her before.
Until 100 years ago, it was still customary among the Hut-

terites that a young man who was looking for a wife had to move to a different colony and inform its preacher about his willingness to get married. The preacher then wrote down the candidate's name and address; he was told to come back on a certain day in the spring or fall. During a church service, the head of the community introduced him and other Hutterites willing to marry to all single women of the colony. Most of the candidates for marriage saw each other for the first time on that occasion. The "menfolk" then made their choice, but the maidens had the right to decline. "A sister shall not be forced against her will when a brother is presented to her to whom she does not feel attracted, since she is also free," as it is written in the old regulations. However, those who declined a proposition got another chance at the next date, half a year later at the earliest. The Hutterites had to abandon this regulation about 150 years ago in Russia under the pressure of the worldly authorities, to whom, even then, this procedure seemed too rigid.

Yet in spite of everything, the God-fearing colonists insisted on their claim that neither lust of the eyes nor lust of the flesh should play an inappropriate role in their marriages. Those who want to marry should ask not their flesh but rather the community that arranges for the marriage through the preacher as the representative of the Highest. And because "what therefore God hath joined together," man cannot "put asunder" (Matthew 19:6), there is no divorce among the Hutterites.

It is exactly this quotation from the Bible to which the groom's father refers during the "speaking": "What God has started should not be opposed by us men."

This is an effective argument. It would be a sin to oppose the works of God. But the bride's father Johannes has not yet given up in this transaction. He makes a surprising offer of compromise by asking his future son-in-law whether he might be able to put the wedding off for another year. The reason: As his oldest daughter, Sarah is a big help in the household with cleaning, sewing, and doing the laundry. Mother Elisabeth would be reluctant to do without her oldest child. "We still need Sarah around the house for a little while since we have twelve children," the bride's father says.

This "compromise" must seem to poor Josef like a rejection. He looks for support from the back of the chair, grabs it with both hands, and disconcertedly looks down at his Sarah, who hides behind a tear-drenched table cloth.

Father Johannes tries to give a little comfort: "What is one year? It passes like nothing! You wake up on Monday, and it's Saturday already." The biblical Jacob, as the Holy Scripture reports, waited for even seven years for his Rachel. What is one year in comparison? To the groom Josef it's an eternity! He has waited for this day for one year, saved his subsistence for the red candy heart, written love letters and certainly dreamed of his Sarah many a night, if he has been able to sleep at all. And now he is supposed to go back home empty-handed and to wait for another eternal summer, autumn, winter, and spring until haying is finally over? Even for a Hutterite with all his serenity this is too much.

Josef Gross wipes his sweaty palms dry on his thighs and takes in a big breath for his final attempt: "My dear Johannes," he says with a pale face and his hands folded, "I implore you, please give her to me!"

Nobody is able to resist this honest directness. Everybody present is moved, and even the eyes of the strict Johannes become watery. Superfluously, he now asks his future son-in-law whether he has carefully thought everything over, whether he is a good judge of his own intentions, and whether he has asked God for help and support for the hard task ahead of him. Josef nods. He also shows that he is very familiar with all pertinent Bible passages, in particular with Corinthians 7, where it says, "It is good for a man not to touch a woman. Nevertheless, to avoid fornication, let every man have his own wife, and let every woman have her own husband." Josef also knows the letters to the Thessalonians by heart: "For this is the will of God, even your sanctification: that ye should abstain from fornication: That every one should know how to possess his vessel in sanctification and honor; Not in the lust of concupiscence, even the Gentiles which know not God" (1 Thessalonians, 4:3-5). Josef knows these passages intimately.

To a Hutterite Christian, marriage is a necessary evil, and I really wonder how this poor guy will be able to handle all that biblical ballast when he spends the first night with his Sarah in a couple of days. How profoundly disturbed must be his relation to sexuality (in this circle, the word alone is almost obscene) and to his own and his future wife's body, since we always hear the same sentence over and over again during the service and at prayer time: "Our body is evil, cunning, and full of lust — it is our worst enemy." If I were in Josef's place, I would simply die next to the tall and slim Sarah whose thick, pitch-black hair, covered by "hat" and "cloth," probably reaches down to her knees. I wonder how the two of them can do justice to the biblical command "Be fruitful, and multiply" (Genesis 1:22) with so much opposition to lust and so much contempt for the body.

Because the Hutterites have a rule for every situation in life, this problem is taken care of as well. In 1536, the preacher Ulrich Stadler from Brixen in Tyrol wrote in his "Good and Comforting Letter About Original Sin and Other Useful Things": "If man had remained pure and good as God created him, the insemination would take place without lust and evil desire. However, this is not the case. But God sees through the fingers at the marital task for the sake of our perishable body and also for the sake of the children and thus does not punish those who fear him and act with chastity." Therefore, there is a small and narrow loophole for Sarah and Josef in a marriage with many if's and but's.

Today, the bride's father, Johannes, has given nothing away for free to the poor "speaker." He has kept him in suspense for two hours in these fake negotiations whose outcome was determined from the beginning because we can be sure that Sarah has talked with her mother and father about her wish to get married before. She certainly wouldn't have let Josef come without her parents' prior consent. But it is, after all, part of the process to make it difficult for the wooer so that he realizes what "precious matter" is at stake here.

Finally, Johannes asks his daughter, "Do you want Josef?" It takes a short, hesitating moment until the one who is addressed meekly produces her first and only word tonight behind her cloth of tears: "Yes." And it sounds as if she felt almost guilty. After we have kept silent for a while in the Hutterite manner, Johannes looks at his future son-in-law and says, "Well, then, for God's sake — take her." A sigh of relief spreads through the rooms. The deal is finished! Then Sarah and Josef serve schnapps, and all of us drink from the same cup and wish the couple a "good life together."

Since the actual wedding, the "joining together," always takes place in the husband's community, the preacher here can only perform the engagement and "put them next to each other." In a short, 30-minute service on Wednesday morning, the servant of the word briefly and to the point swears and curses against the much-despised fornication and lust of the flesh. As a warning, he writes 1 Corinthians 7:29 in the groom's family record book: "They that have wives be as though they had none." After the Puritan schoolteacher's sermon, he asks both groom and bride to step forward in front of the podium and says, "It is the brethren's understanding that one wants to accept the other as a gift from God. However, since nothing is decided yet and neither has heard from the other, I ask you now, my brother, first: If you want to take the sister without reservation and in good faith, then say it so that she can hear it." This time without any hesitation Josef answers, "Yes!" Then again the preacher: "Because matrimony contains much sorrow, since there is not only joy but also pain throughout our days, and because women are the source of all kinds of frailty, I ask you, do you want never to leave Sarah in joy or in sorrow until the Lord will part you? If this is not too difficult for you, you may answer yes." And again, there is a determined "Yes!" Sarah, too, is asked by the preacher whether she is willing to accept Josef "without reservation and in good faith," which here means without any outside influence, and, with tears, she pronounces her "Yes" as well. After Sarah and her Josef have agreed to be a "righteous and obedient married couple," the preacher gives them his engagement blessing, and then we can celebrate "Hulba."

However, the anabaptist engagement party is a sheer tragedy and an incredible disappointment. We sit in the dining hall for hours and sing one melancholic song after the other:

"If you want to have a lover, / One who is not full of gloom, / You must love Lord God, the Father / For He is the only groom."

The men sit on the left, the women on the right side, and only Josef and Sarah sit petrified on a wooden bench next to each other and hold sweaty hands. During the short pauses between songs, everybody gets a coffee cup filled with peanuts which the housekeeper himself pours out of a big jute sack into everybody's palm. When the climax of the "Hulba" celebration is reached, a bottle of "Lethbridge Pilsner" is placed in front of everybody. The children drink cola.

During the celebration back in Russia, the preacher used to place a horse's skull in front of the engaged couple in order to drastically show them the transitoriness of all flesh. "All flesh is grass, and all the goodliness thereof is as the flower of the field," writes Isaiah in verse 40:6. In the age of the automobile, the engaged couple fortunately does not need to go through this ceremony. The sad songs still remain.

"Think of this, you human kin, / Of that time when death has come, / Think all you, so full of sin, / When the final bell has rung:

Today we are alive and strong, / Tomorrow we are in the grave, / Earthly honor that we have, / Death will prove it to be wrong."

At eleven o'clock sharp, the brethren of the court rise, and the preacher wishes everybody a good night. But not everybody goes straight to bed. The unmarried and unbaptized adolescents move with the engaged couple to the remote room in which Sarah and Josef first met a year ago playing "I see what you don't see." But now they don't sit shyly across from each other but closely side by side, as if one needed the other's help in breathing. Their faces look more relaxed and less unnatural now that the strict old men are no longer present. Sarah even laughs, and I can see her beautiful, shining teeth for the first time in days. The young folk, girls and boys mixed, sit at the feet of the newly engaged couple. Everybody's eyes are fixed on the couple of the day, and all get their fill of looks at the happiness presented here.

Andreas's and Georg's mouth organs magically appear from their pockets, and, in one second, I am in the middle of the Old West:

"Hey, get down the fiddle,
and get down the bow,
kick off your shoes
and throw them on the floor,
dance in the kitchen
till the morning light -
Colorado Saturday night."

In the rhythm of the "hopping" country sound we clap our hands, stamp our feet, and shake off all the tension of the last few days. The repertoire of "songs of the flesh" seems inexhaustible, and Johnny Cash ("Buffalo Baby") and Tania Tucker ("Texas when I die") are in everybody's mouth —

heaven knows where the adolescents have heard all of them. Are there hidden radios in Waterton as well?

Shortly before midnight, the door suddenly opens, and Heinrich, Samuel, and Andreas, the three ladies' men from Wilson, are given a hero's welcome. After dark had set in, they secretly left their ark and drove the 80 miles to this place in a station wagon borrowed from a neighbor. Although it will cost them several "Germans" afterwards, such a back-room Hulba, just like the excessive communion orgy a few weeks ago, is certainly worth the price. In comparison to the kitchen show then, the program tonight is much more quiet. Without alcohol in abundance, they are just in a good mood and glad to spend a few hours without grown ups, until toward one in the morning winekeeper Johannes appears behind the window with a flashlight and strictly sends us to bed: "Go home now," he shouts, "and each find his own nest!" Obediently we go to bed, each one into his own, and the engaged couple, too, must sleep in separate nests until the wedding next Sunday.

The large double bed is already fastened tightly on the groom's truck, and with it the rest of the dowry which, according to the good old rule, the bride's colony must furnish: "8 yards of bedding, 10 yards of woolen blankets, 2 cups, 2 saucers, 2 pots, 2 knives, 2 forks, 2 spoons, 1 pair of scissors, 1 sewing machine, 32 pounds of down feathers." In addition the couple receives a new bible, a new hymn book, and the "Justification" by Peter Riedemann. In Josef's community up in the north of Saskatchewan, a room has already been furnished next to the apartment belonging to Sarah's parents-in-law; this room contains a new clock for the wall, a dresser, a table, two chairs, and a footstool. When Josef's and Sarah's two "Kischtn," their two trunks in which they keep their personal belongings, are added, the future married couple's furnishings are complete.

Early the next morning, the wedding party prepares for the 600-mile trip to the groom's colony. Sarah will soon feel at home in the new ark, for life in the community of Kyle consists of much praying, quick eating, and going to bed early as it does here. There, too, Sarah must fulfill her community service: "Kuchwuch," kitchen week, "Melkwuch," milking week every six weeks, and "Backwuch," baking week every three weeks. Over the course of the years, she will have a dozen children like her mother Elisabeth, who will then come the long way on the colony's truck for each birth in order to help her daughter for a month. Working, praying, eating, sleeping — one finds the same rhythm wherever there are Hutterites. It won't be long until Sarah will feel at home with her Josef.

Before the sadness of parting can set in, the preacher quickly says, "In heaven we'll all be together again." Then the truck slowly rolls down the driveway and disappears behind the hill.

The awareness of having to say good-bye as prescribed by the godly rule, is deeply rooted in every Hutterite. This people's 450-year history is characterized by separation and eviction. Again and again, the anabaptists had to say good-bye to brethren and sisters who died as martyrs; again and again, they were driven away from the country that had just barely become their home. "No man who, having put his hand to the plough, looks back is fit for the kingdom of God," Jesus says (Luke 9:62); thus, sadness and melancholy may not be. Those who have God in their hearts and therefore the certainty of receiving heavenly reward are always ready to leave everything and everybody here on earth when the time has come.

But it is not outside violence only that keeps driving the Hutterites on in this earthly valley of sorrow; the inner order keeps the people constantly moving as well. For once a community has grown past 125 souls, new land must be bought and a new colony be built. In Waterton, this was the case four years ago: The community had grown so rapidly that its members had started to step on one another's toes. Both Big and Little Schools threatened to suffocate due to the multitude of children. In the dining halls, it became more and more difficult to find a spot on the long and narrow wooden benches. In the shoemaker's shop during the making of soap, in the smithy — nowhere was there enough work, and the individual had less and less to do. I have heard rumors that there had even been tensions concerning the distribution of leading positions because there had now been several colonists in Waterton who had no responsibilities in any area of the work. This created bad blood among the chosen ones.

In addition, one brother did not know exactly what the other was doing, the supervisors lost control over their herd that had become too big, and mutual care and supervision diminished noticeably. The people increasingly avoided community life. After the meal, they went into hiding within their own four walls. Indifference began to spread. Neighborly love was on the decline.

The clever ancestors had quickly understood that the size of a social group decisively affects its members' behavior. And because Hutterite life presupposes a very intensive relationship among the brethren and sisters, the communities were not allowed to grow past a certain size. Over the course of time, the number 125 had proven to be the upper limit in a colony's growth; then the process of social separation of the cell had to begin, a process which the Hutterites call "leaving one another" or, in English, "branching." Since the Hutterite birthrate averages 10.4 children per family and thus constitutes a rate common only in third-world countries, far exceeding the low birthrate in North America, today the chosen people multiply faster than even India's or Brazil's population. Every 15 to 20 years, the population in the fertile colonies doubles, and they must separate.

The brethren's community of Waterton, for example, already has six predecessors in Canada and in the U.S. In 1870, the Darius People, who had come from Russia, founded Wolf Creek Colony in South Dakota. Shortly before the turn of the century, one half of the community "branched" out to the newly built Richard farm. After the First World War, with its anti-German excesses, they settled at the Wilson colony, in Alberta in Canada 30 miles north of the border with the United States, in 1918. Twenty years later, the Wilsoners built their first daughter community, the Pibrock colony outside of Lethbridge, and they split again in 1961. This time, 65 brethren and sisters had to move to Waterton, while the others remained at Wilson. Six years ago, when Paul's Katharina had her seventh child, Sarah, who will start school this summer, preacher Elias counted and found that the critical number of 125 had been reached; on the following Sunday during the "Stiebl" meeting, he informed his brethren that again it was time for "leaving one another."

Thus the search for new land was begun. Thursdays in town, the brethren from other communities were asked about land for sale somewhere in the neighborhood. The real estate ads in the *Lethbridge Herald* were read and brokers contacted. Since treasurer Elias had kept the Thalers together over the past 15 years, there was enough money for an $800,000 farm near the small town of Carmengey 75 miles northeast of Waterton. The soil there had yielded good harvests, there was enough ground water, and it was a good location for a new farm. At first, this appeared an ideal place for a daughter community.

But when word about the land sale had gotten around among the local population, there was a storm of protest against the threatening Hutterite settlement. Hurriedly, a grass-roots initiative was formed, and 400 farmers from the entire district went to the province's capital city of Edmonton in order to demonstrate against the "Hutterite invasion." In many newspaper articles that old Elias has carefully kept in his desk, we can read what it was that angered the farmers so much about the Hutterite minority: "Hutterites are only second-class citizens, for in order to be first-class citizens, people must serve their country wholeheartedly. If our society is not good enough for the Hutterites, they should go where they came from," the *Lethbridge Herald* quoted an angry farmer.

Another farmer insisted that, personally, he had nothing against the Hutterites as individuals. "The individual Hutterite is certainly the best neighbor one could wish for: always helpful, always friendly. But their colonies don't contribute to society." That means in plain language: The chosen ones don't send their children to public schools, are not interested in public community life, and don't become members of the Lions Club or the hockey or curling association. They consume far too little, and when they need something, they don't buy it at the local stores but drive 60 miles to the town of Lethbridge in order to get it cheaper from a wholesale dealer. The result: Community life falters, the schools must close due to a lack of students, the stores go bankrupt, and the town dies. And everything is the Hutterites' fault.

There have been many similar cases around Carmengey, where three other colonies had been established besides the planned offshoot from Waterton. More than 5% of the farmable land had already come into Hutterite hands in this area, as compared to only 1% in all of Alberta.

However, what the farmers didn't want to see was the fact that, in other areas in which there are no Hutterite settlements at all, similar developments can be observed. For it is not Elias and his brethren who change the socio-economic balance of the region but the general migration from the country to the cities. In 1941 the population of the three prairie provinces of Alberta, Saskatchewan, and Manitoba was at 2.4 million, 62% of which lived in rural areas. By 1966 the population had risen to 3.4 million, but then 63% lived in urban areas. From 1941 to 1966 the number of those living on farms decreased from 1.4 million to 760,000. Between the Pacific and Atlantic oceans, the small farmers sold their land because they could not and did not want to live off a few acres of land by working hard, 70-hour weeks as their ancestors had.

In the age of technology, agriculture has become a big business in which only large enterprises can survive because only they have the capital needed for the purchase of profitable machinery. The Hutterites are not the cause but the beneficiaries of this agricultural revolution, but everywhere they want to settle down, they are the scapegoats held responsible for its negative consequences.

In 1974 the people were — and still are today — particularly upset because the conservative provincial government headed by the newly elected prime minister Peter Longheed had eliminated the last remaining legal discrimination against the Hutterites by abolishing the "Communal Property Act" a year before. This law, enacted in the war year 1944, made it illegal for the colonists to found communities that were larger then 6,400 acres and within 40 miles of another Hutterite settlement. Also, the chosen ones were not allowed to purchase land that had not been offered for sale to private farmers at least 60 days previously. This law was supposed to help the returning veterans become reintegrated into the country's economy during the post-war period. Thirty years later, the government judged this "Lex Hutterites" to have been superfluous for a long time. It even violated the "Bill of Rights" put through by the Canadian prime minister John Diefenbaker in 1960; with this bill, the ethnic minorities of the second-largest country in the world were granted greater importance.

However, the conservative farmers in the province wanted nothing to do with the "multi-culturalism" propagated by liberal politicians in the capital cities of Ottawa and Edmonton. To the farmers, the black-clothed colleagues from Waterton seemed to be a threat because they were so entirely different, because they reversed all of the traditional farmers' values and norms and yet seemed to be content people who were successful farmers on top of it. They pitied the "poor Huts" who abstained from all fun in life, and, at the same time, envied them for their peaceful way of living. They laughed about their old-fashioned, self-made shoes with ties and admired the modern combines of which they themselves could only dream. "We must fight the Hutterite way of life," an angry farmer told reporters during the protest demonstrations in Edmonton, "and if nothing else works, we will forcefully make them give up their communism so that they will be able to enjoy our country's freedom as we enjoy it."

Nevertheless, all threats and protests were in vain. The Hutterites from Waterton legally purchased the land, paid a good price, and began to build the new "ark." The construction crew moved into temporary barracks in which they ate, prayed, and slept. Every Saturday night they returned to the old colony in order to honor the holiday together. Sometimes at night, drunken rowdies came on their motorcycles to slash a few tires or to smash some windows, and then they disappeared again. Fortunately, more serious incidents were avoided.

In the late fall of 1975, the new ark was ready. Everything was as it was at home: there were the six drawn-out houses for living, one row in the east, the other one in the west, the kitchen in the south, and the school in the north. However, the Rockies had shrunk a little and no longer presented the mighty and seemingly threatening view that it did at home by the thundering Waterton River in the foothills. The material for the new construction had cost half a million dollars, the milking machine, the power generator from old US Army supplies, and the cooling equipment for the kitchen being the most expensive items. The shoemaker's shop and the bookbinder's house were supposed to be established during the course of the following year, and the home community was under the obligation to perform all repairs and bookbinding jobs until then.

Now the colonists packed their scarce belongings. Since it was still unknown who would move to the new community and who would remain in the old, everybody got ready to leave. There was actually hardly a person who did not hope to be allowed to stay here in old and familiar surroundings. Sarahbasel, the treasurer's wife, who had had to "leave the others" three times during her 72 years, prayed especially not to have to move, so that she would be able to die in good old Waterton.

On a Thursday afternoon, her fate was decided as well. Everybody was ready to leave, and the baptized brethren met for their last council session together. They gathered in order to divide their community's property — the six tractors, the cattle, the sheepskin which had not been sold, the sausages in the freezer, and the freshly butchered ducks. Anything that did not exist in duplicate was weighed against other items. Thus, the self-made dough mixer went to one party and the chicken-plucking machine to the other. The school teacher wrote everything down in great detail in accurate German handwriting.

When it had been agreed upon which half would now go to the Waterton colony and which to the Carmengey farm, the people themselves were divided. This was a complicated task, for people can't be mathematically split up as easily as cows, sheep, or frozen ducks. Family relations had to be considered, and the structure of age and the size of both groups was supposed to be similar. Most of all, both population groups needed to be able to keep a colony alive independently. Both the old and the new farm needed a preacher, a housekeeper, a bread-cutter, somebody who could handle cattle, and somebody who could head the smithy; and, of course, a strong hand was needed in both communities to keep the young under control and in order.

Michael Gross, then first preacher of Waterton, first wrote his and his substitute's name next to each other on the green chalk board of the school. Now it was discussed which family should be put next to which preacher in order to establish a just social balance in both groups. At the end, there were 60 names on one side of the board and 65 on the other. Now both preachers had to draw a small piece of paper out of the schoolteacher's hat. As the older one, Michael drew first with closed eyes and got a paper on which the words "New Farm" were written. Thus he and his 65 followers were chosen by God to move to Carmengey, while the group around Elias was allowed to stay. Before the men closed their meeting and went out to tell the result to the impatiently waiting relatives, they knelt down and thanked the Lord for his wise decision.

With the speed of lightning the fateful news spread in the colony, and while some unpacked their bundled belongings, the others loaded their boxes, chairs, beds, and tables on the three waiting trucks. After the farewell lunch with zwieback, "Schutenhonkelich," and coffee, they said goodbye to each other with weeping, and each person said to the other the comforting words, "In heaven we'll be together again." Sarahbasel, however, was glad that she had been spared this move in her old days.

Within four years of the separation from the "Carmengeyans," the Waterton colony has again grown by 27 children, four of which Paul's Katherina herself brought into life. Fifty percent of the loan of $100,000 taken out when the new settlement was built has already been repaid by both communities. New tractors and combines have filled the gaps that were opened by the separation. Today, the treasurer is already pondering the next "leaving one another" in about ten years. According to his calculations and in the face of rising real estate costs, he must save approximately one quarter of a million dollars per year so that by the middle of the 90's the necessary funds for a new farm will be

Pages 152-153: *Forming a row, the women cut weeds out of a field of sweet peas. They wear light bonnets for protection from the sun.*

available. Thus he saves the dollars with a stinginess which is in the interest of all. Although all material things are despised, the community's budget is as present in his mind as the Sermon on the Mount or the gospel according to Luke. The contradiction between mammon and God (Luke 16:13) dissolves in the service of the community into pious money-grabbing in the interest of all.

To the Hutterites, every kind of human behavior always exists in tension between the common good and self-interest. Those who serve the interest of the whole through their work do good even though they may violate the laws of the world. If "Chicken-Jerg" secretly keeps a few hundred hens more in his cages than are actually permitted according to the regulations of the "Albertan Egg Marketing Board," then this is a violation of earthly laws but a good deed before God. On the other hand, if he fries one single egg for himself without having asked the cook for permission, or if he puts community money from the sale of the frying chickens into his own pocket, then this is a grave sin and a crime against God. The common Hutterite saying "Community'd be at its best, were it not for self-interest" tells us that, even for a chosen one, unselfishness certainly is not a thing that can be taken for granted, especially since everywhere the evil tempter, "as a roaring lion, walketh about, seeking whom he may devour" (1 Peter 5:8).

These roaring lions enter the colony in luxurious limousines; they have a dark tan, wear sunglasses, and chew gum with their predacious teeth. These salesmen are common Yankee caricatures who come here daily in order to make their business deals with the Hutterites. Most of the time, they park their Chevies or Buicks in front of the treasurer's house, and they don't hesitate to intrude even at 8:00 o'clock at night while we are singing the ballad of some brave martyr who suffered for the Hutterite cause somewhere at some earlier time.

"Howdy folks! My name is George!" a huge fellow bellows into the room without even a trace of embarrassment. Between 30 and 40 women, men, and children stare at him as if he were a rabid bear coming down from the mountains, and George asks whether they are having a meeting. "No," comes Elias's dry reply, "these are just my children and grandchildren." The word "grandchildren" is the giant's cue, and he opens his black leather bag and grabs a handful of pens from an animal feed company. "Animals love VIGOR" is printed on the plastic pens that the man now hands out to each boy and girl with a broad grin. "Thank you," the children reply with embarrassment and do not look at their benefactor. The man sits down on a stool that has been pushed over to him and asks Elias, "How are you today?" Here, the question sounds tacky. This "Englishman's" formal politeness becomes grotesque and untruthful. To me, he looks like a 17th-century white colonial master who cheats the natives with colored pearls and honeyed words, thus hoping to secure their goodwill. Everybody knows that this man has come in order to get rid of his duck feed; the housekeeper's well-being does not matter to him as long as Elias's state of health allows him to sign the order form.

The stable weather situation which is now discussed ("Nice summer this year!") has nothing to do with the salesman's intentions either. Without worrying about anyone's reaction, he asks his blunt questions as he does with every customer. Here, however, he doesn't reach anyone. With his eyes turning into narrow slits, Elias waits for this "Englishman" to get to the point. The ducks are fine, he answers, but why shouldn't they be under Paul's conscientious care? But until butchering in October they could still use some feed, and so the old man orders 2,500 kilograms of VIGOR. With the speed of lightning, the feed salesman produces a form, fills in the desired amount, and gives it to Elias to sign.

Because he is not used to writing Latin letters, the treasurer signs his name a little clumsily as "Elias S. Wurz," the initial "S." referring to his wife Sarah. Before he was married, there was a "J." standing for his father, Johannes, instead of that "S." Sarah, too, had her father's name in her own until Elias took her for his wife more than forty years ago, and now her name is E. Sarah Wurz. Of course, the man's name comes first since the man must lead the woman at all times.

Elias now gets a receipt for the order. But he gets something else as well, "a personal present," as the salesman calls it. This "little gift" is a nice four-color pen made of shining metal. Above his white full beard, Elias blushes a little, mumbles a "Thank you," and, with a quick and somewhat nervous motion of his hand, puts it away in a drawer of his oak desk. Is he embarrassed to be given a present in front of the community gathered here? The personal possession of such a writing utensil could be justified by the fact that the housekeeper will use it in service of the community and not for self-interest, but where should the line be drawn then?

In Lethbridge I have seen how the representatives of all branches of agriculture from tractor salesmen to herbicide agents approach the Hutterites in town in order to palm off their products on them. The Hutterites are generously invited to go out to eat (the meal, of course, is paid for by a hospitality line item); they are given presents such as gas lighters, flashlights, and even binoculars if they are likely to become customers. And how corruption-prone must such a housekeeper be who has one dollar subsistence in his pocket and is supposed to make the initial choice of two or three combines that cost $40,000 each? How will he react if the salesman promises him one or two tenths of a percent as a "personal rebate," a thing which is said to happen occasionally? Nobody would notice if he put the $400 bribe into his own pocket, a fortune to a Hutterite, a tip to a salesman for agricultural machinery. But God can see everything, and man will have to account for each and every cent. This certainty is likely to help withstand many a temptation of this kind. Four hundred dollars may be the equivalent of 10 to 15 years of subsistence, but they are not worth the purgatory.

This summer, I, too, am heavily tempted. The Waterton reservoir, with its cool and clear water right behind the hill in the northeast, is like a magnet during these dog days with temperatures of up to 35 degrees Celsius. Swimming, however, constitutes a difficult question. When children and teenagers frolic in the water in their Salvation-Army swimsuits from the 1960's, boys strictly separated from girls at two different waterholes far apart from one another, the teacher looks the other way. It is true that swimming certainly is a type of lust of the flesh like ice skating or the baseball games which the English teacher at Waterton organizes against Paul's will with her students on the pasture behind the schoolhouse. To Paul, any physical activity which is not useful for the "community" is highly problematic.

It is then with a fairly bad conscience that I quietly leave the bookbinder's house every morning one hour before wake-up and, without a sound so as not to alert the dogs, sneak past the henhouse over to the lake. The feeling of doing something secretly in God's ark stimulates my imagination every summer morning. My lake, which reflects the pale morning light between the softly sloping pastures, now seems to me like a lover with whom I unite day after day under the stern look of God. Stark naked, I swim a few hundred yards and leave a bubbly trace on the mirror-like surface until both banks are the same distance from me. Then I float on my back, listen to the quiet, and dream after the buzzard couple that flies in spirals in the upcurrent of the foothills.

It is a very special feeling for me to be all by myself without the schoolteacher, without the preacher, and without the critical looks that normally follow me from morning to night wherever I go. After six months among God's chosen people,

I still long for my world. When was it that I last went dancing? When was it that I last touched another human being?
How much I would like to really curse and cuss, damn it,
just once! There are days on which I really have to force myself to attend the service and the prayer. This eternal talk
about fear of God, pain in hell, and heavenly bliss — sometimes I can't stand it anymore. Sometimes the hair on my
neck starts to stick out when I am stuck between the hog-
man and the smith, bombarded by the community's
screeching songs. I would love to follow the school children's
example and pick my nose until it starts to bleed so that I
could leave and be outside. I have to admit that, on bad
days, the sermons seem to me like brainwashing, and being
constantly crammed with encouragements to loyalty and
faith day after day gives me the feeling of being spiritually
raped.

The longer I am here, the shorter becomes the distance
between me and the Hutterites. I am increasingly taken over,
and the preacher asks me more and more often whether I
have now realized that only the Hutterite way of life leads to
salvation. They warn me that I won't be able to use the excuse of not having known anything about righteous Christian life when Judgment Day comes around. "If you don't
want to be a Hutterite, Miechel," Paul tells me over and over
again, "you must suffer double punishment in hell."

So the saints of Waterton want to make a Hutterite of me,
and nobody can blame them. They couldn't show me their
affection in a clearer way than by asking me to become one
of theirs. If I were able to walk the narrow path, I would be
one of the very few in North America to convert to the Hutterite faith from the outside. Five or six people of the world
have tried it so far, all of whom gave up sooner or later and
went back to where they had come from. Faced with these
unsuccessful attempts, the brethren have completely abandoned their missionary activities in the New World, activities
which constituted the center of their work in faith up into

the 18th century. Now those who want to be converted must come to the colonies by their own choice. The thought of having to stay here forever makes me afraid. Slowly, the security of community life turns into anxiety for me, and I feel exiled, caged in, and cut off from my world. And there are bitter reproaches: Have I gone too far with my plan to find out everything exactly and to experience through my own body and soul what it means to lead a Hutterite existence? Is that intention at all possible for a man of the world, and am I not asking both the Hutterites and myself for too much? And how am I going to get out of here again this coming winter, when my year is over? Won't leaving lead to serious disappointments if not to a complete break? Will Elias and his followers curse me for all time to come? Thus my feelings sway from heavy anxiety to giddy weightlessness as I float here on my back in the middle of the mountain lake with the buzzards circling high above me.

It is no coincidence that, during those weeks in which I develop the first resistance against the chosen society, I get to know more closely one Hutterite who is in the role of the outsider as I am. He is Peter E. Wurz, called "Patch"; he is preacher Elias's son. Peter is a "poor child," as the people here say, a mentally heavily retarded boy, very tall, almost a little thin, with piercing, light-blue eyes. The 18-year-old's movements are uncoordinated, and he has trouble keeping his balance. Sometimes he falls down the length of his entire body, and the gaps between his teeth are witnesses to many a serious fall in the past. But Patch is tough. When he wants to go somewhere, he yells, "DA!" ("There"), which is one of the few sounds he is able to produce; then he starts to stumble forward even though this is bound to cost him some new bumps.

When I first saw him, right after my arrival at the Waterton colony, I couldn't help thinking of Frankenstein and was afraid of him. His piercing look and his unpredictable behavior made me very insecure. I had never seen people like him, for in my world, the Peters live behind tall walls, are kept quiet with the help of tranquilizers, and spend their days in a twilight in rubber cells. The Hutterites, however, do not need mental institutions. They let the "poor children" lead their own and different lives, a practice which is very unusual for a society in which being different is normally taboo.

Patch loves to be where there is something to see: During soap-making, between the big, steaming cauldrons, for example, or when Paul feeds the ducks by shoveling them barley, in the middle of 1,500 gabbling Sunday roasts. This is fun for him. Sometimes he shows up in the middle of Sunday school, where, waving his arms and uttering a loud "DA," he sits down next to me and looks astonished. The children may then grin a little and are happy about the welcomed interruption, but teacher Paul acts as if nothing has happened and continues to beat the prayer rhythm on the podium with his hand, as usual trying in vain to get a little emphasis into our tired murmuring.

The Hutterite motto of "Everybody gives what he can, and gets what he needs" applies to Peter as well. He can't work, but still every year he gets his new pair of shoes, his "four yards of trouser material" and his gallon of flower wine at the beginning of the month just like the others. Without much sentimentality, one of the women who has "Kuchwuch" feeds him in the kitchen at noon. And because he cannot walk very well, his mother Rebecca serves him breakfast and supper in bed. "As ye have done it unto one of the least of these my brethren," says Jesus, "ye have done it unto me" (Matthew 25:40).

The natural way in which the Waterton colonists treat their least brother Peter helps me gradually get over my fear of him. By being around him every day, I learn to understand the boy. In his big eyes I slowly discover a mysterious kind of life and a removed awareness which fascinates and attracts me. Now I even feel very comfortable when he sits next to me on the grass and watches me repair a rotting fence around the pasture or change a tire. He can watch me for hours without making me nervous. Once in a while, he holds up his right index finger and says his deep and momentous "DA," and then we both have to laugh without exactly knowing why.

I also like to tell him a little about my homesickness or the lake behind the hill, and I feel that nobody understands the problems I experience here better than Peter. He is also the only one who dares to simply put his hand on my shoulder or touch my face without any special reason. But how limited am I that I don't allow myself to return this gesture of affection and tenderness? Is it that I am afraid of the others? Is it that I am afraid of myself? Dear Peter recognizes my inhibitions with one blue look. He laughs, and I feel understood.

There are two other "poor children" in the Waterton colony. Among Peter's five siblings, there are two, 15-year-old Anna and 12-year-old Jakob, who suffer from the same disfunctions as their older brother. The three remaining siblings — Christian, 25, Tura, 23, and Rebecca, 14 — are completely normal. Their father Elias and their mother Rebecca are second cousins. Once in a while, such marriages occur in Hutterite circles. In very rare cases, the married couple's relationship is that of first cousin, which, according to Canadian law, is illegal. The Bible, however, reports similar cases, and thus the chosen do not consider such marriages between relatives anything offensive or unnatural. Then they say, "What God has started should not be opposed by man."

For several decades, however, the leaders have been listening more and more to the worldly doctors, who warn against the adverse results of strong inbreeding. Considering the fact that the present 25,000 to 30,000 Hutterites all descend from approximately 300 individuals who came from Russia to America 100 years ago and were at that time closely related to one another, one is surprised that the number of retarded is not greater. Exacerbating the problem here is the rule that, while in principle marriages between the Darius People, the Teacher People, and the Smith People are permitted, they are only rarely performed.

Peter's parents did not listen to the doctors' advice to have themselves sterilized after the first retarded child or to practice birth control. Where children are still seen as true gifts of God, birth control is blasphemy. Thus the preacher and his wife consider their cruel fate a test by God, a special burden and therefore a proof of God's favor, for the more difficult and rocky life on earth is, the happier the heavenly existence will be. "Live this life in joy and laughter, / There is only pain in death; / But a life that's filled with sorrow, / Gives you joy in your last breath," we read in the Hutterite "Song Book."

The outside world examines the problem of Hutterite inbreeding in many different ways. Out in the world, a terrible rumor has it that the colonists pay young Canadians up to 100 dollars to bring fresh blood into the communities. Newspaper ads to that effect are supposed to exist as well. If there were only a tiny bit of truth in this, I would certainly have noticed it. My abstinence proves the contrary, since they very consciously keep the girls away from me. When there are visitors from other colonies, I am the only unmarried person who is not permitted to sit together with the boys and girls at night and to play harmless games of hide-and-seek. The elders are afraid that I, the worldly sinner, could fall in love with a Sarah or a Rachel. Such shame cannot even be imagined!

Naturally, science too takes an interest in the phenomenon of "Hutterian inbreeding." To science, the Hutterites living in isolation are a tidbit for social studies, for, with the exception of the Amish in the East and Midwest of the United States, there is no other group among the North American population that has kept its genetic homogeneity as consistently as have the Hutterites. For example, "Growth and Inbreed of a Human Isolate" is the title of a study conducted by the University of Cleveland in Ohio; in the study, 667 married couples of the Smith People were measured. It was found that, on the average, the sons resulting from marriages between second cousins were one and three quarters of an inch shorter than those whose parents were not so closely related to each other; for daughters, the number was two inches.

A study conducted in the 1950's by Wayne University in Detroit examines "Hutterite Mental Health" and asks whether, in cases of manic depression and schizophrenia among the brethren and sisters, genetic factors could play a role. However, the scientists do not reach definite answers in this area. On the one hand, the occurrence of psychoses (schizophrenia in particular) in the colonies is only one third of that in the state of New York while, on the other hand, depressions are supposed to occur more frequently among the Hutterites than among the average population. However, it seems doubtful that the cause lies in their biological heritage rather than in their way of life and faith.

A society which is characterized by a harmonious social order, which exists without competition and pressure, which suffers no economic uncertainties, no unemployment or lack of care for the elderly, and which thus provides an all-around social and spiritual security for life from the cradle to the grave — such a society must also be different from the world around it in terms of its mental conditions. Since schizophrenics can be found in particular among socially isolated individuals, it is not surprising that the Hutterites, who perceive their lives as communal existences, are not as likely to display symptoms of schizophrenia. On the other hand, the reason for the Hutterites' being more prone to depressive behavior may lie in the fact that, from the time they are young children, they learn to always look for guilt in themselves rather than in other people. And, with such high moral standards, there are plenty of causes for self-reproach and feelings of guilt. After all, the Bible is full of both.

If a community member shows signs of mental problems, he or she is first sent to town to see the doctor, as is any other sick person. In serious cases, in-patient treatment may be accepted. But if there are no quick results — and to a Hutterite who doesn't know much about the world and has almost never spent the night outside of the community, almost every day is too much — the patient is brought back to the community and treated with Hutterite medicine. According to the chosen, the symptoms of a mental disorder most often reflect "broken nerves," and a "nervic" will not be isolated or discriminated against, as would happen out in the world, but has the right to special consideration and affection.

During the course of the illness, the brethren and sisters encourage the sick to participate in colony life as much as possible. Family ties are not ruptured either, so that female patients of the colony may even give birth. The community people try never to leave suicidal depressives alone and make every attempt to prevent situations that may seem unpleasant to the sick.

Thus, the sociologist Joseph W. Eaton, a professor at the University of Pittsburgh, describes a depressive old man who was so afraid of being alone that his five grown-up sons took turns sleeping in bed with him. In another case, the Hutterites avoided any talk about weddings in the presence of their schizophrenic sister because she always reacted violently when the topic was brought up. "The Hutterite social order may not preclude the onset of mental disorders but it creates a highly therapeutic atmosphere for their treatment," the scientist concludes in his study. After they are healed, the former "nervics" are not stigmatized for the rest of their lives but can again be elected to office and perform tasks just like any other brother or sister.

Overleaf: *Harvest is a hectic time in Waterton. The men thresh the last wheat, the women put up preserves, and the children gather potatoes from the field.*

Aside from psychiatry, there are of course other scientific disciplines whose representatives are interested in the "Hutterian Brothers." So far, 17 academicians owe their doctoral degrees to "the longest-living communist society in the Western world," and thus there is hardly an aspect of Hutterite life that has been spared by the worldly-wise doctoral candidates. The historians studied "The Golden Years of the Hutterites: Witnesses and Ideas of the Communal Moravian Anabaptists During the Walbot-Era, 1565 to 1578"; the communications experts ("mass communication") examined the depiction of "the Hutterite Land Purchase by the Canadian Press"; the theologians took on "The Ideological and Institutional Reflections of the Benedictine Ideals Among 15th Century Hutterites"; regional planners inquired about the "Relationship Between Architecture and Communal Life Among the Anabaptists."

Helen Martens, Ph.D., from the music department at Columbia University, shows with great astonishment that the Hutterites have been able to keep the tunes of their songs from the 16th century intact without a single note having been written down, but only through the tradition of listening — "which is remarkable!" And John A. Baden, doctor of political science at Indiana University, analyzes the tensions between the progressive rationalism in the Hutterite economy on the one hand and the radical adherence to tradition in their social and cultural life on the other. In his work entitled "Management of Social Stability — a Political Ethnography of the North American Hutterites," doctoral candidate Baden concludes that a key to the secret of the "sect's survival strength can be found in their remarkable ability to adapt to the requirements of a highly-developed technological society and their political distribution of power."

How political power is distributed among the Hutterites is something I myself have experienced during this summer. In the New York colony, southeast of Lethbridge, a new preach-

er will be elected. The community has grown to more than
100 members, and they now need a second servant of the
word so that, when the next "leaving one another" takes
place in a few years, each group will have its spiritual shepherd. Thus, the preacher from the New York colony calls up
the venerable Johannes, the elder from the Darius colony of
Wilson, and says, "I need an assistant." Johannes, in turn,
relays the message to the elder preachers in the area. He
"phones into the round," as the Hutterites call this procedure, in order to ask his colleagues to come to a meeting at
the brethren's community of New York as soon as possible.

It is shortly before the second hay-cutting, when the Au-
gust sun has turned the non-irrigated grazing land to burnt
yellow, that the election of the "assistant" is supposed to
take place. Preacher Johannes has given me permission to
be present at this important event although the unbaptized
have no business being there — not to mention the men of
the world. In my case, the elder makes an exception: "So
that you see that we do everything in a Christian manner —
we have no secrets." On the following Thursday I ride on the
egg truck to Lethbridge; there I switch to the hog truck of
the New Yorkers, which takes me to the community where
the election will be held the next day. As a Hutterite, I can
very well do without public transportation.

When I arrive, there are already about 20 trucks and vans
parked behind the community's schoolhouse, and about 20
silver-beards sit together in the kitchen having lunch, the
chosen of the chosen, gathered together with cheesecake
and coffee. Their average age as well as the average number
of their grand-children and great-grandchildren is around
70, and some of these old men's parents had been born in
the Ukraine. They can trace their ancestors back to
Carinthia or Swabia, and the years of the expulsion from
Moravia, from Transylvania, from Wallachia, and from Russia are so vividly remembered that these childhood experiences might have been their own.

The grey men here consider themselves the guardians of the old rule and the keepers of their people's traditions. During this informal gathering between pots and pans, they thus already speak about "how faith is doing in the country." There are those who complain about the girls who have recently started to tie their kerchiefs in a way which shows more and more hair on the forehead, a behavior which, with strict interpretation, violates 1 Corinthians 11:6, which reads, "For if a woman be not covered, let her also be shorn." Others observe that the boys do not obey in the ancestors' spirit as much as they used to. "Bars and gambling houses and saloons is where they go when they are in town," the elder laments, and suggests, "They must be beaten soundly just as my father did it with me" according to the way of the ancestors! Everybody present nods in agreement.

In particular here at the New York colony, Johannes finds many a cause for complaint. Even I notice the causes immediately. It is not only the girls who violate good Hutterite manners, with their kerchiefs pushed to the back of their heads; the boys, too, shamelessly wear tight pants and colorful shirts as well as — may the devil take them — prideful cowboy hats whose rims are turned up toward the sky. In front of the houses there are small flower beds enticing the eye.

The lawn in the yard is kept at golf-course height by weekly mowing instead of being mowed twice a summer as it is in the elder's colony.

Where such worldly actions lead, Johannes Wurz knows exactly: "To eternal hellfire." Again, the preachers nod in unison. Jakob, the preacher of the accused community of New York, joins the nodding with a red face and a bad conscience. He promises to be more strict and, from now on, to ban the little garden plots where an occasional radish or strawberry plant for private consumption can be found. The women shall be asked not to order any more colorful material from the wholesale dealer, "and woe unto those who wear them if..." the "styled" pants do not disappear very soon. One more time, the elder raises his admonishing index finger: "We are the guardians and must see to it that no worldly trash is carried in through the gates of Jerusalem."

Now the guards at the gates of the New York community are supposed to be reinforced with a new watch dog, and this is the reason for today's gathering. At night behind the closed doors of the preacher's room, the old men take counsel about who should be recommended as a candidate for the position of guardian, who is going to "run during the primary."

"Primaries" are held only among the Darius People, while this practice does not exist among the Teacher People and the Smith People. There, any baptized brother of the colony may be elected.

After three hours of deliberation in the back room, they agree on three candidates: the shoemaker Johannes, the smith Leonhard, and Georg, the chief of the pigsty. Each one of these has been judged according to the high standards which Paul clearly specifies for those "who wish to hold such bishop's office": "A bishop then must be blameless, the husband of one wife, vigilant, sober, of good behavior, given to hospitality, apt to teach; not given to wine, no striker, not greedy of filthy lucre, but patient, not a brawler, not covetous; one that ruleth well his own house, having his children in subjection with all gravity; for if a man does not know how to rule his own house, how shall he take care of the church of God? ...Even so must their wives be grave, not slanderers, sober, faithful in all things" (1 Timothy 3:2-11).

The candidates Johannes, Leonhard, and Georg are good family men; they have faithful and temperate wives (each having only one) and drink, as far as is known, only their monthly quart of wine; they haven't had a brawl since their baptism, and those who don't have any money can hardly be its lovers. The next morning, the elder Johannes thus writes their names on the chalk board in the schoolroom before the solemn "Preacher Election Service." Although this is Friday, we wear our Sunday best: the men, their "Pfat," their white shirts underneath their Sunday jackets, and the women, the long, dark dresses which are made out of a finer material. With Stone-Age, stern looks, the preachers sit on the long bench behind the podium directly under the chalkboard, and when I look at these grey guardians of the holy grail of pure teaching, crazy associations enter my mind: Conference of Nobel-prize winners at the beginning of the year 1900; 1st class special salon car of the Hesse-Nassau Railways; the president's conference at the Berlin Humboldt University in preparation for the Emperor's birthday. These impressions may be caused by their Sunday costumes, which include the "Preacher's angle," a wide and long coat with a cut-off swallow tail which, according to my memory, the prominent men wear on old photographs from the last century.

But my fancies are completely out of place here. They cast a light which characterizes my earthly way of thinking. For here it is a matter of a godly procedure which presupposes the pious participation of everybody present in order to be successful. Therefore, we sing:

"God, you mighty Lord, / It is in all Your
pow'r,/Your people You send forth / With
mercy every hour;/We beg and ask You now /
For strength and for wise words, / That I with
my own mouth / Will spread Your holy
works./The ones You chose, if You love them/
And their life pleases You, / Then You will
give them men / Who've proven to be true. /
Your word lend for a shield,/ Pillars support
Your throne, / With those Your house they
built / Through You from living stone."

After 30 additional stanzas, the elder Johannes moves with dignified steps behind the podium, uses his big handkerchief to extensively blow his nose, puts one hand in the other, and says, "Dear brethren and sisters! Today we are gathered here for a special reason and for God's glory since we are all charged with caring well for the community so that all things turn out well and that we may live in peace and unity. This day requires us to place an assistant at our dear brother Jakob's side so that Jerusalem will live through diligent guardians and good supervision, through righteous teaching and good teachers, through watchful shepherds on a good pasture."

In a two-hour sermon, Johannes emphasizes the importance of the moment by building a wide arch from Moses, the first preacher of the then-chosen Jewish people, to Peter, the first among the twelve apostles, and finally to the founding father Jakob Hutter. One of the candidates shall now follow in these three men's footsteps "with wisdom but without curiosity, with strictness but without wrath, and with thriftiness but without avarice." Who is it going to be — the shoemaker, the smith, or the hog-chief? As the election procedure begins, all women and unbaptized children must leave the classroom. With the elder's personal permission I may stay in my furthermost corner as an exception.

When the men are finally alone, Johannes sternly admonishes his brethren one more time, and so that everybody can understand it, he now uses not the standard German but the Hutterite dialect: "Brethren! Each one of you should cast your vote not according to human repute, not out of either jealousy or favor, animosity or friendship, but out of pure fear of God! This means: No glutton, no drunkard, surely no tobacco-smoker shall be accepted; we must rather make a pure and unstained sacrifice before God, for the wrath of God is nothing to joke about."

Thus, each man pulls a piece of paper out of his pocket and, in German handwriting, puts down the name of one of the three candidates. According to age, the men walk in front of the podium in order to cast their ballots into the preacher's hat, which serves as the ballot box. Nobody says a word. The votes are also counted in silence by the elder and the brethren of the court, and the results are written on the chalkboard: Johannes 8, Leonhard 10, Georg 8.

The smith has received the majority of votes, but that doesn't mean that he is now elected. This election was only a kind of human primary through which it is determined who will qualify as a candidate in the final decision. For only those who receive at least five votes will be considered at this point. Just as the 11 apostles designated Matthias as the successor for the renegade Jude ("And they gave forth their lots; and the lot fell upon Matthias; and he was numbered with the eleven apostles," Acts 1:26), among the Hutterites only God, not man, decides who should represent Him on earth. Since all three candidates for the position of preacher were able to exceed the five-vote requirement, three lots are made out of three notebook pages. The word "Preacher" is on one of them. The other two are blanks.

Before the heavenly lottery, the "choosing," begins, preacher Johannes kneels down with his men, faces the ceiling, and prays, "We ask you for help, for you, God, are the master of all of us and your eye knows the human heart. We human beings can see only the outside. As you designated Moses, David, and Saul, choose the right man now, too."

Johannes vigorously shakes the hat one more time, and then the three candidates, the younger after the older, take out a piece of paper, return to their seats, and check with pale faces who "will be the one." While the shoemaker and the smith give no indication at all, I can see that Hog-Jerg is nodding faintly. A murmur goes through the hall. Georg Hofer is the new preacher! God wanted it against the human plurality in favor of his rival Leonhard. Now the brethren cannot keep their pious restraint any longer, and everybody speaks with his neighbor, making wild gestures. Only the chosen Georg sits there with a red neck and is silent.

Instead of congratulating the "new one," the preacher-colleagues call him up to the front for "Comforting and Admon-

ishing." Standing up, they form a semicircle around him.
"Be brave, be diligent, and be not afraid," the old men comfort and admonish. They give the merely 33-year-old the
"good" advice to always listen to the older servants and to always reach agreement with them so as not to endanger the
unity of the saints. Paul says himself, "I beseech you, brethren, by the name of our Lord Jesus Christ, that ye all speak
the same thing, that there be no divisions among you; but
that ye be perfectly joined together in the same mind and
the same judgment" (1 Corinthians 1:10). The newly-elected
solemnly promises to follow this advice, which is actually
more of a command, and never to show a "bent finger" to the
experienced servants of the word, i.e. never to contradict
them. It will depend on his further good behavior whether
Georg will be certified as a preacher for life, since he is now
still a "servant on probation."

It seems that, after all, they do not completely trust the
God whose eye knows the human heart; rather, they act according to a very worldly principle: "Trust is good, but control is better." Such a probation period normally lasts three
or four years; after this period, the "certification service"
may be held during a gathering similar to the one today.
Similar to the baptismal ceremony, this service requires that
the certified preacher-to-be must answer the following questions (among others) asked by the elder: "Do you wish to
seek your obedience and be used within the country and
outside as is needed, in good times and bad times, as God
the Almighty decides? Do you wish to be faithful in your
service toward God and His community even in death, since
we are particularly destined to die through fire and sword
for the sake of God's word?"

Both questions really refer more to the reality of the 16th
and 17th centuries than to that of the present. In those
times, the preachers were often sent as missionaries, as
"messengers," from Moravia and Hungary into the German-
speaking countries in order to solicit support there for the

Hutterite cause. Today, any missionary activity is difficult for mostly practical reasons. How can the command "Go ye into all the world, and preach the gospel to every creature" (Mark 16:15) be in keeping with the prohibition against making an image of oneself? These days, one just doesn't get too far without a passport picture.

The only Hutterite missionary station is the Owa colony in Japan. Here there are a good dozen Japanese who have gathered around the preacher Eisiki, called "Cousin Eisiki." A few years ago, he visited the Wilson community and, with the assistance of an interpreter, was baptized by Johannes Wurz and made a preacher. Today, the Canadian brethren support the Japanese Hutterites with considerable donations, but nobody really knows what happens with the money.

The third question to which the candidate for the position of preacher must answer "yes" is more appropriate for our times than is the mission command: "Do you also wish to conduct brotherly punishment and admonition righteously and eagerly in order to discipline the brethren and sisters so that the community will flourish through your work?" The "servant of the word" is not only the preacher but also the highest judge of the community. He must see that the Holy Scripture's commands and prohibitions are being strictly adhered to, and, in those cases in which violations occur, he must maintain law and order with the severity prescribed in the Bible. "Punishment is more necessary and must be more than the daily bread," one reads in the community rules, "for when there is a lack of daily bread, the body perishes. But where there is a lack of discipline and punishment, the soul perishes."

If a member of the community is in danger of losing sight of the righteous path of Christian virtue, various ways of disciplining him or her are available to the preacher and to the brethren of the court at his side. For example, the supervisors must first "speak with and encourage" a hog-chief who does not take the prescribed care of his animals by keeping precise feeding times or who does not take the necessary and timely precautions when the sows farrow. This "encouragement" happens in a very unofficial way and without much ado, for example, when one coincidentally meets the brother outside his door. Then the preacher may ask him whether he might be overworked and whether he needs additional help so that hog production can be increased again.

However, if this talk does not affect the animals' low weight or the young pigs' rate of death, and if the hog-chief starts to enjoy his wife's and his older children's wine ration, he then is asked to appear in front of the council of the brethren of the court and is formally "admonished": "This is nothing but encouraging and enticing a person to the right or keeping the person from evil," the community regulations say. In most cases, such a summons is enough to bring Brother Lightfoot back to his senses again. The danger of his soul suffering damage is averted before greater harm can be done.

However, the Hutterites are human beings "made of flesh and blood," and it thus occasionally happens that a man does not regret his mistakes in time but continues to live for his sinful flesh instead of his soul. As before, he drinks mother's wine, oversleeps and misses breakfast, and maybe even privately sells two young pigs at half price to a worldly neighbor and then spends the money on drinks at the inn during his visit in town. Such cases have occurred and are considered a serious violation of the law. Theft of "God's property" out of greed and self-interest, combined with "heavy drinking" and "neglect of brotherly duty and responsibility," has serious consequences when the laws of the Bible are applied. "But now I have written unto you not to keep company, if any man that is called a brother be a fornicator, or covetous, or an idolater, or a railer, or a drunkard, or an extortioner; not to even eat with such a one," Paul writes to the Corinthians (1 Corinthians 5:11). In plain Hutterite, this means the sinner's preliminary ban and excommunication from community life.

At the end of a public "service of punishment," during which the sinner must wait outside, the preacher calls him into the classroom. It lessens the punishment if the guilty brother now asks for "severe visitation," for a harsh punishment, which the chairman will promptly grant him. The banning verses he uses are as follows: "I now pronounce your punishment in the name of Lord Jesus Christ and with God's power. You shall not share nor participate in the glory of God, but rather I deliver you to Satan for the destruction of the flesh, that the spirit may be saved (1 Corinthians 5:5) as long as you produce a heart which is ready to repent so that God will look at you with mercy again; and now go and bring your grief before God." Just as the preacher has the power to seal the union with God through baptism, he can temporarily or permanently terminate it through the ban.

From then on, the banned may not participate in communal life any longer. He will get his meals in the children's dining hall after everybody else has eaten. If he is married, he may not sleep with his wife anymore but must spend the night in the sleeping room of the Little School, which is only used after lunch by the children. He is prohibited from shaking hands with a brother or a sister, for a handshake is a sign of peace to the Hutterites. He is also immediately without work and cannot leave the colony. A banned Hutterite is practically a dead man, for how should he live in the community without his fellow human beings' company?

The pressure applied on him through this prohibition of contact must be worse than jail or dungeon even though the ban is enforced for only a relatively short time. After a few days, the convict may approach the preacher in order to "honestly and seriously ask through pleas and wishes to live again in peace with God and the community." The more serious his violation, the more often will the preacher decline the penitent's wishes; normally, however, the community's leader displays an initial willingness to oblige after the second or third approach. "Let her be shut up from the camp seven days, and after that let her be received in again" (Numbers 12:14) is the Lord's advice to Moses. The Hutterite legal system accepts this advice as well.

After one week, the brethren of the court meet again in order to discuss whether the renegade has now done enough penance for his crime. If the answer is yes, the community is asked by the preacher at the end of an evening prayer whether they agree to "lift the apostolic ban from the brother." If there are no objections, they "remain silent for a little while," as is recommended by the regulations, and then the preacher says, "Thus we take your silence and consider it your agreement with us."

The fallen brother, who has been waiting outside, now enters the room, kneels down in front of the preacher, and asks for forgiveness. Because the ban has temporarily severed his union with God and his community, he must now be baptized again; this is done without water and by the preacher's hand on his head. While the preacher touches his head, the servant of the word strikes his name from the book of death and again writes it in the book of eternal life in the name of the Almighty.

The sin has now been erased, and, because it is commonly known that God is more happy about a sinner who finds his way back to the true faith than about one thousand righteous men, the faithful community people now have reason to be content. Those who thereafter continue to distrust the repenting sinner and cannot forget his forgiven sins commit a sin themselves by creating dissent and animosity within the brethren's community.

But woe to the one who has been accepted again and violates the order another time, to the one who can't leave alcohol or who continues to sell community property on the black market, or who even turns his back on the colony and begins a new life out in the world! Such behavior results in the most serious Hutterite punishment, called the "cutting off." Those who are sentenced in this way are normally banned from the ark "for eternity" and may not even set foot on the community land any longer: "God judges those outside. 'Put away from among yourselves that wicked person'"(1 Corinthians 5:13).

Today, Samuel and Barbara Tschetter are outside. Three years ago, they left their colony because Barbara's father, housekeeper Michael Hofer from the New York colony, did not want to consent to their marriage. He believed that his daughter should not move away but should stay to help her mother with the work. Besides, he thought that Samuel wasn't the right husband for his child. Since man should not be opposed to what God has started, Barbara and Samuel used a visit to town in the winter of 1976 as their opportunity to run away. They got married a little later and today live in Lethbridge, Sylvan Road South, in one of the town's many faceless row houses. They have already brought two little children into the evil world. The father now works as a packer at the stockyards, and the mother stays at home.

When Barbara and Samuel Tschetter approached me on Main Street behind the Victorian post office building a few weeks ago during one of my visits in town, I saw a very ordinary Canadian couple standing in front of me. He wore jeans, and she wore her hair long and uncovered. Still, they were not quite ordinary, for they spoke the dialect of my Hutterites although they had a slight English accent. I was very surprised that they even dared to speak with me, a chosen one at least by my looks. This surprised me so because, as people who were "cut off" or had "run away," they were strictly prohibited from having any contact with their former brethren and sisters. But maybe they felt that something was wrong with me. Standing in front of the central mail box, Samuel thus overcame "his reticence" and asked, "And to whom do you belong?" When I found out who he was, I became very insecure. Under no circumstances did I want to be seen by preacher Elias or schoolteacher Paul as I was talking to the banished. Therefore, we agreed to meet in the public library in the early afternoon.

Hidden behind tall bookshelves, the two told me how they survived as Hutterite outcasts in the strange world.

The initial time had been hard, the vivacious, 26-year-old woman said, "but now it's going all right." When the egg truck brought them into town, they had one dollar of subsistence in their pockets and the shirts on their backs. With these they began a new life outside the community, which, to them, had become a cage. They spent their first nights in a Salvation Army emergency room. There, they also got something to eat and, even more important than bread, the worldly clothes which were the first outer expression of their new lives.

Since renegade Hutterites are known to be cheap and good workers, it wasn't too hard for Samuel to find a job, in spite of the general unemployment. He found work as a packer with the town's largest feed company. After the first monthly paycheck, they moved into a run-down hotel at the edge of town, using the false names "Mr. and Mrs. Ferguson." Their fear of being found by their former brothers was still very strong. As a matter of fact, they were wanted everywhere by the colonists at the time, for many suspected that Samuel had abducted Barbara against her will. The community people could not believe that the baptized girl had wanted to leave; such a thing had never happened among the strictly religious Darius People. In their communities, there are by far fewer withdrawals than among the Teacher People or the Smith People.

Only when the announcement of the wedding of two refugees appeared in the "Lethbridge Herald" a month later, did the Hutterites give up their search and decide to "cut" Barbara and Samuel "off" from the community of the saints.

But of course, it was impossible for the young couple to remain hidden in the small provincial town. In spite of her jeans and parka, the girls of the New York colony spotted their former sister one day at the supermarket. "There she goes, the evil daughter!" they shouted, referring to the song about the evil daughter from Hamburg. "You should be ashamed of yourself to leave your father, your mother, and the community in such a way!" the women yelled. It is said that their scorn was so strong that some even spat on the floor in front of the outcast. At that moment, nobody remembered the verse by Matthew: "Love your enemies and pray for them which persecute you" (Matthew 5:44). The Hutterites' excitement was just too strong; their blood boiled. There she was, a chosen creature of God who dared to simply go her own way out of the holy Jerusalem into the sinful Babylon!

Certainly every Hutterite has tasted the forbidden earthly fruits at one time or another; the contents of the "Kischten," the private trunks, at home in the bedrooms give clear proof of that. As I have said before, every girl has photographs, candy hearts, lipstick, and perfume locked away, and the boys guard their cowboy paraphernalia with the same loving secrecy. What a great challenge must it be then if two actually do those things of which the others don't even dare to dream, and if Barbara doesn't keep her lipstick hidden under lock and key but paints her mouth with it, "the whore!" And if Samuel shows off openly in the streets with his cowboy boots without having a bad conscience, what a provocation! The only thing that remains then is the righteous confidence that "those who turn aside unto their crooked ways the Lord shall lead forth with the workers of iniquity" (Psalms 125:5).

However, the oldest preacher, Johannes, did not want to wait until Judgment Day. He could not stand to see Samuel and Barbara master their lives among the terrible — the killers, sorcerers, and whores. He was afraid that their example might serve as a model among the weaker sheep of his flock. Thus, he did everything in his power to make the excommunicated couple's life a hell already here on earth. When the preacher finally found out that Samuel worked at the feed mill where the Hutterites are good customers, he put massive pressure on Ed, the manager: Either Samuel would be fired or an almost completed 100,000-dollar deal between the colony and the factory unfortunately would have to be canceled. On the next day, Sam was out on the street, and this in the middle of an economic depression. For almost a year, the couple survived on Barbara's pay, earned by cleaning at a hotel. Just in time, before she gave birth to her first daughter, Sam got a steady job at the stockyards, which is the city's monopoly and therefore couldn't be put under pressure as easily as had been the competition-driven feed producer.

Financially, things were going quite well, the two told me in the library, but they still didn't feel at home after four years out in the world. "The people, they just go their own ways," Barbara says, "and we are very often alone." Since leaving the colony, they haven't been back home. The contact with the family has been completely cut off by the ban. Even if her sick mother were to die tomorrow, Barbara would not be permitted to attend the funeral; this burdens her the most. It was probably more out of desperation than conviction that, two years ago, they became members of a Mennonite sect that also proclaims to be the only true one. Once a week, its members get together in private apartments for song and prayer — a weak substitute for the lost community.

Theoretically, the way back into the community is open to any renegade, since "every sin and blasphemy shall be forgiven unto men" (Matthew 12:31), but this is hardly possible for the couple anymore. Since the Hutterites do not consider their marriage valid (the worldly marriage certificate being, in their eyes, only a piece of paper), they would have to live just as before their running away — that is, as single persons in their home communities, which are 50 miles apart. The two children would stay with their mother but would have to bear Barbara's maiden name because they are illegitimate. Whether some day, after much repentance and many requests, a new marriage might be possible, and whether, after much discussion during the "speaking", the bride's father might still say "Take her," no one could know for sure. During the 450-year history of the Hutterites there just hasn't been such a case.

The story of 45-year-old David Hofer is just as unique in its own way. When he left his colony 28 years ago, the horse-crazy man just wanted one chance to relieve the pressure of his enthusiasm for rodeos. Down in Colorado in the arenas, he even rode wild bulls until they were foaming with anger. But then his girlfriend, whom he had met at a festival in Wyoming, became pregnant and gave birth to his illegitimate child, the first of four. Now David didn't dare to go back home, and the only thing left for him was the bottle. In the 1960's, he was jailed for the first time for driving while intoxicated.

Today the short, stocky man, a cross between Gunsmoke's Festus and John Wayne, is a regular at the jail in Lethbridge. So far, he has had to spend a total of seven years in jail for insulting an officer, assault, theft of a total of 72 cows worth 12,000 dollars, and armed robbery of a jewelry store. All were crimes committed while he was drunk. During the times between release and conviction, the chronic alcoholic resides in a Cadillac ready for the junkyard and parked in one of the town's back alleys.

Every Hutterite knows this fallen member of the chosen people. And when David staggers through the streets on Thursday, on Hutter-day, the Hutterite parents tell their children, "Look, there goes David! He ran away, and now the devil is getting him!" For teacher Paul in the German school of Waterton, David's fate is also an important part of the curriculum. It serves as a warning to his students that "wolves and sheep don't belong together" and that the wolf gets those sheep that leave the good flock. The same is the case, he says, with the pigeon, which always falls victim to the hawk when it leaves the flock.

However, not only individuals have left the chosen people. It has happened before that entire colonies have been banned from the heavenly community. One example is the Teacher People colony of Monarch, which is located directly on the highway from Waterton to Lethbridge. Driving by that place, one notices right away that something is wrong. The houses are in poor condition, the paint is falling off, the door to the cowbarn is hanging crooked on its hinges, and grass is growing over the footpaths. While a Hutterite community normally looks as clean and fresh as new, prepared "as a bride adorned for her husband" (Revelation 21:2), this colony resembles more a half-deserted gold diggers' settlement. Every time we come by here in our egg truck on our Thursday trip to town, we start talking about the "renegades."

The stories that I have heard about the Monarch community are colorful and contradictory. Only one thing seems to be clear: On November 22 in the year 1938, the first preacher of the Big Ben colony, Jakob Mendel, was taken out of office by the conference of all Teacher People preachers for bearing "false witness." They accused him of having registered and then sold for 600 dollars the patent for a rock-gathering machine which he had constructed himself.

Mendel, who believed in acting in his brethren's community's interest, did not accept the judgment but continued to preach to part of the colony, namely his relatives. This constituted a schism within the community. The adversaries did not talk to each other any longer, they ate their meals in separate places, and their children were taught in two different classrooms. Neighborly love was dead, and the community went to hell. In 1942 Jakob Mendel declared his willingness to split the community's property and to leave with his followers. The other party, however, did not want to give any "heavenly wealth" to the banned preacher. So the ex-preacher went before a worldly court and won: He built the new farm of Monarch next to the road to Lethbridge with 30,000 dollars from the colony's treasury.

I have been wanting to visit these "lepers" for a long time, but it has not been possible because of the ban. However, one day in the late summer, when, by way of exception, I am allowed to drive the truck home from town by myself because Chicken-Jerg is in bed with the flu, I simply turn left and park the truck next to the dilapidated kitchen of Monarch.

The women behind the window panes are so surprised that they can't get their mouths shut. They must assume that this is the first visit of an outside Hutterite since the community was started, and now they probably hope that, with my appearance, the ban has finally been broken after 40 years. Unfortunately, however, I am not a courier from the elder or from heaven, but only a curious "Germaner" who would like to speak with the outcasts in order to hear their side of the story.

The women are all excited and take me to preacher Samuel Mendel, who is a nephew of the notorious and now deceased Jakob whose rock-gathering patent started all the misery. Samuel is 66 years old; deep lines are carved into his face between the pinched eyes and the grey beard. Different from the other Hutterites whom I have gotten to know so far, this man is not really interested in me. It is enough for him to know where I come from and what I want. All the other questions about parents, profession, faith, and television are not asked here. Instead, he gets cracking and tells me at great length and in great detail about his worries and troubles, and it seems as if he hasn't had the opportunity to talk for a long time.

"Our community is at its end," he says in a straightforward way, and his eyes begin to water as he tells me how very much he feels deserted by God and his former brethren. The colony has only 20 members, the last cow had to be sold, there are leaks in the roof of the pigsty, there are no more geese, and since Chicken-Andreas's death, the children have had to take care of the fowl. "And our great God, he just watches how the community dies and does nothing," the old man says hopelessly.

The Almighty also looked on and did nothing as even the German school, one of the pillars of Hutterite life, was closed. Because there are only six children left here, the authorities decided that, for reasons of efficiency, they must ride the yellow school bus to the public elementary school in the neighboring town of Fort Macleod every day. They have even brought hashish home with them, the preacher Samuel says. It is then no wonder that, after graduation, the kids turn their backs on the community and move to town. Three of the preacher's four sons have already left; only 25-year-old Daniel still remains.

However, this quiet young man is in a hopeless position. He despises the faithless world and is despised by the majority of his own people. Unlike other Hutterite adolescents, he cannot "walk around" to other nearby colonies in order to find a wife; for him, there is no "girl-hunting." All doors are closed to him since no community would let their daughter join the outcasts.

"God must help if I should ever find a wife," he says. Then, in what almost sounds like disdain, his mother in the adjoining room quotes the eternal bachelor Paul: "It is good for a man not to touch a woman" (1 Corinthians 7:1). In her youth, in a situation similar to her son's, she decided in her desperate state to marry a first cousin within the community. There just was no other husband available. Daniel, however, doesn't even have this opportunity. His oldest cousin has just turned 12, and whether she would be a good wife for him is not certain either.

Now he probably wonders rightfully why he is punished by the Hutterite majority for a crime in which he personally had no part, having been born 14 years after his grandfather was banned. Even the elder of the Teacher People considers this a valid argument, but the compromise he offers to Daniel can hardly be accepted by him. If he wants to get married, he will have to leave his farm forever and move to his bride's community. Before that, he will have to be "rebaptized" because his baptism was performed by a deposed preacher and thus is invalid in the eyes of the others. Daniel thinks he cannot do this. He has made his union with God and not with men, he says, referring to Matthew. The situation is therefore quite hopeless, and as I say good-bye after half an hour, the preacher weeps.

My short visit at the outcasts' community of Monarch has shocked and scared me. Should strict faith be allowed to have such consequences, and should it be allowed to make the innocents' lives unhappy and make them liable for their fathers' sins? Where, then, is the commandment of neighborly love? Does it exist only among people of the same convictions, or does it also apply to the testament of those who think differently, — even enemies, as Matthew specifically commands? The Monarch people just want to be good Hutterites, and their costumes, their teachings, and their food are the same as those in Waterton, Wilson or any other community. Why don't the preachers forgive and follow their idol Jesus Christ also in mercy? Must repentance be forced onto a minority's sixth generation so that the majority can be kept in fear and discipline? Does, in this case, the end justify the means, and doesn't the holy community therefore commit a sin in its method of dealing with its sinners? These are the thoughts of a heretic going through my mind as I drive the egg truck home. I have an uneasy feeling in my stomach. I don't want to abandon my sympathy and love for the Hutterites, which I still feel inside myself, but my doubts are growing.

It is on this evening that the bomb explodes after my arrival at the colony. During supper, I notice grim faces and begin to feel rejection. The people avoid looking at me; the general mood is bad. At first I think that somehow they have found out about my forbidden visit to the outcasts' community. Maybe the people in the hog-truck saw me turn off the road. After supper, this suspicion turns out to be wrong. The thing is much worse: On my bed in the bookbinder's house, there is a letter from Hamburg written by a female colleague of mine. This letter has been opened.

It is certainly not the first letter which has been opened and then given to me. A concept like privacy of the mail is unknown to the Hutterites since there is neither a private sphere (except for the trunks) nor any other kind of secret. If a letter arrives here and the person to whom it is addressed is not present, then somebody else reads what the aunt or the uncle has to report. Hutterite letters are very rarely meant to be read by the addressee personally; most of the time, they are messages from colony to colony. The following sentence is an example of a common greeting: "Many regards from Jakob Wurz and his community." What follows then is much interesting information regarding the weather, the brethren's and sisters' health, and the community's "spiritual state," which, most of the time, is "at its best." Often, and as a matter that goes without saying, people here ask me, "Well, Miechel, what does your mother write?" Whether I want to or not, I then must read the letter to the entire community. Fortunately, the Hutterites don't quite understand handwritten German, in which the Latin alphabet is used. Many very common expressions — for example, "accordingly," "somehow," "possibly," or "really pissed" — are totally foreign to them.

But the letter lying on my bed now is typed very legibly, and even if details of its contents may not be comprehensible to the Hutterite reader because of the modern German expressions, there is one word that I assume has caught their attention — the name of *Playboy* magazine, for which my colleague from Hamburg has written an article. Now I understand why the people here were suddenly so different, why they didn't look at me, and why they avoided me. It was the name of this "prostitute's rag," which is here synonymous with sin, death, and devil. Old doubts regarding my credibility and integrity have been awakened again. Now I am no longer the marriage swindler, bankrobber, or spy from the Vatican; in the eyes of the faithful, I must now be almost the devil in person who has sneaked into the community in order to cunningly tempt God's people.

The frosty and stern way in which the brethren of the court call me to task that same evening corresponds to my interpretation. "Who wrote that letter? Are you friends with that person? Will you stop writing to her? Are you ashamed?" This kind of inquisition forces me to lie. I admit that I am ashamed of the letter. I declare that I hardly ever had anything to do with the author (who is a good friend of mine). I promise to break off all contact with her immediately. I maintain that I have never held pornographic writings in my hand because I, too, believe they are devil's trash. I lie through my teeth and feel miserable doing it.

That night I wish I had never set foot on Hutterite soil. What I would have given to snap my fingers and all of a sudden be on a plane back to Hamburg! Never before had I felt more like a stranger among these people. We were even closer on the day of my arrival. Eight months of slow and reluctant attempts to get to know and become familiar with one another now seem to have come to nothing. I will have to start at the very beginning, but how can a new beginning be successful if I have to continue to be afraid of further encumbering letters which will compel me to more lies and self-denials?

The preacher concludes my two-hour interrogation with an interpretation of the letter to the Ephesians, Chapter 5, Verse 3: "But fornication, and all uncleanness, or covetousness, let it not be once named among you." In this context, Elias Wurz reads to me the Hutterite interpretation from an old schoolbook: "We must avoid any kind of impurity, for in the Bible, this vice and sin follows right after fornication, and although all sin makes man impure, we still must give thought to the fact that, even though a man does not satisfy his lust with the company of women, he can still soil himself, which is something we should not continue to discuss because of honor."

Later that night, I suddenly find myself lying in one of the big beds of the Hotel Kempinski in Berlin, and, although it is still night, the traffic noise from Kurfürstendamm Street is of such roaring intensity that it awakens me. Lying next to me, like a mummy in a Hutterite costume, is Rachel, the bread-cutter's beautiful daughter from the Wilson colony. Her mouth is serious, but her eyes look at me as they had in late winter during the shearing of the sheep. For a long time, we lie next to one another, immobile, like two mummies; I am naked, and she is wrapped in seven skirts. The night passes, but along toward morning, I untie Rachel's kerchief. I open the knots of the thick pig-tails and slowly loosen them without ceasing to look at Rachel's eyes. My breath stands still. Never before have I seen a Hutter-girl with her hair undone. Now Rachel lies next to me in the splendor of her hair and smiles. Slowly and tenderly, I bend over her and sing to her the biblical "Song of Solomon" that I read during many a lonely night in Canada.

"Behold, thou art fair, my love; behold, thou art fair; thou hast doves' eyes within thy locks: thy hair is as a flock of goats, that appear from mount Gilead. Thy teeth are like a flock of sheep that are even shorn, which came up from the washing; whereof every one bear twins, and none is barren among them. Thy lips, O my spouse, drop as the honeycomb: honey and milk are under thy tongue. Thy two breasts are like two young roes that are twins, which feed among the lilies. Thy navel is like a round goblet, which wanteth not liquor. Thy belly is a heap of wheat, encircled with lilies. Thou art all fair, my love; there is no spot in thee. "A garden inclosed is my sister, my spouse; a spring shut up, a fountain sealed. Thy plants are an orchard of pomegranates, with pleasant fruits; camphire, with spikenard, Spikenard and saffron; calamus and cinnamon, with all trees of frankincense; myrrh and aloes, with all the chief spices. A fountain of gardens, a well of living waters, and streams from Lebanon. Awake, O north wind; and come, thou south; blow upon my garden, that the spices thereof may flow out" (Song of Solomon 4;7).

"This is in the Bible," I soothingly say to Rachel, who is trembling for fear underneath me. But the noise from Kurfürstendamm now becomes so much stronger and so much more roaring and threatening that she can't hear me anymore. Her eyes had begun to laugh during my love song, but now they are filled with fear again; her soft mouth has become hard and taciturn. In an agile manner, she turns away from me and leaves our bed; before I can reach for her, she is gone.

This is how I wake up in the bookbinder's house, alone as usual, awakened by noisy tractor engines that are being repaired over at the smithy. I have a headache and am sick deep down in my stomach. My body fights the social pressure, to which I am being subjected more than ever before. I don't feel like going on with this; I am finished and I decide to pull myself away from the community by simply staying in bed for the next few days. I don't want to see any Hutterites anymore, and it turns out that the feeling is mutual.

There are no visitors as there were several months ago when at night the room was packed with sympathetic people who were there because of my little flu. Today, two school boys named Andreas and Jürg bring me food in a bowl in

the morning, at noon, and in the evening; they politely ask
how I am feeling, but that is all. Even Paul doesn't come although it had become a dear habit for him to fix an old notebook or a torn bible at night and then to talk about God and
the world. No, nobody comes tonight, with the exception of
the two food-carriers. I think we must now take a break
from each other, the Hutterites and I, since what we have
been asking of each other has not been exactly easy. It may
also be that the brethren and sisters leave me alone in order
to punish me for the evil letter from Hamburg; maybe this is
some kind of ban.

However, the chosen people don't know a man of the
world like me. Right now, being alone is not painful; on the
contrary, it liberates me from the narrow-minded Hutterite
faith. Here, within my four walls, I have the opportunity to
really dream as much as I want for three days and three
nights; I can dream of Rachel's doves, her flock of sheep,
and the two young roes that feed among the lilies.

AUTUMN

A Blissful Death with Coffee and Zwieback

arvest time is approaching, and the colony wakes up from the calm of the summer. Even before the bell tolls, winekeeper Johannes gets behind the steering wheel of his white station wagon, his white horse, to go to examine with an expert's grip the grain's ripeness out in the fields. In the smithy, the men take care of their threshers and grain cutters, which have been waiting behind the henhouse for a long year and are now getting ready for action. Together with his students, teacher Paul organizes a great clean-up in the huge sheet metal barns, and the women bake zwieback to keep in stock, for who knows whether there will be enough time for that during the next days and weeks.

The Lord's beehive is humming again; early in the morning, the colonists are all excited. They move faster and with greater determination, and the air is filled with a very unusual tension. Again, the community awaits its annual test, and harvesting becomes more than just mowing and threshing. As always and everywhere in Hutterite life, earthly and heavenly matters as well as the temporal and the spiritual cannot be separated. Full barns are not only the result of human capability but also the heavenly reward for a righ-

Opposite Page, Top: At the beginning of every month, housekeeper Elias distributes the wine which is made out of dandelion blossoms. Each member of the congregation older than 15 gets one liter of "flower wine" which is filled in bottles and carried home by the children.

Bottom: The trunk is a woman's only private world. It contains the bare necessities of life but also some wordly kitsch, nail polish and colorful photographs, all things which are actually outlawed at the colony.

teous existence. The well-tended fields may be full of opulent grain, but if a thunderstorm ravages the area, all effort may prove to have been in vain from one day to the next. The Hutterites know this to be true from personal experience, and so, for just such occasions, they sing the following words at the evening prayer:

"The fields, they are a sorry sight, / The fruits, they suffer damage; / The moisture causes them much plight, / Through wetness they may perish. / The blessing, Lord, that You have shown / Comes down to earth from Your high throne / But it may vanish soon.

Our evil deeds, they are the cause, / Our life that is so wrong; / This brings Your wrath and our woes / Which plague us for so long. / Since we don't search for Your good grace / Through penitence for sin's disgrace, / the heavens, they must weep."

This year, however, God treats us mercifully. He keeps back the evil night frost and heavy autumn storms and lets the warm autumn sun shine brightly on the land for weeks. Punctually at the beginning of September, the grain-cutters go out into the fields; they are called "Swodders," a term which originated from the English word "swath." Because the growth period is short here in Canada, the grain must be cut before it has fully matured. Then it ripens on the ground for nine days, forming long rows — the "swods." Only then can we begin with the threshing.

"We" includes (as it did during the planting season in May) the broad-necked and strong preacher's son Christian; Georg, "Chicken-Jerg's" oldest son, who, for Hutterite blood, is quite shy and almost frail; and stocky Andreas, the treasurer's youngest son. In addition, the young ones Elias and Andi have joined in over the course of the year since they had to (and wanted to) leave school after their 15th birthday;

like me, they are now simple hands and help wherever help is needed — which means practically everywhere.

During lunch and supper, the two boys and I substitute for the main crew; we sit on the hydraulically cushioned seats on the three combines and creep across the dusty fields, back and forth, endlessly. The fire-engine red monsters eagerly eat their way through rape, oats, barley, and winter wheat, let the threshed-out kernels ripple into the five-cubic-yard grain tanks behind the driver's seat, and then shoot the finely chopped empty straw out the back.

"This is going just fine," I say to myself during my first round on the rape field which I had raked with my harrow into a nice and even Barbary carpet four months earlier. But before long the machine suddenly starts to stutter and cough heavily. The revolution counter falls to zero. I have driven much too fast into a heap of rape, and now the thick lump makes my McCormick 450 choke, or "shupper" as the Hutterites say. The threshing drum separating the kernels from the ears is stuck. I must stop at once and shut the machine off; otherwise, the belts will run hot. This happened to Hog-Jerg (Johannes) four years ago when he turned the ignition key off one moment too late. Immediately, there were flames shooting out from under the hood. Johannes hardly made it out of the cab to safety. The $20,000 combine burned out completely. Today, its remains can be seen down by the stream, standing as a rusting memorial.

Fortunately, I've managed to turn off the engine before the disaster. Now I follow the instructions which the winekeeper sent with me into the fields this morning: I open the hatch covering the threshing drum, which is all wrapped up in thick, greenish-yellow rape bundles. With one hand, I slowly pull the stubborn plants out of the immobilized machinery, which is a tough job to do. Above me, the sun is burning down; below me, the engine emits its heat; and I can hardly breathe the dusty air filled with diesel fumes any longer. Only after Andi and Elias have passed by me on their combines for the second time (because they were grinning and gloating over my misfortune, I couldn't feel much of the community spirit), has the rape lump been pulled out and the drum freed so that I can start the engine again.

That day, I "shupper" two more times before Christian finally relieves me at around three o'clock. He and his colleagues from the main shift must now work for the next twelve hours without a break except for supper, for which Johannes picks them up with his "white horse." At that time, between six and seven, we replace them in the rape again.

Since the climax of the harvesting battle has been reached, work must now go on around the clock: from the morning at around eight — as soon as the sun has dried the grain, moist from the night — until between one and four in the morning, when the dew forms again on the heavy ears. For Christian, Georg, and Andreas this is a 14- to 16-hour job which brings even these tough "menfolk" to the brink of exhaustion.

For me, too, the day is far from being over after my rape duty during supper. Now I work the nightshift in one of the big barns, supervising the delivery of the grain which shepherd Georg and smith Jakob bring up in their trucks, driving back and forth between the colony and the fields. As long as the bin is still relatively empty, the grain is just dumped out by the loaders; with a tractor-loader, I push it into the far corners. As the heap of kernels grows into a yellow mountain over the course of the night, I must roll in the "Ogger," which is a long, red pipe aimed high in the air; in it, a motor-driven spiral rotates the grain directly from the truck up to a height of 10 to 15 yards. With this machine, I can systematically pack the bin from rear to front up to the sheet metal roof with at least 20,000 bushels. Filling the bins carefully is important in this year of good harvest, for storage areas are scarce, and each and every dry corner must be used efficiently. Thus my work requires intuition and good skill. Down to the centimeter I must guide the backing loaders to the front of my "Ogger" and, (at just the right moment), must yell "HO!" which means "STOP" in standard German. Then I carefully open a hatch in the back of the truck so that the grain flows out evenly just like a fat flour mash. The flow of the grain must correspond exactly to the capacity of the transporting spiral; if there is too much, the grain runs onto the cement floor, and if there is too little, we waste precious time. Then the next transport must wait in front of the bin, the threshers can't be emptied, and the machinery of harvesting must stop. It is clear that I have been given a job with great responsibility, and I try hard not to disappoint the community again after the affair of the opened letter from Hamburg destroyed much of the Hutterites' confidence in me.

But because we all have the same goal in mind during harvesting, we become a little closer again — a thing which seemed impossible to me two weeks ago. At least the Hutterites take into consideration that I, the sinner, am obviously on the road to recovery here in God's community. "Those who work do not sin," they say, and indeed, after the last grain delivery at 3:30 in the morning, I have no other desire than to drop into my bed no matter how dirty and black in the face I may be. There is no thought of Rachel or Hotel Kempinski tonight.

And since I produced my first pair of shoes last winter, no work has ever given me as much satisfaction as this harvest, which is the harvest with which I have come to identify, as I did before with my own articles in the newsroom. Having participated in the planting of what I now harvest with the others — our daily bread, the fundamental aspect of our lives — what could be more important? Meanwhile, I have come to know the fields, I know where the moist depressions are in which I got stuck with my harrow in the spring, and I know where the difficult slopes and the dried-up stream bed are. I am familiar with this Hutterland, familiar with its moods and with its colors at each season of the year: Snow-white in the winter, earth-colored in the spring, green as grass in the summer, and yellow as straw in autumn.

All of this restores my faith in the people, people who just want the best for me and who cannot know how bad I therefore feel at times. Their honest hearts fear for my eternal soul as they imagine me immersed in the Hamburg hell-hole up to my neck, sinking steadily. Maybe they are not so wrong after all. They want to pull me out before it is too late and save me for eternal life at the feet of the Lord. Can I really blame them for trying to do that?

Our harvest lasts exactly fourteen days; then the fields are clean and about 400,000 bushels of dry grain with a total value of more than 1 1/2 million dollars are stored under the roof. This has been the best harvest for Waterton since the community was founded 18 years ago. The bins are therefore full. Wheat is even temporarily stored in the smithy and the washhouse, for nobody knows where else to put it.

This year, God has had mercy on His people. It is therefore no wonder that I see only happy faces these days, since He has given ample reward for an entire year's toil. Soon the treasurer can put a nice chunk of Thalers into the colony's savings account, which, as we know, is so important because, about 10 years from now, the Hutterite growth limit of 125 people will be reached again; then, they will need to buy a new farm, which is likely to cost three or four times as much as the Carmengey colony cost four years ago.

The preacher is also glad that the blessings of harvest turned out to be so ample, because he considers the filled bins to be, above all, proof of heaven's favor, as well as an indication that he has performed his duties as a guardian to the Lord's satisfaction. In his Thanksgiving sermon on the Sunday after the completion of threshing, however, there is no word of complacency. Instead, Elias uses a text from the prophet Hosea as he speaks about the spiritual relationship

between planting and harvesting: "Sow for yourselves righteousness, reap the fruit of steadfast love...you have plowed
iniquity, you have reaped injustice, you have eaten the fruit
of lies" (Hosea 10:12,13). The connection between this life
and the next life, the preacher says, is just like that between
the planting and the harvest. Those who stay on the right
path here on earth without lust of the flesh, lust of the eyes,
and pride, without inns, tobacco, and self-interest, will reap
eternal bliss and happiness in heaven. This life and the life
in eternity after death are inseparably interwoven; a mistake
in this life may result in inevitable damnation after death.

After the sermon, old Elias thus gives out only one bottle
of beer per person for the "Habtschinka," the custom of a
Thanksgiving meal originating in the Ukraine, in order to
prevent any heavy drinking, which was probably customary
on such occasions in the old homeland across the Dnieper
River. In celebration of the day, the Sunday roast today is
stuffed with a mash of rice, bread soaked in milk, some
onions, salt, pepper, and ground liver. "Stuffed Duck" is
what this dish is called, and it tastes better than can be de-
duced from the description. With the exception of the beer
and the duck stuffing, this banquet is in no way different
from any Sunday meal. The standards are modest here; had
we not been talking about this "Habtshinka" for days, I
would hardly have noticed anything special about today, for
it goes without saying that we are silent during the meal,
and the hidden little rituals regarding the best pieces of the
roast are performed with the same determined friendliness
as on every Sunday at noon. It is part of the regulations that
four persons share one animal. However, since a duck has
only two delicious breasts with dark meat, each eating quar-
tet must come to a silent agreement which shows how Hutterite justice and equality can be practiced even at the table.

I share the roast with smith Jakob, Hog-Johannes and
Joschua, the ruler over the cows. Because I am the
youngest, I must wait until the others have cut off a piece of

meat with much determination and without much etiquette. But although both Joschua and Jakob love duck breast as much as I do, there is a breast piece for me every other Sunday. One of the two then does without his favorite bite, is happy with the drumstick or the shoulder pieces, and looks forward to the coming Sunday.

However, harvesting is far from being finished with the Thanksgiving celebration. It is the garden's turn after the fields. Here the burden of work lies mainly on the shoulders of the women, the children, and schoolteacher Paul. In the meantime, the men plant the land with winter wheat before the first snow falls. Only one day after "Habshinka," on a Monday morning, Paul rings the kitchen bell for the women to gather. They are then driven up the hill into the cornfields on the big trailer of the garden tractor. There is much talk and laughter, as is always the case when the women work together. Whether during spring cleaning, weed-pulling or now at garden work, it always seems as if a merry old-fashioned costume club were getting together.

At one time, I asked Paul's Katharina whether she would trade places with a worldly farmer's wife. The round person then only shook her head heavily, answering "never"; she said that a worldly farm wife has too much work. At first, such an answer from a mother of nine comes as a surprise; but if one takes a closer look at the organization of work for a female Hutterite, Katharina's reaction becomes plausible. For it is the company of the sisters that takes many burdens off the individual woman's shoulder in spite of the Hutterite blessing of many children. With the exception of 2-year-old Andreas, all of the Hofer kids have already left their home and either are in the Little or Big School or have joined the people. Once every six weeks, Katharina and a colleague cook for the entire community and milk the cows for a week. Once every three weeks on Friday, she is in the bakery with five other sisters baking bread, zwieback, and "Schutenhonkelich." Every Monday for two hours, she does the family's laundry in the technically modern wash house. About once a week during the summer, she must do garden work, and during the winter, she sews clothes, a project with which both of her oldest daughters, named Rachel and Maria, are able to help considerably. Even with all this diligence, enough time remains for lunching and chatting.

In spite of her submission to man and her lack of a voice in community affairs, determined Katherina does not consider herself powerless or even oppressed. She knows how she can influence her husband and, for this reason, does not need "to stay home all day." "What I tell my Paul," she says, "he does most of the time." According to her, he plants not one potato without asking her advice first.

When I tell Katharina that, out in the world, women are beaten by their husbands, she shakes her head in disbelief. Such things are unheard of here at the colony. If her husband beat her, she would immediately go to the preacher, and he, in turn, would admonish Paul at the next service in front of the entire community, including his own students. His punishment would probably be to kneel for an hour and a half. As she says, "the embarrassment would be unspeakable!"

Katharina and her sisters harvest mountains of ripe ears of corn; for days, the tractor delivers a big load of "Gugurutz" to the kitchen down in the valley at noon and in the evening. The old women sit there at long tables in front of steaming cauldrons and preserve the corn in glass jars for the winter. Tomatoes, cucumbers, pumpkins, green cabbage, and red beets are treated in the same way and are stored on long wooden shelves in the basement. Also here in the basement, bundles of onions and garlic hang from the ceiling and emit an intense and spicy odor.

Here, too, the gracious God has rewarded the Hutterites' industrious weeding and righteous way of life with an overwhelming harvest. Very soon Paul does not know anymore where to put all the "Bageliana," "Kratsowitz," and pumpkin.

Soon all preserving jars are full; he then has a small truck loaded with "garden stuff" to sell door to door to the farms and small towns in the area. This form of small trade is called "Peddeln" by the Hutterites (from "to peddle").

With Martha, Susanna, Tura, Rebecca, and Anna — five girls between 15 and 20 — Paul and I begin our first peddling tour. Just like a frightened little boy whom his mother has sent into the dark basement to fetch some wine, Paul starts a song as soon as we have left the driveway of the colony:

> "God, make us confident and calm, / God, let us travel without harm, / Please keep us safe and sane; / And in Your mercy stay with us / And save us from all pain."

With loud Hutterite voices we sing, driving on Highway 810 toward the Rocky Mountains past the harvested, stubbly grain fields.

After about five miles, we enter the first farm place. Here lives neighbor Meyer, whose land the Hutterites cultivate as good neighbors when their own fields are taken care of. After the red mailbox, Paul turns left and stops directly in front of the house on the small farm. Instead of getting out, we stay in the car and wait until somebody comes. The girls are all excited and push one another away from the windows in the rear. The devil knows what there is to see out there on this very common western farm. However, everything is exciting out here in the world, even the Meyers's ugly prefabricated house with its colorful curtains in the kitchen window and two rustic plastic lanterns on both sides of the entryway. The flower bed next to the house, with its roses, geraniums, and asters enticing the Hutterites' eyes so very much, also draws admiring attention. "Look, how beautiful," the girls say, and Paul nervously honks.

Finally Mrs. Meyer, a vigorous country woman, comes out. I could imagine her in Pomerania if it weren't for her jeans and tight blouse whose three top buttons are open.

Paul ignores that and, without trying to hide his Hutterite accent, asks in English, "You want corn?" The woman orders six dozen ears for six dollars to serve at her grill party next weekend. The girls jump out of the car at once, open the hatch, and count the ears into three woven willow baskets. When I want to take one in order to carry it to the house, they reject my offer almost harshly: "We'll take care of that!" The girls do not want to pass up the opportunity to carry the goods into the customer's kitchen themselves. How much there is to see inside! Fine crystal glasses in a hutch! Above the sofa the oil painting of a mountain panorama at sunset ! The glowing screen of the television set atop the brass-covered chest of drawers! It is terribly beautiful to look at all of this in passing and to enjoy the scary thought of what it would be like to live as Mrs. Meyer with her own farm but without the community, with TV and without martyr ballads, and with vacations to Hawaii but without permanent residence in Waterton, the outer courtyard of paradise.

But before the mental game can be played to the end, Paul is there and tells them, "Turn quickly now," hurry up! Mrs. Meyer counts out the six dollars into his hand. Conscientiously, he puts the money into his deep pockets, which are rightfully called "sacks" because they are so big that, if need be, one could make 25 kilograms of potatoes disappear into them. Then he chases the excited girls out of the house and into the car, and off we go to the next farm.

By late evening, we have sold a hundred dozen ears of corn to more than fifty customers. Paul has had to run the gauntlet through the temptations of worldly pleasure every time we deal with a customer. The worst was a quick-shop near Fort McLeod, a small town 30 miles north of the colony. The owner, an opulent Indian with a broad face, ordered ten dollars worth of corn and gave each one of us some ice cream. Of course, Paul thought of the admonishing words of Sirach right away: "Presents and gifts blind the eyes of the wise" (Sirach 20:29). But before he could follow the implied dictate of these words from the Bible, the friendly owner had already handed him an ice-cream cup. Now the teacher could not go on driving right away, but first had to eat his portion.

As a result, his female company had enough time to fully inspect the fast-food place. The girls were particularly fascinated by the pinball machine in the corner. "Lady Black Jack" was written above the picture of a full-bosomed girl dressed in black nappa leather. Two young Indians made the shining balls spin. Lights flared up and went out again, bells rang, and the numbers on the counter below the lady in black reached astronomical heights. Silently, the girls formed a semicircle around the machine; there were the same big eyes devoid of understanding that I had seen in the faces of their male counterparts in front of the television wall at the Lethbridge department store.

Ignorant of the world, 20-year-old Tura then asked me on our way home whether the points displayed on the pinball machine indicated the dollar amount that was won. When I explained to her that people did not play the game to win money, Tura wanted to know why the Indian boys would then spend 25 cents per game, a fourth of one subsistence. "For fun," I answered, and Tura was silent; until our arrival in Waterton nobody said a word.

At home, the worried mothers have been waiting for us. "My heart has been pounding up here," Paul's Katharina says and puts her hand to her strong neck. She is always worried when Paul leaves the community; all women here feel as she does since they don't leave the colony as often and are therefore not as "experienced about the world" as their husbands. After supper, Paul takes the peddling's proceeds to his brother-in-law Elias: One hundred dollars for one hundred dozen ears of corn and a dollar fifty in tips. The treasurer sticks the bundle into his thick wallet and carefully locks it in his desk without counting the money.

This fall, the Hutterites go out to peddle the garden surplus quite a few more times; it is always gardener Paul who accompanies different groups that assist him in selling the produce. With the exception of the little children and the old people, everybody gets to go twice. Peddling is fun for all of them, and only Paul sweats blood, in particular when his underage students are with him.

But at times, he probably has terrible worries, even about his fully grown brethren. A few weeks later, when he wants to drive home as quickly as possible after successful potato sales in the Lethbridge area with the preacher's son Christian, Smith Jakob, and myself, we pass the university, which is located on the outskirts of town. The university is a drawn-out, monument-like block made of glass and concrete on a hill across the bed of the Oldman River. There is much speculation about this university among the Hutterite brethren. It is the center of all worldly knowledge in which the people "study themselves pale and yellow" and research the world's secrets without caring much for heavenly wisdom. When the word of the Bible is not respected even in this place of learning, the brethren suspect there cannot be Christian and civilized behavior in other areas either. Once a brother told me he had heard that the dormitory's sewer system had been clogged for years without anyone knowing the reason. Finally, all drainage pipes were pulled up and a gruesome discovery was made: Rumor had it that hundreds of aborted children in the pipes had clogged the drainage. That the three brethren accompanying me also know this story gives one a good idea about the Hutterite view of the world.

While we are driving past Lethbridge University, Jakob suddenly asks me whether non-students can be on the grounds of the university. "Sure you can," I answer in Hutterite; this encourages Christian to suggest to Paul that just once they might dare to take a brief look at this hole of corruption. At first, the teacher refuses because just the thought itself produces "towering" fears in him. But the others push him; their curiosity makes them itch. They just want to see "what's going on in there," nothing else. By the time we reach the next intersection, they have persuaded Paul to turn around and follow the campus signs down into the valley.

We leave the car in a big parking lot. The Hutterites stand in awe in front of the main entrance: "Siberian," they say, deeply moved by the mighty entrance, which is at least 20 yards high. Respectfully, Jakob touches the concrete's rough surface and looks straight up; he is probably checking whether everything is exactly vertical. A brief expert's debate follows, during which the Hutterites' own experiences in building enter the discussion. Yes, when they were building the cow barn, they had poured a concrete wall for the dung pit, three yards high and as straight as a soldier. But their own work at home is nothing compared to this massive gate, the three chosen ones admit, not without a certain amount of admiration. Solid work counts among experts, and what kind of prayer book they use is not so important for a change.

While we four men in black stand in amazement at the university entrance, the students come and go without being noticed by my brethren. It is only when a girl with long, blond hair approaches us that they listen up. "Are you the group from Jerusalem?" With a smile, she asks us whether we are from Hebrew University; we are surprised and say nothing. In the streets of Lethbridge, the Hutterites may not be an unusual sight anymore, but here on campus our appearance is so special that the student thinks we are a group of Talmud teachers from the Holy City. She simply cannot believe that she is dealing with "real Hutterites" that come from a colony only 40 miles away.

In the way of most North Americans, she immediately offers to help us. Her name is Susan; she is a sophomore majoring in anthropology. The Hutterites stand there as if they had been struck by lightning. "What have we started here?" their frightened faces ask. "As soon as you stand in front of this sinful tower of Babylon, the girls start talking to you out in the open." Every rumor seems to be true. But Susan doesn't give up. She almost forces her help on us by quickly opening the university's glass door; like a friendly doorman, she asks us to come inside. I take the lead, since it is easiest for me after nine semesters at the mammoth University of Bochum. The endless halls, the walls covered with posters, the batteries of empty plastic cups on the window sills, and, most of all, the grey young faces — I clearly remember all these things from the time when I was a student. Paul, Christian, and Jakob, however, cannot believe their eyes: Such a long house! So many "shtudents!" Paul thinks of his 32 school children at home and asks how the "schoolteachers" here can handle so many students. That there are 150 teachers for 1500 students here is simply amazing to him. Who wouldn't lose his orientation among so many people? "One doesn't know the other anymore," he says, "and the people are like strangers." Indeed, the word "community" does not apply here.

But our young guide is proud of her university. She shows us a lecture hall which is so big that the teacher at the podium in front can be heard only with the help of loud-speakers. We see a cafeteria which holds four times as many people as there are in Waterton. Susan also shows us the library. "Three stories with nothing but intelligent books full of worldly wisdom," Paul remarks, "and the Bible, the book of books, already contains everything man must know."

Of course, we finally want to inspect the infamous student dormitory, which is housed on the three lowest floors. Indeed boys and girls live here together very closely; even though they do not share rooms, they are still separated only by a narrow hallway. The kitchen and lounges are shared by both sexes. There is no strict supervision. It is then clear to Paul "what's going on there at night."

During the day, however, life in the dormitory seems quite harmless; it is even a little sober and simple. In small grey study rooms which don't seem to be suitable for extensive orgies, the students sit like monks and cram for upcoming exams. A boy in the kitchen who is eating egg ravioli out of the can tells us at Paul's request that he can afford to have meat for lunch only once or twice a week. His parents, small farmers from the north, do not have more money for him. Such conditions don't fit the image of the unrestrained, luxurious academic life; they much rather remind my three brethren of the ancestors' hunger years during the Thirty Years War in Hungary.

After the tour, we leave the university through the impressive main entrance and have very mixed feelings. At this point it is difficult to say whether this visit has contributed to enlightenment or whether it has only caused additional confusion, since the things we have seen simply cannot be properly evaluated by the Hutterites. The rumor of the dormitory's drainage pipes clogged by fetuses has certainly not been refuted by today's impressions, much as the general meaning of the entire "university business" remains totally unclear.

Teacher Paul simply sees no use in higher education. According to his unshakable conviction, a young person must learn how to read and write in order to be able to study the Bible and copy it. And if that person has mastered the multiplication chart, it suffices for Hutterite life. He refers to the trustworthy words of the Bible: "It is not needful for thee to see with thine eyes the things that are in secret" (Sirach 3:22). Besides, he looks at my example and sees his prejudice against the "big heads" fully confirmed: "Well, Miechel, you went to school for nineteen years. Now you know everything but can't do anything," he once told me right after my arrival at the Waterton colony when I tried without success to steer a tractor with trailer in reverse gear into the smithy.

In the half a year since then, my skills have been constantly improving through the practical life of a Hutterite. Actually, no day passes without my learning something; I don't perceive everyday farm life as routine work. Maybe I haven't been in Waterton long enough, but, on the other hand, Hutterite work life may also be too varied. I consider only the new cow barn: I put up walls with the others, I did carpentry work, I poured the concrete floor, I did electrical work, I put on the sheet metal roof, I welded the metal stalls for the cows, and I put in the windows; I learned almost everything while doing it. Whereas special schools and training prepare people for such work everywhere else in the world, here a look over the neighbor's shoulder is sufficient for a person to learn a trade.

However, the most important thing that I learn from the Hutterites is not an artisan's skills but something very different, something much more important: The ability to live with death. Death is not a subject of taboo inside the colonies. It is always present and always talked about. The little children sing about it before they learn to walk, and the old people talk about Friend Death as if he were a brother. Dying is the peoples' goal in life here, both the end of a cumbersome pilgrimage and a new beginning. Released from the sorrows of earthly existence, the brethren and sisters believe they will one day be ready to begin a new and heavenly life which, to them, is the "true existence" because it is a "purely spiritual" life, without the "body's filth" and the "temptations of the flesh." What kinds of delight and pleasure await the chosen ones (and only them) in heaven exceeds all human imagination. Still, the old Hutterite texts

Pages 210-211: Teacher Paul and the school children on their way to the garden. During the summer months, Paul demonstrates to those entrusted to him that the bad weeds must be kept low so that the good fruit can grow. This, he says, is a rule that applies to human beings just as it applies to vegetables.

describe life after death in very concrete pictures which are composed of quotations from the Bible and medieval salvation fantasies.

In the "Book of Articles About Life and Death" from the late 16th century, we read in the chapter "About the Heavenly Delights of All Righteous": "Speaking to the people about heaven's bliss is as if somebody who was born blind speaks of many different beautiful flowers which he has never seen. For heaven is a place and dwelling of holy people blessed in God. Yes, there we find the most gold-wonderful and unspeakable and unthinkable delight which lasts for eternity. O how beautiful is the heavenly Jerusalem whose throne is made of wonderful precious stones, of emerald and sapphire, as bright as transparent glass, and in her streets the Alleluiah is sung from morning until night. O what a wonderful heavenly kingdom that is, in which all of God's saints, clad in pure white silk, rejoice with the Lord. And there will be no more night, and the sun will not be needed any longer for the Lord himself will be their light. The righteous then will also be light and shine into the Father's kingdom. They will no longer suffer hunger or thirst, for there will be no more death. There will be neither sorrow nor pain, but there will be Alleluiah in all places and joy after joy.

In this place itself, there will be unspeakable joy resulting from many a thing: Firstly from the inside, the joy of a pure heart; then, from the outside, the joy of the glorified body; and finally, from all around, the joy of the beautiful new heaven and all God's creatures as ornaments. Out of this comes the most pleasant rejoicing. In this place there is everything one could ever desire and nothing frightful, but there is in all things plentiful contentment and honest pleasure and great bliss and safe rest and perfect life."

With this kind of future, the friends and relatives of the carpenter Josef Tschetter in the Riverside colony, only 30 miles from Waterton, have good reason to celebrate, for the

87-year-old has finally, after a lengthy illness, left this life. Like lightning, the good news of the old man's death spreads throughout the colonies. In Waterton, the telephone rings at 7:30 while we are in the process of spending the evening singing a beautiful martyr ballad at old Elias's place. The host picks up the receiver and answers the phone with the usual short "Yo." For about two minutes, he constantly repeats this slightly grouchy-sounding "Yo" and then puts the phone down. Returning to his regular spot on the bench between his six sons, he briefly says, "Cousin Josef from Riverside is dead."

The women near the oven look at one another with big eyes and start to talk among themselves with great excitement and even euphoria, not as if there had been a death at Riverside but as if a sister there had given birth to quadruplets. The men react to the news with more restraint, with a sober "Yo" and a fatalistic "That's the way it goes." This, however, does not mean that they are moved less by the death of the carpenter from the neighboring colony. Elias, for example, had been good friends with Josef since the days during which the Hutterites left the United States immediately following the First World War. But now he and the other menfolk distract themselves with planning and organizing. They designate the people who tomorrow will go to attend the "corpse," which is what the Hutterites call a funeral. Relatives and close friends, of course, have precedence over others. But because practically everybody is related to everybody, at least half of Waterton's adult population will travel to the sister colony of Riverside the next day in two crowded vans. The construction of the cow barn is interrupted, doctor's appointments are postponed, and class at the German school is cancelled. For a "corpse," Hutterites leave everything in order to take part in a brother's or sister's earthly farewell.

At the Riverside community, cars are parked up to the driveway, so we must leave our vehicle at the edge of a dirt road nearby. I can see license plates from Saskatchewan, Montana, and Washington, "from all over the place," as Elias proudly explains to me. From the still distant house of the deceased comes shrill singing. The windows of the house are foggy on the inside. I can see only many blurred dotted kerchiefs. Elias opens the door, and a dark and steaming mass of people welcomes us. Tightly squeezed next to each other, between one and two hundred Hutterites with hot, sweaty faces sit around the dead man's bier, excited by the importance of the event. I feel anxious and get claustrophobia. More screechingly and passionately than is usual, the community people repeat the verses after the speaker has sung them, and even the men make it through the long songs of lament with high falsetto:

"All life that we so cherish, / All flesh passes with you, / Whatever lives must perish / If it shall once be new. / To be renewed eternally / This body must now rot away. / Then a great splendor is declared / And for the righteous is prepared."

It takes us a while to find a seat in all this commotion. Elias notices my insecurity and takes my hand in a fatherly manner. The men make room for us up in front on the first bench right next to the bier by moving even more closely together. My hands start to shake because of all the excitement. I am sitting so close to the dead carpenter that I think I can smell him. His hollow eyes are closed so tightly that they seem to be glued shut. The corners of his thin, blueish mouth are low and serene. His forehead and cheeks and protruding nose have a yellowish shimmer. Nothing has been powdered here, nothing beautified with make-up. A pale corpse lies here, and nobody is afraid of looking into death's unpainted face. Only the position of the arms has been slightly manipulated; with a small white handkerchief, the hands have been tied together on the stomach; the elbows rest on two rolls of toilet paper. No false piety can be found here. Josef wears a simple white shirt, the "corpse clothes," and black Sunday trousers. Every decrepit Hutterite is prepared and has his dying clothes in his trunk. They are an inch wider so that he can be sure they will fit him; in that way they aren't so "stylish" either, for fashionable clothes are things one does not like to see in heaven or on the Hutterite earth.

Dead Josef can show himself down here, as well as up there, with good conscience. In celebration of the day, his daughters even knitted white socks for him. The women across from me on the other side of the bier place great importance on Josef's outer appearance anyway. After each song, they comb his thin beard and tug on his shirt in order to flatten yet another wrinkle. With their handkerchiefs, they lovingly swab the grease away from the dead man's forehead, dry the back of his nose, and stroke his hands.

Nobody shies away from the dead, and there is absolutely no one who shows any signs of disgust. Nor is anyone here bothered when "lunch" is served right next to the corpse during a break from the singing. This lunch consists of coffee, honey, jam, and the "funeral zwieback," which seems to be slightly sweeter than the regular one. The enamel pot gives off its steam right next to the dead man's head, and the jar with the jam is next to his right foot.

At first, I am unable to swallow one single bite. Somehow, I constantly have a moldy and greasy taste in my mouth, the physical manifestation of my concept of death. At this moment, I remember my deceased father, to whom I had to say good-bye in the cold morgue of a hospital. Under glaring neon lights, he lay in a sterile room with beige tiles; on his breast, there was a sign with his name, address, date of birth, and date of death. The possibility of a mix-up had to be eliminated. I was permitted to be with my dead father for ten minutes; then the nurse came and asked me whether I was done. He said that he was sorry but that he had to go home. Because I was unable to answer him, he pushed the corpse into the next room and put it back into the darkness and cold of his freezer box. There it rested alone until the funeral.

How I would have loved to give my father a Hutterite funeral, a warm and humane farewell in the community's company with serene and shrill songs and coffee and zwieback! The Hutterites know about death in the world. "A man dies the way he lived," they say. Thus it is also the rule that they don't take their old people to the hospital in town; if they close their eyes forever a few days sooner without intensive care and artificial life-saving devices, it is all for the better.

It was also carpenter Josef's last wish to die in his own bed. When, in the evening after a heart attack, he felt that the end was near, he called on the entire community to gather. As one of his sons tells me, he "took leave" by shaking the hand of each and every one of them, including the children; then he "asked that nobody hold any grudge against him for anything," sent warm greetings out to "all righteous in the land," and then "fell asleep with a peaceful face, very quietly and with no pain."

This peace of the dead person is what gladdens the living for two days and two nights during the "Wachten," the wake. They just can't see enough of and they feel attracted to this body of the carpenter whose soul they have commended to the Lord's arms already. Rarely does a tear drop here at the bier, but again and again I hear the people lament: "Josef is fine now! If we could only be where he is!" Endlessly, we sing about the heavenly joys in which the carpenter's soul now probably indulges:

> "This will be a joyful living, / Many thousand souls are there / In the glory God is giving, / Serving His throne everywhere; / Where the seraphs live and sing, Song of songs they now begin, / Holy, holy, holy host, Father, Son, and Holy Ghost."

I still remember the songs well when I think of the wedding. The dream of life after death is a suitable topic for any occasion. Just as on the night before the wedding, we now get a bottle of "Lethbridge Pilsner" and a cup of peanuts in order to keep up our strength. Only the old people go to bed around midnight. All others stay up, keep the guard, and sing until they are hoarse. The preacher sits in the corner with the Song Book; he is next to a little lamp which is so weak that we can see the moon's pale light coming through the windows. The dead man can hardly be seen anymore. Sometimes he seems to float in the air; then again, he looks petrified. I am dead tired; during the course of the night, my eyelids often drop. Stuck between my neighbors, I now and again tip over for a short time. Old Elias, too, snores once in a while on my right side.

During the night I can't help thinking of Katharina's story; she is the cook and midwife at Waterton. One night, she took a miscarriage wrapped in blankets over to the cemetery all by herself in order to bury it there. She told me this story in great detail on our way here. This is how I found out that there are strict regulations for funerals as well. If a child is stillborn, there is no ceremony at all. "We just cover it with earth," Katharina says, "so that the coyotes can't find it." For those babies who die before their fourth week, the community only sings the hymn "O Lord, blissful farewell"; for those up to the age of six months, there is a wake of one night. Only those who are older have the right to a real Hutterite funeral with a two-night wake.

At dawn, the carpenter comes and brings with him the custom-made coffin of spruce. Its length is 5 1/2 feet, and it is laid out with sawdust according to the old tradition. We carefully put the corpse into the litter. This is when I touch a dead body for the first time in my life. Twenty-four hours earlier doing so would have been something unimaginable for me, but in the meantime I have become more familiar with the carpenter's corpse, which now no longer causes feelings of fear for life in me. The unpleasant taste in my mouth is gone as well. I am glad to finally be able to do something and lend a helping hand after a long night of sitting still. As we lift the corpse I can feel the shape of the backbones, and the cool hands feel like parchment. I almost want to help the women as they put the dead body into the right position in the litter, as they comb it, swab it, and tug around on the clothes. The rolls of toilet paper, which, up until now have been used to support the elbows, have become a headrest under the neck. At the feet there is still some room; this is where Josef's Bible, torn from many readings, and his old Book of Songs come to rest — not as a present to be enjoyed in life after death, but out of respect for the holy books that can no longer be used and that nobody wants to just burn in a garbage can.

Another long morning filled with hoarse singing passes before we all march into the dining hall for the "corpse sermon," the funeral service. Our faces are grey and fatigued as we follow Josef's sons, who carry their father's coffin on their shoulders. At least 500 Hutterites have gathered here; I can't overlook the ocean of white-dotted kerchiefs on the left side or the sea of black jackets on the right. A narrow passageway in the middle of the room separates the sexes; it is just wide enough for the coffin. The preacher stands in front and first begins a long song:

> "O the old tale is the same, / That a man is dead and gone, / Some of them are killed and slain, / Dead of broken necks are some; / Then the stroke kills most of those / In the drinking, gambling pose, / Some in slumber without worry'ng / Will not wake up the next morning.

> Fire, water, earth, and air, / Lightning, thunder, war, all ill / Must become our murderer / As it is God's Holy will. / No one can escape from death, / Varied are the different

ways; / Our time on earth is gone / Like a shadow in the sun."

In the sermon that follows, the leader declares with a deep and sonorous voice "that we who have gathered here have the duty according to the rules and traditions to bury brother Josef, who lies here before us and whose time is over and has run out." He says that the dead man still has ears, but that he cannot hear these words any more than can "a table, a chair, or a bed." Therefore, he prefers to address the living "since we are still in the time of grace and can still hear with our ears and correct our behavior and repent."

The coffin, the servant of the word explains to his audience, shows how fleeting and unimportant earthly wealth actually is; whether "emperor, king, nobleman, or Jew," nobody can take more into the grave than Josef. Why then "live for the Thaler like everybody in the world?" he asks, then pauses for a long time. The Hutterite disdain for everything material cannot be expressed more convincingly than it is in the face of death. Out there, outside the community, he continues, where the peoples' lives become meaningful only through the massing of dead matter, the reality of death must turn into a threat. Therefore, people intoxicate themselves by eating and drinking and "hoarding up Thalers" and suppress the knowledge about the cruel and inevitable end. A community man, on the other hand, does not need to fear death since he has nothing to leave behind here on earth. There remains only the body, which, throughout his life, was his "worst enemy" and the tempter of his soul. The preacher continues, saying that, death having arrived, the man finally gets rid of his body; as on a bird's wings, he now rises up to heaven, to the highest court, in order to give testimony about his life down on earth. "O the sinners will begin to wail and lament," the preacher warns, with a stern look searching in particular the eyes of the boys and girls in the last rows. "Yes, there will be fear, terror, chattering of teeth, weeping, and different kinds of pain and sadness. And the devil with his fiery eyes and his black body will step up in front of the godly judge's chair, and he will say, 'Judge of Justice, give me this one because of his sins. He did not want to obey you but has always been ready to do my will; therefore, it is only right that he share damnation with me.'"

Referring to his text, the preacher describes the place of damnation, "hell with its cruel and terrible torture," in great detail and not without enjoyment: "Hell is a pit filled with fire, prepared for the godless, and full of pain and without peace. Those who enter it can never leave it again. There is neither quiet nor order but always fear and terror, and only weeping and lamenting. There is not only the greatest heat but also the worst cold, one great misery and suffering, a fire that can't be extinguished, an awful darkness, a worm that never dies, a pool with snakes and fire and the devils' terrible faces and eternal bitterness. In short, the absence of all good things!

Yes, and the souls of the damned will become the devils themselves, never-tiring hangmen who do not fear anyone. The damned will be full of sorrow and covered with unspeakable pain. They will be food for the fire but will never be totally consumed by it. They will bite their tongues and will never satisfy their hunger, for they will be hungry like dogs. Their drink will be the most bitter dragon gall and snakes' poison; their clothes will be roaches and worms, and their songs will always be screaming and yelling 'Woe, woe, and woe!' Their eyes will be filled with tears, and they will gnash their teeth; their lips will be filled with stink, and their ears filled with the screams of the devils. Their hands and feet will be tied with fiery bonds. All parts of the body will be on fire, but none can burn to ashes. They will ask for death, but death will escape them; their end will draw near over and over again but will never arrive.

For the lords and kings as well, God made the fire of pain deep and hot, and their rooms will be filled with fire; there is much wood which the Lord's breath will ignite like a hot river of sulphur. And they will curse the mothers who gave birth to them. Then the damned will say, 'O blessed and worthy of salvation are those who are not stained with cruel sins, those who did not live in lust and joy, in worldly pride and stupidity. Of what use to us now are pride, lust of the flesh, precious clothing, a life of luxury, and the lust and joy with which we vainly filled and consumed our life? Now these things pass like a shadow, like the smoke. All we have left is sorrow and eternal fire.'"

With big, surprised eyes, respectfully and faithfully like children in their story-telling grandmother's lap, young and old alike follow the descriptions of the inferno. There is no other topic that can so fascinate a Hutterite soul; never before have I seen so much naiveté and guilelessness in the faces of the righteous candidates for heaven than at this moment. "Whosoever does not receive the kingdom of God as a little child," Luke writes, "shall in nowise enter therein" (Luke 18:17). I am very convinced that nobody in this room will be sent away from the Pearly Gate. Without this simple belief in good and bad and in heaven and hell, Hutterite life cannot be imagined at all. It is the scripture-founded naiveté that gives this people the strength to hold on to its traditions; simplicity also keeps its spiritual innocence. "We are children of God: and if children, then heirs; heirs of God" (Romans 8:16-17).

This self-inflicted refusal to come of age may seem terrifying to an enlightened person. At this funeral I feel both forsaken by God and forsaken by the world. If only I had a bit of the carefree sense of security of the Hutterites, who preserve their childhood from the cradle to the grave. If only I knew as they do what is right in life, and if only I could listen to the stories of hell with such gullibility, as if each were no more than the tale of Little Red Ridinghood and the bad wolf! I feel so terribly old next to 75-year-old Elias who listens to the sermon with surprise as if he were hearing it for the first time.

Two long hours of sermon pass before the coffin is finally closed after one more song of 30 stanzas. The men carry it outside to the "Garden of the Dead," which is surrounded by a simple wooden fence painted white — the cemetery at the edge of the colony. There are neither crosses nor head-stones, and I see no flowers on the square lawn in whose center a rectangular hole has been dug. Without a trace, the chosen disappear from their valley of sorrow — earth to earth, ashes to ashes. With two ropes, the dead man's two sons lower the coffin into the grave; the hole is very quickly filled again by us menfolk. As early as next summer, this spot will be covered by rapidly growing prairie grass just like all other gravesites here.

"God created man out of the earth and turns him to earth again," the preacher quotes from Sirach 17:1. As a final salute, we have taken off our hats. Now there are finally a few women who can't hold back their tears. These are the dead man's sisters and daughters crying now. As strong as their faithful joy of death may be, they will painfully miss their brother and father as long as they must live here on earth. After a brief moment of silence, the preacher turns away from the grave and leads the congregation to the kitchen for the final "funeral lunch."

Eating potato soup with belly meat, we don't talk about dying anymore. We sit at long rows of tables and tell about the harvest that has just been finished, which is the primary topic in October. The men inquire about the yields of new brands of seed, which carry beautiful names such as "Sun-dance" and "Field Blessing." Excited about the costs that are too high and the prices that are too low, they are farmers just like all other farmers in Canada. Among the women over by the windows, the talk centers more on the garden — the weight of pumpkins and the quality of potatoes. What interests them the most, however, is the latest family news:

When will Martha from the Waterton colony finally marry her boyfriend from the Carmengey colony? Has Anna from Wilson finally given birth to her child? Is old Christian well again? Although meals are normally silent, today the Hutterites are unusually talkative in this dining hall. Maybe they first must let off some of the earthly steam after the long hours of singing around the coffin, talking now about real and worldly events instead of continuously shouting with joy about the bloodless life after death.

During this merry funeral lunch, I make the acquaintance of Andreas Wurz, a preacher from Montana; the brethren have told me many stories about him. His body bent by grief, the 84-year-old man is a living legend among the Hutterites, one of the last martyrs who, during the First World War, had to suffer the most cruel torture for the sake of his faith.

Whenever Andreas visits a colony, nobody sings ballads about the ancestors' sufferings from the thick songbook at night; the almost deaf and half-blind man tells about his own fate: It was on a Saturday morning in the year 1917, the man with the grey beard recalls, that the military police got him and a few other young men of the Rockport colony in South Dakota out of bed and put them in jail in Mitchell, which was 50 miles away. After a short interrogation, the police took their fingerprints and made them sign a piece of paper by which they committed themselves to "service without weapons"; the unsuspecting young men, however, did not understand the contents of the paper because, at the time, their knowledge of English was still very poor. Afterwards, a police escort took them to the town's railway station. There, a large crowd had been waiting for them. Andreas heard shouts such as "Hutterite Huns" and "Go to hell, go to the Kaiser!" "They beat us with clubs and bayonets," the veteran of faith remembers.

On the military train, drunken soldiers forced their way into their compartment and cut off their hair and beards.

"We didn't do anything. We were just praying that it wouldn't get any worse." In the barracks at Fort Lewis, however, it got much worse: "In the camp, they took me to a big building to the captain. Says the captain, 'You're gonna wear a uniform!' Says I, 'I won't wear a soldier's clothes!' Says he, 'Take your clothes off!' Says I, 'I won't take them off!' Says he again, 'Get undressed!' Then I tell him, 'No, I can't wear no soldier's clothes. I am a Hutterite, and we don't believe in fighting wars.'"

After Andreas bravely and firmly refused to put on a uniform, the soldiers knocked him to the floor, tore his clothes off, and put him in the uniform of the army infantry. Now private Wurz received the order to carry waste wood off the drill square. Andreas, however, again refused to carry out the order and, with bleeding head wounds, was taken to the fort's jail, where the guards beat him until he fainted. When he regained consciousness, they dragged the pacifist to the washroom and threw him into a bathtub filled with ice-cold water. Four men held Andreas's head down until he started to breathe water. "Then I thought: 'Now you must drown. Now the great God will take you.'" But the soldiers pulled him out of the tub at the last moment; they asked him whether he now wanted to follow orders, and because the exhausted Hutterite only shook his head in silence, they again pushed him under the surface of the water "until I passed out."

For an entire week, the fighter in faith had to go through the water torture twice a day. They refused him food; instead, the guards beat him up in between treatments. One day he was placed at a richly set table. Andreas didn't believe his eyes and thanked his God for "food and drink" as a Hutterite must do. But when he wanted to start to eat, his guards laughed and took him back to the cell with his stomach empty. "If you are a chosen one," the soldiers asked him then, "why does your God let you starve to death?"

Twenty-three-year-old Andreas could hardly crawl after three weeks in the US Army. His eyes were almost swollen shut from the beatings; his pulse was dangerously low. The half-starved man somehow managed to smuggle a letter to the colony out of the barracks. Alarmed by the prisoner's report, his preacher sent a petition to the president of the United States in Washington. It was successful. Andreas and many other brethren in faith were fed at Fort Lewis. When they had regained their strength, they were released and sent to work farms on which many "C.O.'s" (Conscientious Objectors to War) did their substitute service. In other military camps and jails (such as Leavenworth, where the brothers Michael and Josef Hofer died under mysterious circumstances), Hutterites were still mistreated many months after the end of the war; it was in April 1919 that the last prisoners were released and returned home.

When the severely tried Andreas Wurz came back, the Rockport colony had already purchased new land in Alberta in Canada. Only after the Second World War did the brethren dare to come back to the United States. But still today, 60 years after his tortures, Andreas is "afraid" when he meets a man in uniform on the street in town: "Then I am frightened." In his dreams, too, his tormentors from the past appear again and again. To him, America has hardly changed since the hard times of his youth. "The world remains the world," the old man says.

His children and grandchildren, however, cannot completely understand their old father and grandfather. They already feel dangerously secure here on earth, and the grandfather's experiences sound to their ears like stories from a different world. To be sure, the war in Vietnam ended only a few years ago, but the substitute service the young Hutterites from the United States had to complete as gamekeepers in some of the country's national parks was a welcome change from the colonies' routine; some of them liked it so well outside that they didn't return to the communities after the end of the service but stayed in the world for a few years. "Young people," the old man complains, "they don't know anymore what it means to fight for your faith with your life; they've got it too good. A comfortable life has never produced good Christians."

Secretly, some of today's preachers would be glad if they could re-institute the suffering and pain of the past, at least to a certain degree. If only just a few Jesuit persecutors sent by the Catholic empress Marie Theresa or some military police of the US Army would suddenly appear in front of the community's gates! As Hutterite history proves, the morals, the seriousness of faith, and the willingness to make sacrifices were greatest during those times when the evil world showed its supposedly true face. Then the flock gathered more closely around the shepherd. It is this closeness that is missing everywhere today, in many a preacher's opinion.

A very current conflict with the outer world must seem to them almost like a gift from above; almost every day, the country's newspapers write about the "Tax War" between the Canadian fiscal authorities and the chosen ones. This controversy seems to have become a substitute for the ancestors' religious wars. The Hutterites stubbornly refuse to pay income tax to the federal government, because the military is financed with the tax money. With the motto "income tax is blood tax," the elder of the Darius People, Johannes Wurz from the Wilson colony, marched into a battle which has been fought in the courts for years.

Instead of obeying the civil code, the Darius brethren prefer to follow the articles prescribed by Peter Riedemann, who says the following "about taxes": "Because the authorities are instituted and put in office by God, paying taxes is also instituted and required. Thus we are willing to pay interest, rent, toll, or whatever it may be called because we learn from our master Christ, who says, 'Give to Caesar what belongs to Caesar and to God what belongs to God.'" Therefore, the Hutterites pay communal income and property taxes as all other citizens do. "However, we do not give anything for wars, strangling, and bloodshed in those cases where the money is specifically designed to be used for this; we do this not out of blasphemy or spite, but out of fear of God so that we do not share in the sins of others. Whenever our conscience troubles us, we must and want to obey God more than we obey man," Riedemann demands.

Paying more than communal taxes would not only be sinful, in the opinion of the chosen ones, but it would also be unjust: Since the Hutterite people do not lay claim to old-age pensions, unemployment insurance, welfare, or orphan support, they do not need to contribute any taxes for those things. "We pay for ourselves," the elder Johannes Wurz says. "We need no welfare." However, the revenue service so far has not budged: The country's 67 Darius communities owe the state 45 million dollars. In 1960, the Teacher People and the Smith People gave in to the pressure of the authorities; since then, they have been remitting approximately 25% of their income to Ottawa. The orthodox Darius brethren, however, did not submit to the fiscal office and went before the Canadian Supreme Court. "How can a Hutterite pay income tax if he doesn't earn one single penny?" they asked the judges, who then ruled in their favor. But this decision soon turned out to be a Pyrrhic victory: If taxation on an individual basis is not justified, the tax authorities argued, the colonies must be considered a cooperative, but in this category, taxation is 46% and thus more than twice as much. The outcome: Each community received notice that it must pay nearly a million dollars in additional taxes, which would result in most of the communities' being on the edge of financial ruin, not to speak of the consequences on Judgment Day.

The decision was appealed, and the suit has gone on for years. The justice system has its problems with the case since it does not fit traditional law. Here the judges deal with an economic cooperative which, in the eyes of those who run it, constitutes a heavenly corporate body founded by the Holy Spirit and answering only to the Almighty. The purpose of the people living and working in the colonies is not to earn money but to gain salvation. And every penny in the housekeepers' cashbox belongs not only to the community people but also to God. How can you tax God? Not without logic, the Hutterites class themselves with other churches that have tax-exempt status and do not have to pay even property taxes.

When the final decision will be made is still uncertain. Preacher Johannes is determined not to commit a sin via tax dollars. "We are not going to pay," he says stubbornly; among his people, secret deliberations have already begun over how to react in case of legal defeat. On the one hand, there are those who don't want to do anything and are willing to suffer the resulting compulsory collection of the tax debts; there is plenty of expensive machinery on the farms. On the other hand, there are brethren who favor a new emigration, this time maybe to Australia. Last year, one of their worldly neighbors was over there "across the sea" (nobody here knows exactly where that continent really is) and came back with the most fantastic stories. He said that there is virtually unlimited cheap land, the growth period is much longer than in Canada, and the winters are so warm that no heating is needed. Yet again the Hutterites contemplate from a distance what appears to be a land of milk and honey. But the legal suit is on, and nobody takes the plans for emigration very seriously.

They also say at the Waterton colony that somehow the Lord will take care of the problem and prepare for the harvest next year. The last winter wheat must be in the ground before the first frost freezes the land to stone. The women are fully occupied as they open and dry pumpkin and sunflower seeds so that, in the winter, the men in particular will always have roasted seeds in their pockets for snacks, a habit which the ancestors brought over from Russia. Also, the soap for the long winter must be boiled. Katharina, the head of the kitchen with her scratchy, piercing voice, is in charge of this process; not even preacher Elias dares to contradict that voice here in the wash house. "Making soap is women's work," he says and follows her instructions: "Take 50 pounds of lard, 12 pounds of lye, 7 pails of rain water; boil it for two hours and add a little salt."

With big wooden spatulas like the ones I've seen used by pizza bakers in Italian restaurants, we scoop the grease from the last six months out of the old oil barrels. God have mercy! This stinks so much that I will not get the foul odor of decay out of my nose for days. First the grease is poured onto a scale and then into water heated from underneath; afterwards, it is mixed with lye and stirred for hours so that nothing can burn at the bottom. By way of a chemical process which Elias explained to me but which I still haven't quite understood, a layer of thick, brown soap separates and floats to the surface of the steaming cauldron. With big ladles, we pour the viscous sauce into sheet metal pails and take them to the front of the wash house, where we pour the contents into rectangular wooden frames laid out on big plastic sheets. The frames themselves are two yards long and one yard wide. There the pulp cools off; as soon as it has hardened and turned into real curd soap, the cook uses her butcher's knife to cut the soap block into fist-size pieces. Each colonist receives three of them, which must last until March. What is left over is used by the women when they do the dishes together or when they clean the kitchen, the school, the wash house, and the slaughterhouse. Hutterite soap, by the way, is a medieval all-purpose cleaner which, unlike its worldly counterpart, does not bleach dark clothing or pollute the ground water to any serious extent.

As soon as I have a little time for myself during these busy weeks of autumn, I walk to the dense poplar forest southwest of the colony; the trees form a shining red and yellow seam along the banks of the Waterton River down into the valley. Under this canopy of leaves I feel as good as during the summer in my lake behind the hill of the sheep pasture. Now, however, it isn't a claustrophobic fear that drives me away from the tightness of the ark; I follow an inner peace and quiet which until now has been very foreign to me and which I perceive as a calming of the storms in my mind. All of a sudden, my sleep disorders are gone, and with them the nervousness and inner tension which, on bad days, made me even cough up blood and which puzzled the doctors in Lethbridge so very much. All of these defensive reactions to the tremendous social pressure here in Waterton are blown away.

As a big-city person plagued by progress, I was at first enthusiastic about the alternative of Hutterite life. I admired the community and consciously overlooked all contradictions or justified them for myself in my diary as a necessary evil. For example, I am thinking of the inconsistent attitude of condemning the universities as the devil's breeding ground, on the one hand, and, on the other, using their fruits in the form of the most modern agricultural technologies for the well-being and to the advantage of the heavenly communities. "The Hutterites are just forced to earn money," I said to myself. Because the Old Testament commands them to "be fruitful and multiply," they must buy new land every 15 to 20 years. In an economic sense, they must be "equal to the world" in order to keep up with the competition, for the spiritual foundation would break without a material basis. And it is actually this "spiritual foundation" which is most important here and to which the preachers therefore ironly, stubbornly, and without compromise hold on. The interdiction of the woman, the beating of the children, the damning of the renegades — after all, these are biblical commandments. Who would dare to touch them without endangering the entire system of faith? At the time, the Hutterite arguments made sense to me.

Then came late summer and with it the painful experience of increasing isolation. The brethren and I had gotten too close, and they had to mistake my romantic identification for my willingness to become one of them; their expectations in regard to me, which I constantly provoked, now caused a terrible fear and almost panic inside me. The scandalous letter shortly before the harvest marked the climax of this sad development.

But now, toward the end of October, there are no more peaks of enthusiasm or valleys of disappointment; all that is behind me. The emotional highs and lows have turned into a straight mental line: I have accepted the conditions; I have "delivered myself up" as they say here. Could this lukewarm feeling, this pious fatalism, this letting yourself fall into the community's lap be the much-emphasized Hutterite serenity?

Or might I only be tired of and exhausted from the daily pressure to adapt to an environment which is foreign to me? Am I giving up? Am I already thinking of the approaching end of my Hutterite year? The leaves are already falling, and winter stands in front of the colony's gates; Christmas is only two months away. Do I accept everything that happens to me here because my thoughts have already turned back to the world, to the hell-hole of Hamburg and to Hotel Kempinski? Maybe my state of mind is a blend of contradictory elements which neutralize one another and thus let me find my peace. At any rate, I feel good about myself, not only here under the poplars next to the rustling Waterton River, but also at the daily prayer, the common meals, and the gatherings below the naked lightbulb in treasurer Elias's house every evening.

Now I rarely open my diary, which used to be a confidant necessary for survival in times of personal crises. The letters from home, from out in the world, have lost the great importance they had for me during the past three seasons. Even my dreams, no longer like a heavy and sweet shadow burdening my awakening, are driven away like a specter by the first stroke of the bell every morning. As a Hutterite, today I am not a stranger to myself any longer.

WINTER

Back into the Hell-Hole
with Five Thalers for the Journey

The relatives and friends of dead Johannes keep a wake at his bier for two days and two nights. Over and over they sing "O Lord, Blissful Departure."

inter had been threatening us from the peaks of the Rocky Mountains since the end of September. "The Big Chief," at 9,000 feet the tallest mountain in sight, was the first one to wear a cap of snow. Only days later, the "Black Rock," the peaks of the "Three Sisters," and finally all the rest of the rocky majesties changed color; more and more often, their tops were shrouded by black and grey cloud banks. Very slowly, week by week, the white mass then crept down into the valleys, reached the timber line, devoured like a glacier the dark green of the sparse coniferous forests, and did not even stop at the higher pastures in the northwest. This process the cattle there took with melancholic calm.

Thus nobody is surprised that the heavenly ark is covered with three feet of snow after a stormy November night. In the bookbinder's house, I take a first look out of a window that has been almost completely covered up by drifting snow; the snowed-in colony suddenly looks much smaller and more compact — the buildings have moved much closer together. It is this picture that is fixed in my mind when I remember my first arrival at the Wilson colony on that day almost one year ago when the frozen-meat truck dropped me off in front of the community's cow barn. It was a January day, with snow drifting everywhere. The dark cavities of the windows under the snow-laden roofs, the smoke rising straight up into the air from the chimneys — all was just as it is now. At this moment, my first day with the Hutterites is infinitely far in the past. But even farther away is the time before I came, the time when I was still living out in the world. Like childhood experiences, the little, everyday occurrences of that previous life are now long gone: Going shopping, making a telephone call, reading the paper, traveling, watching TV — all touch me with the strange familiarity of memories of skipping class, playing with marbles, or having my ears boxed.

On the whole, my existence out in the world seems strangely short and fleeting when I compare it with this Hutter-year which now slowly draws to an end; during this year, I seem to have experienced more and lived more intensely than during the 31 years that preceded it. Here a whole new world opened up to me; like a foundling, I was abandoned in a foreign land and had to learn everything from the beginning — not only the Hutterite language, with its old German handwriting, and their way of sitting still and obeying, making shoes and castrating pigs, but also their way of life in which not over-consumption, pride, aggression, and selfishness but rather modesty, humility, pacifism, and unselfishness are the greatest values. In brief, the emphasis here is not on having but rather on being.

After one year in Hutterland I can still confirm only to a certain degree the applicability to Hutterite life of what Erich Fromm writes in his book "To Have or to Be?" "That production must serve the real needs of the people, not the demands of the economic system" applies if one substitutes "colony" for "people." For in the Hutterite economy, the individual is always only a link in the chain of the holy community's production process, a small wheel in the economic machine, turning not on its own but always in concert with and for the benefit of the whole. The "whole" includes particularly the "widows and orphans," the school-age children, and the old and sick who cannot work. Everybody declares solidarity with them. "We then that are strong ought to bear the infirmities of the weak, and not please ourselves," Paul writes in his letter to the Romans (15:1).

Since in the end everything serves God, the strong ones always work hand in hand and never compete with one another, thus satisfying Fromm's second requirement, "that mutual antagonism" be "replaced by solidarity." Personal rivalries within the colony are rare even though the brethren's communities, and in particular the three different groups of "people," are engaged in a brotherly competition among themselves. Who has the best sheep, who finishes threshing first, and who is strictest about the old order? These matters merit close attention, and, once in a while, one can feel a certain complacency when the brethren and sisters become agitated about the supposed mismanagement at a neighboring colony. Such complacency, however, is rare and little human weaknesses, for, in principle, there is solidarity among the communities. If a community has financial difficulties because of a barn fire or an epidemic in the pigsty, the housekeepers from the other colonies meet and, without charging interest, set the leaking ark afloat again.

These "treasurers" also make sure that "sane" and not "maximum" (Fromm) consumption takes place. No Thaler may be spent frivolously, each and every cent being God's property, which the old Elias and his colleagues manage only for the good of the community. This management for the common good, however, does not assume that "all social arrangements"will necessarily result in the "human well-being and the prevention of ill-being" which Erich Fromm envisions. Hutterites are destined to suffer; for the sake of Christ, they endure persecution and earthly pain and thus become like the image of God's son (Roman 8:29). "For as the sufferings of Christ abound in us, so our consolation also aboundeth through Christ" (2 Corinthians 1:5).

The pious colonists' goal is the welfare in heaven that they can reach only through prior suffering on earth. This goal too, is in sharp contrast to that of the "men of the world," who consider good fortune their goal in life, a goal they hope to attain through the constant fulfillment of their desires, i.e. through consumption. But as, out in the affluent society, peoples' unhappiness increases with growing material possessions and their dissatisfaction grows in spite of increasing freedom, the Hutterites radiate an inner serenity and contentment which has been fascinating to me since my first arrival at the colony. Liberated from the compulsory addiction to constant pleasure and divested of the opportunity to do as they please, they seem to be closer to a life of fulfillment than is many a worldly hunter of fortune.

"That the individual" is "an active, not a passive participant in social life" (Fromm) would be confirmed by preacher Elias, who would emphasize the word "man" since women must "keep silence in the churches" (1 Corinthians 14:34) and thus have no right either to participate or to vote in the community council; this restriction doesn't exclude their having responsibilities regarding their work duties. Since Katharina was elected by the "menfolk" to be head cook, no man has interfered with her business, with the exception of the housekeeper's constant reminders to use flour and sugar sparsely. In turn, the male work duties are taboo for the women. Maybe this fact explains why "a new relation... between people and nature, one of cooperation not of exploitation" (Fromm), exists neither in the colonies nor in almost any other part of the world. The Hutterites, too, exploit their land by using artificial fertilizers; year after year, they burden the environment by using more and more pesticides. Their chickens, too, are squeezed into cages and pumped full of antibiotics and hormones.

It comes as a surprise that the chosen ones in particular stand with both feet on the side of "having" when it comes to the area which they consider to be most important: Faith itself. "Faith, in the having mode, is the possession of an answer for which one has no rational proof," Erich Fromm writes. "It consists of formulations created by others, which one accepts because one submits to those others — usually a bureaucracy. It carries the feeling of certainty because of the real (or only imagined) power of the bureaucracy. It is the entry ticket to join a large group of people. It relieves one of the hard task of thinking for oneself and making decisions. One becomes one of the...happy owners of the right faith." Maybe it is this denial of spiritual independence which looms between the Hutterites and me like an abyss across which I cannot jump and do not want to jump, even if failing to do so means my continuing in uncertainty and fear.

My life in God's ark began with blowing snow; to me, too, the arrival of winter means a fresh start. Feeding the cows is again the first thing to do in the morning, since the animals can't find anything to eat on the pastures. Of course, everything is much easier now, from the stacking of the hay bales to the game of skillfully throwing the feed from the loft down into the feeding troughs. Behind me lies a year of physical work; with time passing, I have become not only stronger but also more dexterous. Since the spring of the year, I have been doing repair work in the shoemaker's house, and the lace shoes for boys now turn out better than they did under shepherd Samuel's expert supervision at Wilson. Here in the Waterton community, I work together with hog-keeper Jakob, but this time not as the apprentice whose hand must be held. Now it is the school's graduate Andreas who must learn from the beginning to turn the string for the soles before he attempts to make his first boys' shoes, size 1. I like to give Andy some advice, for example, about how he can get the heels from the old tires to be of equal height so that the "little men won't walk to be cripples."

Because the garden lies buried again under snow and ice until April, schoolteacher Paul now has more time for instructing his pupils in the word of God and the ancestors' songs. During one hour in the morning and again for two hours in the early evening after English class, the colony resounds with the children's high voices. Including the six-o'clock prayer, the Hutterite students must spend an approximate daily total of nine times 60 minutes on the hard schoolbenches, less the time it takes to pray kneeling on the floor or recite memorized Bible verses standing up. How nice were the times when one could hunt gophers for one gum per tail and ride the horses without a saddle, chasing after run-away cows over hill and dale through the knee-high grass and the endless open country. Now it is back to dull studying in the confined, stuffy, and constantly overheated classroom and under the severe gaze of the teacher sitting behind the tall podium whose upper right-hand drawer is the home of "Paul's Dear Rod," which is always ready for action.

Preacher Elias, too, now has more time for his official business, unless some grim frost bursts a waterpipe which he then has to repair in his capacity as the colony's plumber. In the afternoon and at night, he sits completely withdrawn at the desk in his study and copies the old sermons word for word and in painstaking German as his ancestors have done for generations. In one winter, Elias copies up to six sermons, which take up roughly 500 notebook pages. This servant of the word, who was elected only 10 years ago, has already written down at least 60 sermons. It would be his greatest wish to copy with his own hand the complete Hutterite library of 600 different writings before his death; then he would have done his share in the passing on and spreading of the "true faith."

These writings bound in pigskin, some of them from the 17th century, are the only objects in Elias Wurz's household that he really cherishes. Other objects — the hand-made chairs from the grandfather from South Dakota, the old sofa, the knitted bedding — are earthly things, or "temporary," as the Hutterites disapprovingly call all matter; they are as fleeting as one's own body and without use up there in the kingdom of eternal values. It is this kind of thinking which made it possible for a smart dealer in antiques from Calgary to talk him into giving away the beautiful octagonal clock, which was certainly a hundred years old. In return, Elias got a cheap thing made in Hong Kong. Still, the preacher thought he had gotten a good deal, for the new, ugly plastic clock needs to be rewound only once a week instead of once a day, and besides, it has a daily calendar on its face. How "practical."

The Hutterites don't understand how so many men of the world can love everything old. Museums in particular are puzzling to them — for example, the visiting exhibition called "Canadian Heritage," which could be seen in Calgary a few months before. Elias went to see it in the fall when he attended a bull auction with his father, the housekeeper, and winekeeper Johannes. There the three Hutterites were, standing in front of three mannequins dressed as Hutterites in an originally reconstructed Hutterite room. They simply couldn't understand it. They themselves had been turned into objects of lust of the eyes; the Hutterite way of life had become a show. The people of the world really didn't seem to shy away from anything. In old times, the Hutterites were persecuted; today, they are exhibited next to old costumes of the Blackfoot Indians, next to steam engines and muzzleloaders.

The other visitors at the museum were quite surprised to see live representatives of this species of chosen ones next to the Hutterite museum pieces, the dummies behind the red ropes dressed in exactly the same way. At first, people started to laugh, thinking it was all a gag instigated by the museum in order to liven up the building. The laughter stopped only when old Elias was asked by an "Englishman" whether they were "real Hutterites"; in the good old Hutterite tongue, he answered, "Shur sa mir echt," of course we are real.

The colonists appreciate old things only in areas in which they are useful and have proven to be of worth to the community. The almost antique scrapers with which the men scrub the pigs' hairs off during butchering are an example. These are round irons, similar to saucers, in whose center a wooden handle has been fastened by a screw; the edges are extremely sharp. The farmers scraped their pigs with them as long ago as the Middle Ages.

A few weeks before Christmas, the housekeeper takes the scrapers out of his storage room and distributes them among us menfolk. Finally, temperatures have fallen far below minus 30 degrees, the ideal temperature for slaughtering pigs. In the early morning light, I drive the caterpillar to the barn in order to take the animals to the slaughterhouse. The first five of the extra-fattened sows are waiting there, freezing in the snow and shaking as they feel their end draw near. Hog-chief Johannes holds a long knife in his big right hand; teacher Paul and smith Jakob quickly grab a squealing pig and throw it on its back. Its throat is now unprotected, and Johannes sticks his knife into it. In the rhythm of the pulse, the blood shoots out; the throat's main artery has been severed. Laboriously, the poor creature gets up on its feet one last time, staggers, and pushes its nose into the snow drenched with its own blood. The fearful grunting slowly dies away. With a gargling death-rattle, the animal breaks down like a falling tree. Its hind legs move by blind reflex, while the pupils of the eyes turn away to the back. The mouth opens in a silent cry; then a final convulsion of the bloody body ends the agony.

When I observed the same scene in February of last winter, I almost died along with the animal, for the butchering had simply been too much for me to stand; in the meantime, I have lost many an urban over-sensitivity. "If you want to eat meat, you must butcher, too," Paul said to me only a month ago and put an axe in my hand during the beheading of the ducks. The first stroke was pure torture for me, but after the first dozen, the duck heads rolled every 10 seconds. I killed 1,500 ducks within three days without losing any sleep over it. Doing this kind of thing, one quickly develops an almost neutral feeling toward the animal to be butchered. The duck becomes an object made of feathers and flesh which will turn into pillow stuffing and Sunday roasts.

The bodies of the five pigs, now lying on the red snow of the battlefield in front of the barn, must today be made into sausage and ham, the meat supply for the winter. Just as if they were five sacks of flour, I take the dead animals to the slaughterhouse on the front loader's snow blade. Winekeeper Johannes and his men are already waiting next to a boiling tub by the door; each man has a scraper in his hand. I tip one sow after another into the steaming water, where they are briefly scalded so that later the hair can easily be scraped off.

Once an animal is without hair, it is hung by its hind legs; sharp knives quickly make a slit in the body from the bottom to the top. Young girls with big metal pails carry the edible organs, such as the liver, spleen, and kidneys, to the slaughterhouse, in which the women make sausage out of the meat. With a press, the cleaned intestines are filled with ground meat and liver, a process which looks about like an empty fire hose being filled with water. In spite of her age, 70-year-old cook Katharina swings the butchering axe with agility and cuts the ribs into handy freezer portions. Other women stir the boiling lard in the cauldrons in which, only a few weeks ago, the soap was boiled. In here it is as hot and humid as in a tropical rain forest. Condensing water runs down the aluminum walls; there is a damp and warm odor of meat, blood, and excrement. This slaughterhouse climate also seems to heat up the women's blood, for they start to throw cut-off curly tails at us menfolk through the small opening of the door while we cut the meat outside in the icy cold.

From now on, the pigs appear daily on the table in one form or another; for breakfast, as "Sperkele," which are salted and fried porkrinds served with zwieback and jam; sometimes for lunch, as broth with hearty meat in it; or for supper, as ham hocks in jelly, called "Zitala," which are served with a little vinegar or lemon juice.

Christmas Eve brings us pork as well: "Rippna," pickled ribs, served with French fries and preserved red beets on the side. Unfortunately, this is no special meal, given the Hutterite tradition not to celebrate. "To us, Christmas is not eating and drinking as out in the world," teacher Paul tells me on Christmas Eve as we sit in the usual circle at his father-in-law Elias's place and scream out songs of lament of which I already know quite a few by heart. There is hardly anything which makes this 24th of December different from the night before any holiday: We are all clean and fresh out of the tub, the girls pigtails are straight and orderly, and Elias's thick and white full beard is parted right in the middle with an elegant wave. Still, something is in the air today; a certain unrest rises from the children on the floor to us grown-ups on the chairs and benches, and there is whispering, giggling, and the shuffling of feet.

During a short break toward 8:30 at night, the boys and girls all rise at once and go outside. Paul explains to me that they now go from house to house and do their "wishing." I see what that means half an hour later when the young bunch return with full pockets and cheeks red with excitement. "We wish you a Merry Christmas," they shout together, but with "you," they really address not all of us grown-ups but rather and primarily Susanna, old Elias's wife. It is she who, as a precaution, has put a brown jute sack behind her chair and now takes it out. Each child politely steps in front of the "Ankela," the "aunt" — the boys first, and then the girls. The chubby "aunt" gives everybody some candy and a piece of gum.

The housekeeper has given all mothers such a sack full of sweets from community supplies so that each one of them can provide the children with a little Christmas joy. For Hutterite children, a few pieces of candy or a piece of chewing gum is still sufficient. They don't need more to be happy.

In order to eliminate any connection to the worldly celebration of Christmas from the beginning, Paul explains to me during this modest distribution of Christmas presents, the little ones are not allowed to believe in either Santa Claus or the Christ child: "Playing Santa Claus and all that

stuff with the angels, this is no good. We don't do it." Thus
he had also prohibited the English teacher from practicing
Christmas plays or any other pseudo-religious theater. He
was unable to prevent the teacher from giving her students
color crayons for Christmas in spite of the biblical command
not to make an image; with the crayons, they now set free
their excess creative pressure and decorate even the German notebooks and the sacred Hutterite Song Book with
flowers and garlands that Paul definitely feels are a good
deal of lust of the eyes.

There is yet another thing that the teacher hasn't been
able to prevent: The "prideful" postcards that many adolescents get from their girlfriends or boyfriends during Christmas time. For example, Chicken-Jerg's oldest daughter,
Martha Hofer, received from her boyfriend from the Carmengey colony an intensely colorful Christmas card on
which four golden candles stand out in the middle of an
ocean of blood-red poinsettias. In the middle of this glossy
orgy of colors the words "Merry Christmas, Sweetheart, and
a Happy New Year" are printed. The 24-year-old now guards
this worldly kitsch like a precious stone in her trunk, where
she has given the card a place of honor right next to her
wooer's Easter greetings with the porcelain bunny among
the lilies of the valley. Martha finds such trash simply
"beautiful," since it is different from the usual, different from
the white walls, the black jackets, and the naked light
bulbs.

But it is one and the same Martha, in whose trunk a
miniature America is locked away with all the consumer society's kitsch, who sits here at Christmas Eve together with
her sisters and brethren, whose trunks are no different on
the inside; with fervor and devotion, the young people sing
the old tunes of contempt for the world and of the sweetness
of death:

"What good can the world hold / With its
fortune, with its gold, / All our friends, all our
kin / Pass like dust in stormy wind. / Foolish
joy!"

As I look into Martha's madonna-like face, I wonder what
it must look like in her mind. How can both the "Merry
Christmas" of her card, with its golden hearts and red flowers, and this simple, so very ordinary Christmas Eve fit
under one dotted kerchief? Wouldn't these contradictions
have to give the girl a headache from morning to night?

I could ask such a question of myself as well: How do my
well-being in the security of the Hutterite community, on the
one hand, and my plans to return to the world in a few days,
on the other, fit together? After all, I will return to a world in
which, at this moment, mountains of precious presents and
hypocritical wishes are exchanged only so that the usual animosity and jealousy may continue right after the holidays.
What do I want out there among the "wolves ravening the
prey...to destroy souls" (Ezekiel 22:27)? Why won't I stay
here in the outer courtyard of paradise with "the sheep of
the pasture" (Psalms 79:13)?

So far, I have pushed this question aside. One full year
seemed to be such a long time, and I believed I didn't need
to think about the end of my Hutterite time. Now the
farewell is around the corner, and I have very mixed feelings
when I think of packing, of the trip home, and of Hamburg.
What seemed to me like a far-away vision of happiness in
the summer has now turned into almost a threat. Should I
continue where I left off a year ago? Should I wear my reporter's skin again in order to run after news and to run
away from myself? Am I still able to lead that worldy life
after what's been happening to me since last winter? I came
here in order to live together with people to whom "Alternative Living" is no quick fad but a 450-year-old tradition. I
wanted to write a book about these "chosen ones" because I
thought that we "people of the world" know too little about

them and might learn something from them. Now, at the end of my time in the ark of Waterton, shortly before the somersault back into the sea of sins, I wonder whether a book will be all that I will bring back with me from Waterton, and whether I should not make changes in my personal life after everything I have experienced during this time!

Of course, I could stay here and become a Hutterite. Paul, Elias, Johannes — they all offered me this solution more than once. I would need only to be baptized and to hand my possessions over to the community as the early Christians did, to lay them down, "at the apostles' feet" (Acts 4:35). The second condition sounds tempting, but the first condition frightens me. Leaving one's possessions behind, liberating oneself from the weight of material things in order to work in the community together with other people, living no longer for the "I" but for the "We," no longer for having, but for being — all this seems like paradise to me. However, I am unable to live here forever because this Hutterite "being" actually begins only after the end of the earthly existence, i.e. after the death of the body. I am such an enlightened modern that I lack the faith needed for such a high goal in life; I just don't have it. I am looking for self-realization and not for self-surrender as baptism actually requires: The candidate for baptism "cannot be himself anymore but must become an obedient member of the Lord's body without free will." As a man of the 20th century, I find this course to be like going back to the Middle Ages, back to bondage and drudgery.

To the Hutterites, this choice is very different. They need this voluntary denial of their freedoms in order to obtain the serenity which enables them to withstand the temptations of the world outside, temptations which limit and bind the human being in a different way, but also much more strongly, than does baptism. In theory, I have known this for a long time. But it is only among the Hutterites that I have experienced for myself how liberating the reduction of standards can be and how much strength the human being gains by refusing to ask for more than a roof over one's head, three daily meals, warm clothing, and work useful to a community which does not exploit but rather loves its members. Here at the Waterton colony, where a piece of gum and some candy can make the children happy on Christmas Eve, I find that the things that are happening this evening under the Christmas trees of my world seem almost like a loss of freedom. How liberating it is, on the other hand, to notice that one's own self has been placed in the background and is no longer so important, that one's self-imposed standards no longer rise like an invincible mountain which one must nonetheless try to climb. The only thing the Hutterites lack is the difficult choice among the stereos with the best sound, the most advantageous life insurance policies, and the detergents with the most washing power. Martha is lucky that she will have to do without all these things.

The Hutterites are unable to understand that, even with this perspective, I still cannot stay. I use the hypocritical excuse of my visa expiring after one year, which will force me to leave the country. The argument that I am just homesick for my friends, for the familiar streets and smells, and for the sound of the ships' sirens in the Hamburg fog is much more credible because it is also more honest. Of course, I don't mention the fact that I also think of my difficult girlfriend, of dancing all night long, of lying out in the sun on the balcony, and of fresh flowers on my desk. Even over the course of one long year, they have not been able to turn me away from the world, these Hutterites, without whom the world would be so much poorer.

I had come as a sinner, and it is a sinner whom old Elias, his son the preacher, winekeeper Johannes, schoolteacher Paul, and Chicken-Jerg — the entire leadership — take to the airport in Calgary at the beginning of January. It is a sad trip. We don't talk much because we don't know what could be left to say. I realize that, in the eyes of the chosen ones, I am now a runaway who refuses to continue his journey on the narrow path, although he should know the ways of a righteous life after such a long time. My companions simply cannot believe that I want to return of my own free will to Hamburg, where the ships are supposed to be bigger than even the cow barn and where the hell-hole once swallowed the wheelmaker Jerg Schneider's evil daughter.

To be sure, I had never made it a secret that I would leave one day; however, now that the time has come, the Hutterites can't believe it. They feel betrayed, and I feel guilty. Have I been playing with their hope that they might yet convert me? Have I been strictly following their regimented rules of life just because I wanted to fully gain their trust? Have I misused God's chosen people in self-interest? Yes, I played with, deceived, and abused the trust of the naive holy people. And no one out in the world will condemn me for it. On the contrary, the publisher will praise my skillful persistence. My attempt to give up my career and to get to know an alternative way of life will help my professional future. I feel like a traitor!

During our three-hour trip to the airport, Paul makes a suggestion in order to show me a way out of the difficult situation: "You should start a community in Germany." Actually, the thought of founding a community in Germany is not at all foreign to me; in the bookbinder's house, I often gave thought to the question of how one could establish a humane, civilized, yet natural community life together with people who think the same way, a simple and honest life with the emphasis on "being."

I tell the brethren about the young people who, all over Western Europe, are leaving the "sinful" cities in order to lead their lives on a few acres, without self-interest and pride but with much joy of living. "Hippies?" Paul asks skeptically. "People who are honest and are tired of the world," I answer dodgingly. "Where there is no faith, there is no basis," Paul says and feels that this contemporary youth movement certainly can't be made to agree with faith in the

Hutterite sense, although each group could learn much from the other. However, continuing this discussion now would make no sense; the brethren just wouldn't understand and would continue to stare at the straight line of "Highway Two" which takes us north. In spite of our life together, we have remained strangers. The gap between the holy colonies and the sinful world is too wide for me to bridge within one year; to do so would require a vacation lasting my entire life.

At the airport in Calgary, I am suddenly back in the world, the great, big world. Everywhere there are strange people, hectic movements with murmuring muzac. My brethren are as nervous as I am. At first, we can't find our way, but then a merciful black porter shows us to the counter for departures. Before I go through passport control, we say good-bye. In a manner different from their greeting in the cowbarn one year ago and in spite of their disappointment, the Hutterites now shake hands with me. Treasurer Elias fulfills the duty of his office and pulls a five-dollar bill out of his pocket, my subsistence for the long trip — an unbelievably generous gesture considering the old man's stinginess. "Greet your mother from us," Elias says; Paul asks me to write and tell him how "things are going" with me. I am so excited that I can hardly hear their words of farewell. Almost abruptly I turn around and walk through the checkpoint.

In the lounge at Gate 14, the people look at me with disguised curiosity. I am relieved to see that my black Hutterite costume creates a physical distance between me and this jet-set uniformity composed of expensive furs, gold-rimmed glasses, and well-kept jeans. How similar they are to one another, my thoughts go; the people of the world resemble one another just as do the Hutterites in their colonies. Unlike the colonists, however, these poor Mr. Cleans and women of the world take nothing as seriously as their "individuality." The sleepy synthetic music gets on my nerves terribly. Even in the bathroom I am not spared. Among the Hutterites, it was strictly forbidden to listen to music; here, one is forced to listen.

In the Lufthansa jumbo jet there is the same music piping down from the ceiling before take-off. I refuse to take the pills which are supposed to ease the difference in pressure during take-off and also refuse to let the pretty flight attendant talk me into renting the headset (it costs 10 marks — my entire subsistence!). "Death Wish, Part II" is the title of the film which we are expected to watch during the flight. Main actor: Charles Bronson. I really am back among the wolves, I think, and my homesickness is gone.

I arrive at my final destination, Frankfurt/Main airport, after ten hours of flying. The official checking my passport stops in surprise. He asks me to whom that passport belongs. I answer, "It's mine. To whom else could it belong?" "You claim to be the person in the photo?" the stunned man asks and points at my passport picture. Indeed, I am no longer the beardless, long-haired person wearing a T- shirt and smiling into the camera; I don't even resemble him, for I am now a stern-looking Hutterite with his hair parted in the middle. My passport picture and I have nothing in common anymore. When will I again resemble myself?

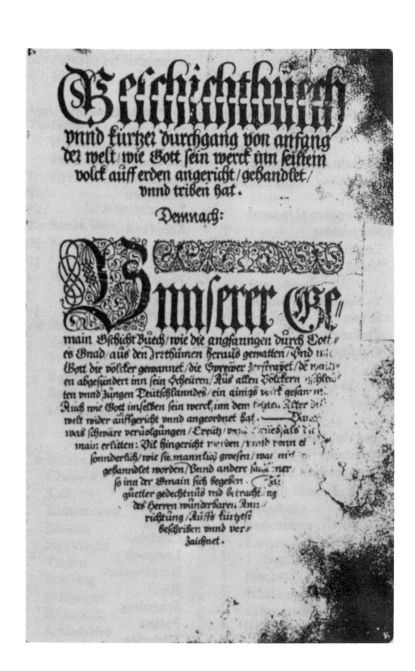

Geschichtbuech

vnnd kurtzer durchgang von anfang
der welt / wie Gott sein werck ynn seinem
volck auff erden angericht / gehandlet /
vnnd triben hat .

Demnach:

Vnnserer Ge-

main Geschicht Buech / wie die angefangen durch Got=
tes Gnad / auß den drthümen herauß gematten / vnd wie
Gott die völcker gemannet / die Spreiber zerstrayet / dē man=
en abgesundert inn sein Scheüren / Auß allen völckern geschlech=
ten vnnd zungen Teütschlanndes / ein ainigs werck gesam=
Auch wie Gott imselben sein werck / inn dem letzten Altter der
welt wider auffgericht vnnd angeordnet hat . ——— Dan
was schwäre veruolgüngen / Creütz vnnd trüebsal die
main erlitten : Vil hingericht worden / vnnd wonn es
sonnderlich / wie sie mannlich gewesen / was mit
gehanndlet worden / Vnnd andere sachen
so inn der Gmain sich begeben . Zu
guetter gedechtnüß vnd betracht=ng
des Herren wunderbaren . Anu
richtüng / Auffs kürtzest
beschriben vnnd ver=
zaichnet .

Title Page of Hutterite Chronicle

APPENDIX I:
A PETITION

To the Hon. Woodrow Wilson,
    President of the United States,
        Washington, D.C.

Our Dear President:—

We, the Hutterian Brethren Church, also known as Bruderhof or Communistic Mennonites, comprising about 2,000 souls, who are living in eighteen communities in South Dakota and Montana (organized as a Church since 1533), kindly appeal to you, Mr. President and your Assistants, briefly wishing to inform you of our principles and convictions regarding military service. Being men of lowly station and unversed in the ways of the world, we would ask your indulgence if in this letter we should miss the approved form.

The fundamental principles of our faith, as concerns practical life, are community of goods and non-resistance. Our community life is founded on the principle, "What is mine is thine," or in other words, on brotherly love and humble Christian service, according to Acts 2:44,45: "And all that believed were together, and had all things common; and sold their possessions and goods and parted them to all men, as every man had need." Hence we differ fundamentally from non-Christian communistic systems, with their principle, "What is thine is mine." We believe the community life, if not based on Christian love, will always fail. Our endeavors are of a religious nature throughout, and we know that very few people are willing to accept our faith, denying themselves and serving God by serving each other in community life, as we do.

We are free from political ambitions and recognize civil government as ordained of God. We honor our civil authorities and in our daily evening prayer meetings, which are regularly attended by all our members, as well as in our Sunday services, we pray for our government. We have always willingly paid taxes on our real estate and personal property, although we were told that our property, being held by a religious corporation, is not taxable according to the law. It need not be said that we do not permit our widows and orphans, invalids and feeble-minded to become a burden to the county or state.

Our community life is based on God's Word, and we could not serve God according to the dictates of our conscience if we were not permitted to live together in our communities. Our members would, by the help of God, suffer what He may permit, rather than consent to leave the community life.

On the principle of non-resistance our position is strictly in accord with the New Testament teaching. Our Confession of Faith shows that we hold the government to be ordained of God for the reason that not all men are followers of the meek and lowly Savior, and that we further believe, the government should protect those who do good and punish the evil-doers according to Rom. 13:1-7. The Church, however, must conform to the express teachings and example of the Master. She is in the world, but not of the world. We have never taken any part in the election of civil officers. Without boasting we can say that our life has been consistent with this principle. To go to law is contrary to our convictions and is not permitted among us. Our young men could not become a part of the army or military organization, even for non-combatant service, without violating our principles.

Our comprehensive Confession of Faith was written in 1540 and printed for the first time in 1565. The voluminous Chronicle of our Church, which gives our history since the year 1530, is mentioned in the article, "Mennonites" in the International Encyclopedia. The principal contents of our Church Chronicle were published by Dr. Joseph Beck, in 1883, under the title, "Geschichtsbuecher der Wieder-taeufer." Our history is written with blood and tears; it is largely a story of persecution and suffering. We have record of over two thousand persons of our faith who suffered martyrdom by fire, water, and the sword. Our Church has been driven from country to country, and rather than to compromise their principles, have fled to various countries until at last they emigrated from Russia to this country in 1874.

We would further say that we love our country and are profoundly thankful to God and to our authorities for the liberty of conscience which we have hitherto enjoyed. We are loyal to our God-ordained government and desire to serve our country in ways and duties which do not interfere with our religious convictions. We humbly ask you, our dear Mr. President, not to lay upon us any duties which would violate our Christian convictions, and we hope, you believe with us, that we ought to be faithful to the teaching of God's Word and the dictates of our conscience, and should suffer what He may permit, rather than to do that which we clearly recognize to be contrary to His Word.

Dear Mr. President, we humbly ask that we may be permitted the liberty to live according to the dictates of our conscience as heretofore. With the vow of baptism we have promised God and the Church on bended knees to consecrate, give and devote ourselves, soul and body and all, to the Lord in heaven, to serve Him in the way which, according to His Word we conceive to be acceptable to Him. We humbly petition our Honored Chief Executive that we may not be asked to become disobedient to Christ and His Church, being fully resolved, through the help and grace of God, to suffer affliction, or exile, as did our ancestors in the times of religious intolerance, rather than violate our conscience or convictions and be found guilty before our God.

For proof that our attitude on the points in question is one of conviction, and not of arbitrariness, we would respectfully refer you to our Confession mentioned above, as well as to our life and history. We desire to serve our country and be respectful and submissive in every way not interfering with serving our God consistently. We are sincerely thankful for having been granted shelter and protection by our government and for having enjoyed full religious freedom up to the present time, and we are quite willing to do something for the good of our country, provided that it is not against our conscientious convictions.

Very respectfully yours,
Hutterian Brethren Church,
David Hofer.
Elias Walter.
Joseph Kleinsasser.

APPENDIX II:
CHRONOLOGY OF THE HUTTERITE HISTORY

1525   Conrad Grebel, Georg Blaurock, Felix Manz and others establish the Anabaptist movement in Zurich, Switzerland.

1529   During the imperial diet at Speyer, Emperor Charles V. introduces the death penalty for adult baptisms.

               Georg Blaurock is executed in Klausen (Southern Tyrol); his successor is the hatmaker Jakob Hutter.

               Hutter visits the refugees in Moravia. Because of their beliefs they were banished from southern Germany, Austria, and Switzerland and were granted protection by the Hussite lesser nobility.

1533   A group of Christian communists choose Hutter as their leader.

1536   Hutter dies at the stake in Innsbruck.

1539   Hutterite prisoners are taken to Trieste and are forced to fight in the sea-war between the Hapsburgs and the Turks.

1540   In his Nuremberg prison, Peter Riedmann writes the "Justification" which, next to the Bible, represents the foundation of Hutterite belief.

1540 through 1556	Continuing persecution drives the martyrs into the forests and forces them to live in caves through the winter.
1556 through 1593	The "Good Years" bring about a blossoming of Hutterite communal living until the war between the Hapsburgs and the Turks destroys many community farms.
1568	Peter Walbot writes the "School Regulations."
1605	Heavy plundering by the Turks.
1618 through 1648	During the Thirty Years War, the Hutterites are favored victims of the Catholic and Protestant lansquenets.
1621	Emperor Ferdinand II expels the Hutterites from Moravia. 186 anabaptists move to Transylvania and establish the first new colony near Hermannstadt.
1755	The Carinthian protestants expelled by Czarina Maria Theresia join the Hutterite communities and strengthen the "chosen people" threatened by corruption.
1757	Jesuit monks burn Hutterite prayer texts and songbooks and force baptisms of new-born.
1767	Escape over the Transylvanian Alps into Wallachia.
1770	Hutterites follow the call of Czarina Catherine II and immigrate to Russia.

1874   Threatened by compulsory military service, the first 250 Hutterites move to South Dakota via Hamburg and New York.

1918   Anti-Hutterite riots during World War I cause the Hutterites to give up their colonies and purchase new land in Canada.

1973   With the abolition of the "Communal Property Act" in Alberta, the last legally sanctioned discrimination of the Hutterites is removed.

               Since the beginning of the seventies the Darius people have been in a tax war with the government because they refuse to give "money for bloodshed."

Notes on the Translation

(For the most part, this translation keeps both Michael Holzach's meaning and his spelling. Advance readers have offered comments summarized below. — *The Publishers*)

p. x, **Hammonia, Harmonia** — Mr. Vogel of the Staatsarchiv Hamburg says the Harmonia (length:100 meters, width: 10 meters) was built in 1867. In 1874 it sailed 4 times from Hamburg to New York under Captain B. Voss. The ship was sold to Russia in 1878. Mr. Vogel says that no ship named "Hammonia" was ever seen in the port of Hamburg. (S.L.)

p. 7 and *passim*, **"Deitche"** — "Germans." Note similarity to "*Peitsche*," "whip." (R.G.) "Refers to the blows as a hot or hard strapping, not a light one. As you can see in the photo (p. 9) , this Lehrer intends to inflict pain." (M.W.)

p. 141 and *passim*, **house keeper** — "*Haushalter*," "House holder." "He holds the responsibility of household needs and necessities." (M.W.)

p. 242 and *passim*, **hog chief** — "Hog Boss." Hutterites themselves use "boss" to refer to those with responsibility. "Even Holzach writes, 'den Boss vom Schweinestall.'" (R.G.) "*Haushalter* or Boss . . ." (M.W.)

p. 35 and passim, **wine keeper** — "*Weinzierl*." Not in charge of wine, but of crops in general — seeding, cultivating, harvesting. . . . The *Haushalter* or Boss is in charge of wine as another commodity for family use." — (M.W.)

p. 215, **decrepit** — "Age-weakened" or "life-weary." (M.W.)

p. 244 and *passim*, **"aunt"** — "*Ankela* is Hutterite for Grandma." (M.W.) "It's also used several times in the context of kindergarten or Little School — there 'aunt' seems to be much more appropriate than 'grandma,' 'aunt' not as a word describing family relations but rather a person to whom somebody is entrusted." (S.L.)

R.G. — Reuben Goertz

S.L. — Stephan Lhotzky

M.W.— Mary Wipf